BURSTING BUBBLES

More praise for *Bursting Bubbles*

'Robert Walters is an exceptionally good storyteller. His writing is eloquent and often impassioned. Wherever you stand, you should read the book. The debate is worth having'
Tamlyn Currin, JancisRobinson.com

'*Bursting Bubbles: A Secret History of Champagne* (Quiller) by Robert Walters is the most provocative wine book I've read in a while'
Henry Jeffreys, The Best Books on Drink of 2017,
***The Guardian* Newspaper**

'A brilliant and appealing book, and the story it tells is fascinating and compelling — leaving me thirsty to try some of the wines that are its subject'
Tim James, *Wine Mag*

'There's much to agree with in this book. It is well written and researched, a pleasure to read and Walters argues his case persuasively. Most importantly, at the same time as it engages in some hand-wringing about the way things are, it communicates a joy and enthusiasm for good Champagne. I wholeheartedly recommend it'
Huon Hook, *The Real Review*

'Written with verve and wit. In addition to a fascinating historical examination, Walters explodes numerous myths, which will amuse any lover of wine trivia'
Tim White, *The Australian Financial Review*

'Reckons with the multitude of Champagne myths in an edifying manner. This is the most readable wine book on this list'
Scott Rosenbaum, 9 Must-Reads for Drinks Industry Pros, Sevenfifty.com

'Shows a masterly command of what is important in writing fastidiously crafted profiles of the top artisans of the Montagne and Cote he knows best'
Michael Edwards, *The World of Fine Wine*, Issue 55

'This beautifully written book is so cheerful and entertaining that one risks not realising how thoughtful and informative it is as well — a risk that I would advise any wine lover to take without hesitation'
Jesús Barquín, Award-winning co-author of *Sherry, Manzanilla & Montilla*

BURSTING BUBBLES

A SECRET HISTORY OF CHAMPAGNE
& THE RISE OF THE GREAT GROWERS

ROBERT WALTERS

Quiller

Copyright © 2017 Robert Walters

First published in Australia in 2016 by Bibendum Wine Co.
3-5 Harper Street, Abbotsford Vic 3067, Australia

First published in the UK in 2017
by Quiller, an imprint of Quiller Publishing Ltd

This paperback edition published in 2018

Reprinted 2019

British Library Cataloguing-in-Publication Data
A catalogue record for this book is available from the British Library

ISBN 978 1 84689 279 0

The right of Robert Walters to be identified as the author of this work has been asserted in accordance with the Copyright, Design and Patent Act 1988.

The information in this book is true and complete to the best of our knowledge. All recommendations are made without any guarantee on the part of the Publisher, who also disclaims any liability incurred in connection with the use of this data or specific details. All rights reserved. No part of this book may be reproduced or transmitted in any form or by any means, electronic or mechanical including photocopying, recording or by any information storage and retrieval system, without permission from the Publisher in writing.

Book design by Philip Campbell Design
Typeset in Janson Text and Benton Sans
All photographs by the author unless otherwise credited

Printed in the UK by TJ Books Limited.

Some of the text in this book first appeared in a modified form in a series of articles in *The World of Fine Wine* magazine.

Quiller

An imprint of Quiller Publishing Ltd
Wykey House, Wykey, Shrewsbury SY4 1JA
Tel: 01939 261616
Email: info@quillerbooks.com
Website: www.quillerpublishing.com

CONTENTS

Foreword *Andrew Jefford* — 10

Disclaimers *Where the author pre-empts several lines of criticism, comes clean about his motivations and forewarns the reader that he is not without self-interest* — 11

Prologue *In which a wine traveller has an encounter with a Champagne from another planet and lets the reader in on a little secret* — 13

Part I *Where we follow sparkling Champagne's remarkable metamorphosis from faulty to fabulous* — 21

Myth I *In the name of the father: Dom Pérignon was the father of Champagne* — 30

Part II *In which we drive along a haunted racetrack in search of a singular grower and discover, not for the last time, that all is not what it seems in the world of Champagne* — 33

Part III *Where we meet the revolutionary parents of modern Champagne – science and industry* — 47

Myth II *First place: Champagne was the original sparkling wine* — 52

Part IV *In which the author travels to the mountain to meet the rock of Ambonnay, tries to get blood from a stone and ends up leaving on better terms than when he arrived* — 55

Myth III *The good and the great: Grand cru vineyards produce the best wines* — 68

Part V *Where we head to 'Rahnse' to visit the cathedral and then travel south to Épernay, for a stroll down the legendary Avenue de Disney* — 69

Myth IV *Silver spoon: Placing a spoon in the top of a Champagne bottle helps preserve the bubbles for longer* — 77

Part VI *In which the wine traveller drives south from Épernay to Avize and discovers that all that glitters is not gold* — 79

Part VII *Where we encounter more threats to Champagne's 'Great Wine' pretensions and find out what conventional Champagne has in common with baked bread, roasted nuts and seared steak*   91

Myth V *Holy Trilogy: Only three grape varieties are used to make Champagne*   98

Part VIII *In which we pay a visit to Pascal Agrapart, and where the author acknowledges that he can sometimes miss what is right under his nose by playing the man and not the ball*   101

Part IX *Where we unearth even more image problems for Champagne (by comparing the 'approach Champenois' with best practice in Burgundy) and where we also learn that the English are the necrophiliacs of the wine world*   113

Myth VI *Blending is better: Champagne is blended in order to produce a better balanced, better quality wine*   119

Part X *In which the author tries to comprehend Anselme Selosse via a blend of pop psychology and historical minutiae and then plays word games with the man himself*   123

Part XI *Where we blend a few things together in order to produce a histoire vraie of Champagne and then explore the extent to which brand has come to dominate land in this famous region*   135

Myth VII *Simple fizzics: Where bubbles come from*   143

Part XII *In which we head south to Vertus and visit a great grower making 'crazy wine' in order to remind ourselves, once again, that Champagne is a wine, first and foremost*   145

Part XIII *The continuation of our histoire vraie, where the author views advanced capitalism through the rosiest of glasses and perhaps takes the friendship too far by comparing the history of Champagne to that of Camembert and free-range chicken*   159

Myth VIII *The shape of things to come: Champagne should be served in flutes*   163

Part XIV *In which we travel from Vertus to the historic market city of Troyes, all the while grappling with the ideologies of Champagne's separatists*   165

Part XV *Where the author discusses the problems with the term 'grower revolution' and then offers the reader a choice between two radically different worlds of Champagne* — 171

Part XVI *In which we visit our first Aube grower and learn what it means to be an outsider in your own wine region* — 179

Part XVII *The final instalment of our histoire vraie, where the true grower revolutions are revealed – and yes, there were more than one* — 191

Myth IX *In the beginning: Champagne is mentioned in the Bible* — 195

Part XVIII *In which we visit a vigneron farmer – or is that a farmer vigneron?* — 197

Part XIX *Where we delve into the remaining key factors that led to the development of Champagne's current batch of great grower-producers* — 207

Myth X *Bursting bubbles: Smaller bubbles are a sign of a high-quality Champagne* — 212

Part XX *In which we visit the last of our growers in the Aube and learn that, no matter how seriously we take it, wine's main work is to make us happy* — 215

Epilogue *A short manifesto in which the author asks you, the wine lover, a simple, somewhat rhetorical question: 'What sort of Champagne do you really want to drink?'* — 223

Notes — 229

Acknowledgements — 237
Bibliography — 238
Index — 239

Hand-drawn map of the Champagne region:

- MASSIF de ST THIERRY
  - CHARTOGNE-TAILLET
  - MERFY
- GUEUX
- "LES BEGUINES" JÉRÔME PRÉVOST
- HAUNTED RACETRACK
- REIMS
- PETITE MONTAGNE
- MONTAGNE de REIMS
- FÔRET DE LA MONTAGNE
- VERZENAY
- VE
- PHARE
- VALLÉE de la MARNE
- HAUTVILLERS
- MOËT ET CHANDON
- POL ROGER
- JACQUESSON
- AY
- MAREUIL-SUR-AY
- BOUZY
- AM
- AVENUE DE CHAMPAGNE
- ÉPERNAY
- CHOUILLY
- CHAVOT COURCOURT
- CUIS
- CRAMANT
- PASCAL AGRAPART
- AVIZE
- ANSELME SELOSSE
- OGER
- LE MESNIL-SUR-OGER
- VERTUS
- CÔTE des BLANCS
- CÔTE de SÉZANNE
- CÔTE
- LARMANDIER-BERNIER
- CONGY
- ULYSSE-COLLIN
- Marne
- N

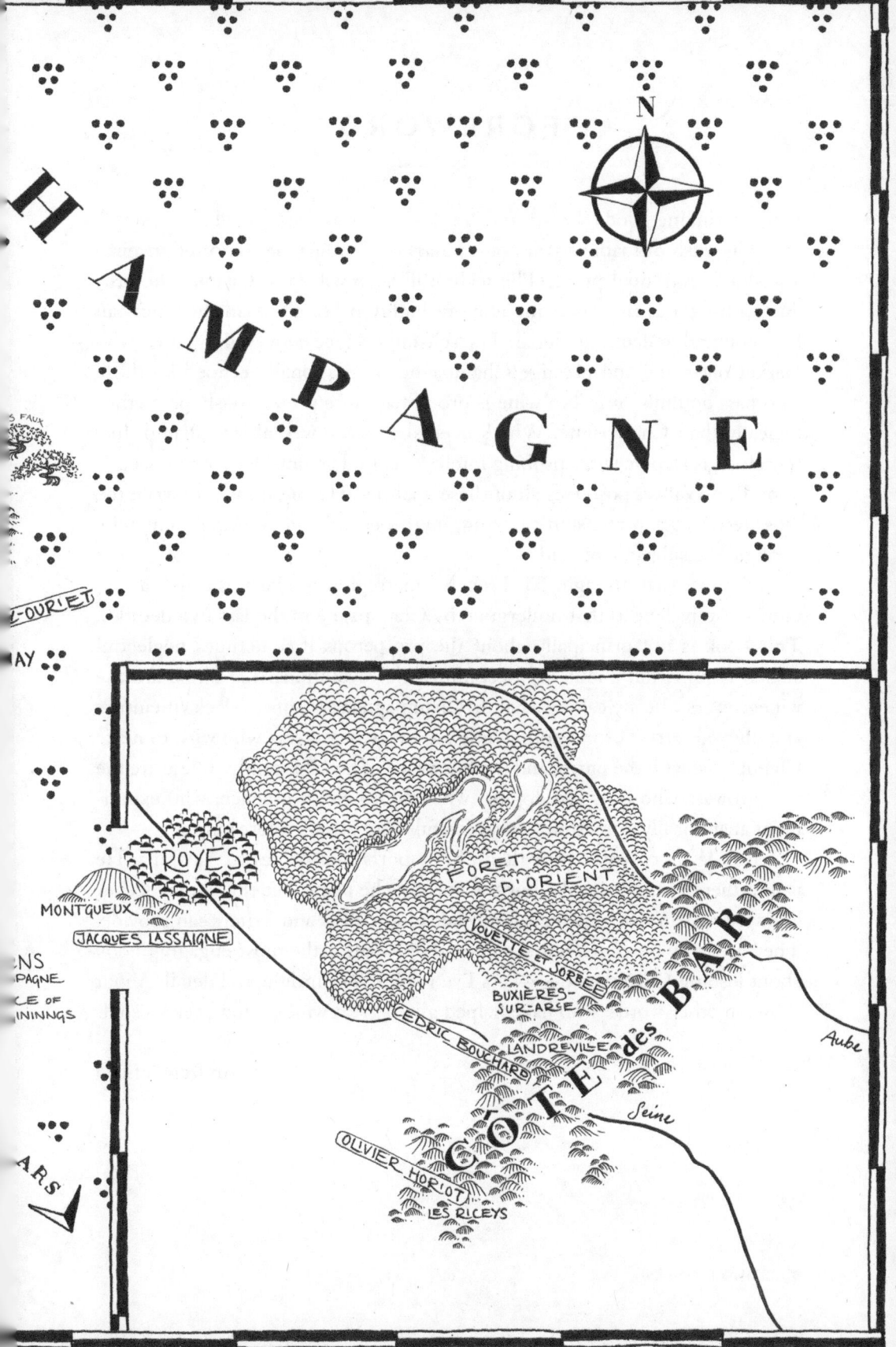

FOREWORD

I enjoy drinking good Champagne, but I don't always enjoy reading about it.

The gush of foam as you pour a glass of Champagne too often inspires a gush of reverential prose. The technicalities involved in Champagne production methods (no fine wine is more highly processed than this one) can be recounted in daunting detail. The self-importance conveyed by those who market big-name and prestige Champagne is occasionally echoed by those who pass opinion on it. No wine is promoted more pretentiously or mythologically than Champagne. What's needed to write well about Champagne, therefore, is laconic wit, a probing intelligence and an outsider's innate scepticism. Rob Walters possesses all of these qualities. He's used them to write the most refreshing, pretension-pricking, myth-busting and amusingly unfrothy book on the subject I've read.

Not just that, though. No French wine region has been through a revolution equivalent to that undergone by Champagne in the last two decades. This book is not principally about the prosperous if sometimes neglectful ancien régime, but about the uncomfortable revolutionaries. These are the winegrowers who are calling a halt to Champagne's easy life of slack viticulture and blurred terroir expression. These are the winegrowers who wish to make Champagne with the purity and truth to place of fine Burgundy. These are the winegrowers who question dogma; who rethink every practice; who experiment anarchically, sometimes unsuccessfully but always interestingly.

Rob Walters works with them; he imports their wines to Australia. He is not, therefore, impartial – but the portraits he paints benefit from a deeper knowledge than that which even specialist journalists and writers can provide. They are truly portraits, not sketches. The result is the most engaging book about leading Champagne growers I've read, full of insight and detail. About those, in other words, who have helped give a great wine region back its soul.

Andrew Jefford

DISCLAIMERS

Where the author pre-empts several lines of criticism, comes clean about his motivations and forewarns the reader that he is not without self-interest.

1: This is not a wine guide

It is a voyage through the history and also the landscape of Champagne, from north to south, in order to visit and comprehend some of the region's greatest artisans. The winegrowers we visit within these pages are those that I have been able to spend some time with and whose wines can truly move me. Real wines. Delicious wines. Wines that I would like even if they did not have bubbles. Yet, there are any number of other Champagne growers that critics speak highly of, whom I have either not visited or whose wines have not excited me in the same way. If you are after a more comprehensive guide to the wines of Champagne, I can recommend Peter Liem's champagneguide.net, Michael Edwards' *The Finest Wines of Champagne* (Fine Wine Editions) and Tyson Stelzer's *The Champagne Guide* (Hardie Grant Books). These guides cover many other growers that are not covered here, as well as all of the quality Grandes Marques (the most famous large houses).

2: The author is not completely impartial

The Australian Labor politician Jack Lang once said, 'In the race of life, always back self-interest – at least you know it's trying.' Let me be completely transparent: I am a wine merchant. I buy and sell wine. When it comes to Champagne, I work exclusively with first-rate grower-producers, and I import the wines of most of the producers covered in this book.[1] I am therefore far from impartial. On the contrary, I am completely self-interested. Having said that, I have not written this book in order to sell more wine – I could have spent my time far more effectively had that been my goal. Rather, I have written this book because I believe that the story of the great growers of Champagne is one worth telling and because I believe that the producers I have highlighted in these pages are making the most exciting wines in their region. I write about them for the same reason I work with them – because their wines are brilliant.

Warning: the author sells wine!

3: The arguments in this book are the author's, and the author's alone

The views expressed in these pages should not be seen as directly representing the opinions of the growers that are mentioned, unless of course I am quoting them. There are in fact a number of instances where my opinions may differ strongly from those of the producers we visit in this book – as is befitting an outsider.

4: This book should not be viewed as an exercise in Grandes Marques bashing

Most of Champagne's *worst* wines are in fact produced by lower grade growers, co-operatives and *small* négociants, not by the large houses or Grandes Marques.[2] On the other hand, the large houses account for the majority of exports, and as such they are the standard-bearers. In many markets, most consumers will never encounter a Champagne that has not been made by a négociant or a co-operative. It is in this context that I have critiqued the négociants and contrasted their culture, and the general practices of the region, with those of the finest growers.

PROLOGUE

In which a wine traveller has an encounter with a Champagne
from another planet and lets the reader in on a little secret

My epiphany came at a simple dinner at the home of a friend, Dominique Denis, in the city of Châlons-en-Champagne almost fifteen years ago. The wine was a bottle of Larmandier-Bernier's Terre de Vertus, the food a slab of thick, earthy, duck liver terrine. My host had simply pulled the Champagne from the cellar and poured it into my glass. It was cool, but not truly cold.

'Shouldn't we chill this?' I asked.

'Don't worry,' he assured me. 'What you are about to drink is a wine first and a Champagne second.'

This was a phrase I was to hear a number of times during subsequent visits to the region.

As soon as my friend poured the wine, I was disorientated. Intense aromatics of earth, salt flakes and crushed chalk rose from the glass. There were none of the toasty, bready, yeasty characters that I thought Champagne was supposed to have; this smelt like the ocean and like rocky soils immediately after the rain. In the mouth, the wine was like nothing I'd ever tasted from the region: a mineral blast that was somehow rich yet intensely savoury at the same time, like essence of mineral water – ferrous and with a long, citrussy, saline finish. It was wonderfully dry and cleansing and had none of the harsh acidity or the syrupy, dosage-driven texture and sweetness that you find in so many Champagnes.[3] And it went perfectly with the food, losing none of its personality or intensity. It slurped up the terrine and broke it down like a river carrying silt.

I was floored. What I had in my glass was not Champagne, or at least not Champagne as I knew it. Rather, this was a remarkably fine, complex *wine*, with the heady minerality that you might associate with a great Saint-Aubin (a high-altitude, rocky white Burgundy commune). There were nutty elements as well that reminded me of the finest northern Italian whites, and a salty, iodine-like tang that recalled the greatest Manzanilla sherry. Yet, for all its complexity and energy, the wine was wonderfully pure and transparent – fresh, tangy, citrussy and incredibly moreish. I guzzled it as quickly as it was poured into my glass.

'Shit – this is good!' I said.

'Always the poet,' said my friend.

At that moment, all my conditioning and assumptions about Champagne came peeling away like layers of old wallpaper. If you are not an experienced wine traveller, you might wonder why I was so surprised by the quality and interest of the wine in my glass. Well, perhaps I ought to let you in on a little trade secret: *not all wine people rate Champagne very highly*. Yes, everyone agrees that Champagne is the finest sparkling wine region on the planet, but in terms of 'Greatness' with a capital 'G', the wines of Champagne are rarely held in the same regard as the finest still wines of the world. You need attend only a few wine dinners or visit the wine cellars of some major collectors to understand Champagne's place in the pecking order. Champagne is the stuff you open when you want to celebrate something, when you're feeling frivolous or when you're trying to seduce. It's something you use to start a wine dinner, just to rinse the mouth out, before getting stuck in to the real stuff.

This was largely how I felt about Champagne prior to that night in Châlons. For years, the little voice in the back of my mind had been telling me that I should have been appreciating Champagne more than I did. Yet, the more experienced I became, the less the wines of Champagne moved me. They seemed to lack the authenticity that I came to associate with truly 'Great' wine, and so they rarely held my interest. And, when I focused critically on the wine behind the bubbles, when I let it warm up a bit and lose some gas, things only got worse. Far too many of the Champagnes I encountered – often very famous, revered examples – tasted heavily manipulated, simple, disjointed, austere, short and sugar-sweet. I could enjoy the 'prestige cuvées' (a winemaker's finest and most expensive wines) as much as the next wine traveller, especially if I didn't pay for them. But these wines never seemed to move me or intellectually stimulate me with the same power as the finest still wines, despite their being similarly priced or more expensive.

Perhaps I was in the minority? I couldn't be sure, although I was certainly not alone. I had heard lots of fellow wine travellers disparage Champagne. The wine groups that I was a part of rarely (if ever) organised 'Champagne only' events or even put on Champagne brackets.⁴ There was also an obvious lack of interest among some of my fellow tasters when the Champagne (invariably served only to kick off proceedings) was discussed.

Yet, something in all this did not sit comfortably with me, which was why I returned to the region: to decide, once and for all, if I had been missing something. More specifically, I had heard that certain small Champagne growers (or vineyard owners) were doing interesting things, and I wanted to see if the wines of those producers might make me think again about their region. The wine that I had in my glass in Châlons answered that question emphatically.

Over the years since that night, I have spent a great deal of time visiting, researching, tasting and thinking about Champagne, and I have often wondered just how I had arrived at such a dim view of it. It wasn't simply what I'd found in my glass. Many factors, most of which we will cover in this book, encourage the idea that Champagne is primarily a festive drink or, at best, a high-quality aperitif that should not be taken as seriously as the great wines of the world. For a start, this is how the region typically markets itself. The largest Champagne producers have always promoted their wine primarily as a celebratory drink. You don't see bottles of Grand cru Burgundy being smashed against the sides of ships or tipped over the heads of victorious racing car drivers; Burgundy is far too special and rare for that.⁵ Anniversaries, weddings, romantic dinners and celebrity parties – Champagne has always been pushed as a bubbly drink for bubbly people.

With this image naturally comes a certain superficiality; it's a challenge to build a reputation for both frivolous fun *and* high quality. The Champenois have attempted to walk this tightrope, yet the results have been mixed when it comes to the opinions of serious wine drinkers.

The web site of Moët & Chandon – far and away the largest producer of Champagne, churning out an estimated twenty-five to thirty million bottles a year – is a perfect example of the double-edged marketing that has both led to Champagne's incredible popularity and diminished its reputation in the eyes of serious wine travellers. On a recent visit, I discovered that the web site opened with a full-screen image of a glamorous woman in high heels passionately kissing a dishevelled, too-cool-for-school type in a nightclub setting. Bubbles rose up the screen, as though I was viewing this lip-smacking encounter through a glass of Champagne. The words 'BE FABULOUS' shouted out from the top right. At two tables, one on either side of our embracing couple, sat a lone man on one side and a lone woman on the other. Both were as glam as the kissers, and both seemed to be having a great time despite the fact that they were sitting alone. Were these the partners the kissers arrived with? The suggestion seemed to be that Champagne would let you enter this plastic world of beautiful people who wear shiny clothes at night. It might even let you swap partners. While the image made it clear that Moët was a FABULOUS drink for FABULOUS people, it was hardly the kind of advertising that we would expect for a serious wine.

The Moët web site trumpets its latest advertising program via a prominent link at the top of its home page. The last time I followed this link, I came to a promotional video starring Scarlett Johansson, Moët's ambassador until recent times. (Johansson has now passed the Moët baton to Roger Federer and has taken on the ambassadorship of SodaStream – the woman obviously has a thing for fizzy drinks.) The site informed me that Johansson 'truly embodies Moët's key values of glamour, generosity, spontaneity and living life to the fullest'. Hm. So Moët's key values have nothing to do with the vineyards with which they work? Or their terroir? Or the quality of their wines?

As the largest producer of Champagne, Moët may seem like an easy target. Yet Moët is not only big; it is also the most prominent Champagne brand by some margin and to a great extent sets the tone for the entire region. Most, if not all, traditional Champagne producers follow the same 'luxury goods' marketing logic: Piper-Heidsieck had Jean Paul Gaultier design a Champagne bottle that was tightly clad in a red leather suit with an inviting zip from top to bottom, Veuve Clicquot commissioned both Porsche and boat designer Riva to design Champagne cabinets and carry cases, and Dom Pérignon had Karl Lagerfeld create a Champagne coupe modelled on one of Claudia Schiffer's breasts.[6]

Should such marketing surprise us? Only if we have collectively repressed the true history of Champagne.

Sparkling Champagne was initially a sweet novelty wine created and sold by trading firms under international brand names. It has always been promoted as a luxury, celebratory drink more than a serious wine. Champagne originally had no pretensions to 'greatness', in the sense that we understand that term in the wine world today. How could it, when it was so often made from still wine that had not sold?[7] How could it, when it was dosed with at least 30–60 grams (and up to 300 grams) of cane sugar? How could it, when it was often doctored with – among other things – brandy, port, elderberry wine, cherry and raspberry liqueur, alum solutions, tartaric acid and tannins?[8] Nor did Champagne historically have any legitimate claim to being a *vin de terroir* (a wine of a specific place – typically, one of the key attributes of the world's most revered wines). Prior to the 20th century, the wine merchants or négociants of Champagne routinely blended the wines of other regions into their sparkling wines and rarely used the term 'Champagne' on the label, preferring instead to emphasise the brand name, along with the designation '*mousseux*' to indicate that the wine sparkled.

In order to discover the true history of Champagne, we will need to embark on two parallel journeys. The first will take us through the history of the Champagne region in order to discover how production of its wine came to be dominated by large négociants who buy grapes from across a vast area of land, blend them to a 'house style' and then market the wines under global brand names – a structure that differs radically from other top French wine regions. On this journey we will learn that it was the négociants of the area, as opposed to the vinegrowers, who created modern Champagne and fashioned the region in their own image, creating a wine culture driven by commercial pragmatism rather than by the search for the highest quality. The relentless commercialism of the négociants of Champagne still dominates a region that, despite the glossy image, is swimming in substandard and over-priced wines.

Our second journey will be through the Champagne region itself, through the landscape from north to south, in order to get to know the tiny band of 'great growers' who have recently surfaced to challenge (in quality terms) the hegemony of the region's much larger négociants. We will visit many of the finest of these 'grower-producers' – the artisans who are producing Champagne's most exciting and authentic wines.[9] This voyage will be a search for authenticity in a region dominated by marketing and advertising and promotion.

The great growers of Champagne have been around for only twenty years or so in any number, and they represent only a tiny fraction of Champagne's production, yet they have fast become the quality benchmarks for their region. This statement may shock those who are familiar only with the region's most famous brands, but in fact it makes perfect sense. When you own great vineyards that you manage yourself, work with higher viticultural standards and lower yields, know what you are doing in the cellar and work with smaller volumes, you are always going to make better wines than your far larger, more industrial competitors. This is especially so when those competitors need to buy a great deal of their fruit from conventionally farmed, higher yielding vineyards that they do not control in any way.[10]

The great growers of Champagne – many of whom we will visit in these pages – are reminding us that Champagne is, first and foremost, a wine, and not simply a luxury beverage. It is a product of the vineyard much more than it is the result of any winemaking hocus-pocus or 'art of the blender' (a term that we will encounter again in the pages that follow). They have proved, beyond any doubt, that when Champagne is grown and made with enough care and dedication, it can rival the very finest wines grown anywhere in the world – even with low or no sugar additions, even when it is not served ice cold, even when it is served with food and in large wine glasses rather than narrow flutes, even when the bubbles have gone. The great growers have created a new category of Champagne simply by growing wines of place, wines of terroir, wines that reflect a type of vineyard work and winemaking that had been completely lost to their region. Their wines have in turn awakened a renewed and powerful passion for Champagne in many wine lovers who, like me, had tired of conventional Champagne and who had, in some cases, completely lost faith in the region. In the pages that follow we will hear the stories of some of the very finest of these grower-producers, and we will visit their vineyards and cellars.

PART I

Where we follow sparkling Champagne's remarkable
metamorphosis from faulty to fabulous

Once upon a time, the Champagne region produced only still wines – wines that were not meant to sparkle. Before the 18th century, if a Champagne had bubbles in it, it was faulty, undrinkable, an abomination. This was a time that has been largely forgotten. A time when the wines of the region were sold almost exclusively in barrel, as bottles were still very expensive and difficult to transport. A time when fermentation was a poorly understood, unpredictable force, especially in a bitterly cold region like Champagne.

The region of Champagne, in the northeast of France, is at the climatic extreme for French winegrowing, with an average temperature today of around 11 degrees Celsius (and a lower one in the past). In this icy, marginal climate, ripeness was a struggle, and the Champenois were typically forced to wait until very late in the season for their fruit to mature. This meant that when the grapes were harvested, the cold weather was already setting in. When temperatures drop too low, wine yeasts become dormant. They stop consuming sugars, they stop their bubbling, and they lie sleeping in the wine until the temperatures rise again. This arrested fermentation is exactly what would occur in the chilly late autumn and freezing winter of the Champagne area; the wines would appear to finish fermenting, and yet there would still be plenty of residual sugar left in them for the yeasts to consume. Regardless of whether they were shipped or stored in barrel or bottle, these wines would begin bubbling away again when the warm weather returned the following spring.

Unbeknown to the Champenois (before the scientific advances of the 19th century), this new fermentation was simply the yeasts reawakening from their hibernation and beginning to feed again on the sugars that were still present in the wine. This reactivated fermentation was not a great problem when the wine was sold or stored in barrel, as it almost always was prior to the 18th century. In barrels, the gas given off by the fermentation could dissipate.

But as more and more wine came to be stored in bottle, this second phase of the fermentation resulted in fizzy and cloudy wines that often forced out corks and caused countless bottles to explode. Even if the bottle survived, the wine itself was often badly affected, becoming turbid and stinky and oily. This was why bottle fermentation was at first viewed as a catastrophe by the Champenois. The renowned wine merchant Bertin du Rocheret called sparkling wine 'an abominable beverage', claiming that bubbles were only 'proper for beer, drinking chocolate and whipped cream'.[11] Locals desperately tried to find ways to eradicate the problem. Although Dom Pérignon is falsely glorified as the 'inventor of Champagne', it appears far more likely that he spent a good deal of his time trying to *prevent* the local wines from sparkling. There is not one iota of evidence that Dom Pérignon made even a single bottle of sparkling wine. Rather, his abbey was renowned for its *still* wines, sold almost exclusively in barrel. Myth I (page 30), offers more details about this famous monk and the many legends that surround him.

It was only in the second half of the 19th century, when the work of Louis Pasteur started to make headlines, that the wine trade began to truly grasp the phenomenon of fermentation. Prior to this, although growers obviously witnessed the furious bubbling of the liquid and knew that this commotion was the key step in transforming their grape juice into wine, they had no idea about the dynamics behind this strange and seemingly magical process. Fermentation was typically described as 'boiling', 'bubbling', 'seething' and so on. The root of 'ferment' or 'fermentation' (the same words in both French and English) is the Latin '*fervere*', which means 'to boil'. The Latin word for 'yeast' is '*fermentum*'. In other languages, including English, the root of the word 'yeast' also derives from ancient words meaning 'boil', 'foam' or 'froth'. One exception is the French word for 'yeast' – '*levure*' – which comes from '*lever*', 'to raise', an etymology that obviously derives from the action of yeasts in breadmaking.[12] Today, we know that the alcoholic fermentation that converts grapes to wine is a process by which yeasts break down the sugars in the juice, producing carbon dioxide and, of course, alcohol, as the main by-products. In the 18th century, the science behind this process still remained a mystery.

And yet, throughout this period, something surprising started to happen: Champagne merchants began receiving ever more requests from their clients for bottled *mousseux*. As we have noted, prior to the 18th century, almost all of the wines of Champagne were sold and shipped in barrel soon after the harvest. Yet, as bottling technologies – superior bottles and corks – slowly became more widely available, some of the region's clients preferred to have these wines bottled as soon as possible in order to keep them fresh. The wines of a cold, northern region like Champagne were usually light-bodied and so quickly oxidised once the barrel had been opened and some of its liquid consumed. This was less of an issue for merchants, who sold full barrels, or tavern owners, who could sell through a barrel quickly, but it was a major problem for wealthy private clients who drank through their barrels of wine much more slowly. These consumers could not help but notice that the wine they were purchasing each year deteriorated over time once the barrel was breached. The solution was to have the wine bottled by their local merchant or in the region itself. Some of this wine naturally became sparkling.

In his book *Burgundy to Champagne: The Modern Wine Trade in Early Modern France*, Thomas Brennan writes, 'Historians now generally agree that it was the consumers of the white Champagne wines who discovered how to turn it into a sparkling wine. Some of them had bottled this wine during the spring, before it had finished fermenting, and it had become "bubbly, foamy" (*mousseux*) in the bottle.'[13] Clearly, a number of drinkers liked this foaminess and requested more of the same. Those doing the bottling somehow worked out how and when to bottle the wines of Champagne in order to deliberately make them sparkle. Bottle early, and you got some bubble when you popped the cork; bottle later, after the bubbles had dissipated in the barrel, and you would end up with still wine in your glass.

The English devised an even more systematic method to encourage the wines to sparkle. Tom Stevenson has shown that it was in fact the English who were the first to make sugar additions to all sorts of still wines and ciders with the specific intention of making the liquid bubbly. This practice is a key element in the famous *méthode champenoise* (Champagne method, now called '*méthode traditionnelle*', or traditional method), yet it was first presented by an English doctor and scientist, Christopher Merret, to the Royal Society of London in 1662, at least thirty years before it was used in the Champagne region – or anywhere else apart from the UK, as far as we know.[14] Cider-making had become popular in 17th-century England, and it appears that the knowledge of how to produce fizzy cider was soon being applied to wines. English merchants were also very keen on heavily sweetening and flavouring the wines they bottled, a practice the Champenois would later mimic.

Bottles of the kind that may have been used for early Champagne (circa 18th century) Thierry de Putter, Collector

At this time, England was the only market with access to strong enough glass (made in coal-fired furnaces and reinforced with iron and manganese) to withhold the pressure of genuinely sparkling wine. English glass was far stronger than the wood-fired equivalent from France; the French called it *'verre anglais'* (English glass), in order to distinguish it from their own, weaker glass. The English also appear to have had far better access to proper corks; the northern French still primarily used wooden stoppers wrapped in hemp in this era – obviously not an ideal closure when it comes to holding the gas in a bottle of sparkling wine.[15] From this, it seems clear that it was the English, not the French, who were the first to systematically create sparkling wine by refermenting still wine in the bottle. We explore this in more detail in Myth II (page 52).

Soon, growing numbers of clients of Champagne were asking for their orders to be delivered in bottle, some as still wine, some as sparkling. The Champenois were reluctant at first. For a start, bottling was wildly risky and expensive, and they did not have the appropriate know-how or technology. For these reasons, the producers of Champagne 'rarely bottled, preferring to ship their wines in barrels and leave the bottling to consumers or wine merchants in Paris and London'.[16] Eventually, they had no choice. In the first half of the 18th century, sales of Champagne's still wines were collapsing in the face of increased competition from winemakers in the south of France (whose wines were cheaper and richer in flavour) and Burgundy (whose wines were more esteemed). The declining reputation of Champagne's still wines played a key role in this collapse, as did the new railroads and canals that made the Paris market accessible to those other wine regions.[17] A series of poor vintages didn't help, either. The cellars of Champagne were soon full of unsold wines, and the growers and merchants of the region now realised that *mousseux* might in fact be their ally.

The birth of sparkling Champagne did not occur because the local vignerons or merchants believed it to be a natural evolution for their region or even because they thought it was the finest wine style the region produced. In fact, there is ample evidence to show that they often believed the opposite. Sparkling Champagne had such a poor reputation among growers and merchants that some of them called it '*vin du diable*' (devil's wine).[18] Rather, sparkling Champagne was born of economic desperation and the rising fashion for a gimmick wine among an elite clientele. Only when faced with these two conditions did the merchants of Champagne finally agree to bottle more and more of their wines as *mousseux*.

These merchants also realised that if their new bubbly wines were heavily sweetened before shipping, they were even more popular, and additions of between 30 and 300 grams of sugar became standard practice. Sweetening wines has a long tradition, especially with wines of inferior quality. The négociants of Champagne quickly discovered that the wealthy classes would pay a significant premium for this new, sweet and bubbly product – which was just as well, as *mousseux* was an expensive wine to produce. With these market realities, the traders of the Champagne region would have been foolish not to focus their attention on capturing and developing the international market for sparkling wine.

From that point on, the Champenois began searching for a process that would enable them to produce sparkling wine reliably. In so doing, the merchants of the region ceased to be simple traders and became true négociants, purchasing still wines from growers and transforming them into bottled sparkling wines. As we shall see, it was simply impractical for the growers of Champagne to produce their own bottled *mousseux*: they lacked the capital, the savoir-faire, the contacts and the appropriate economies of scale. They would continue to rely on the négociants to sell their wines, as they always had, only now, increasing amounts of it would be sold as sparkling wine at very high prices. Over the next 150 years, *mousseux* would become Champagne's point of difference, and it would ultimately prove to be the saviour of the region's wine trade. Even so, it would be almost two centuries before the production methods for sparkling Champagne (as we know this wine style today) were truly mastered and commercialised.

It is impossible to understand Champagne and its history without grasping that it was the traders, the négociants, the business people of the region, and not the growers, who launched and drove the success of sparkling Champagne. The Champagne region was one of France's most economically dynamic areas long before the development of *mousseux*. Its proximity to Paris and the wealthy markets of northern Europe, and its location on the trade routes between Flanders and Switzerland and between Paris and the German states, made it an ideal base for industry and trade. As early as the 12th century, merchants in Champagne were trading directly with many markets across Europe – mostly in textiles, but also in wine. The city of Troyes was a major trading centre, and Reims was where the French kings were crowned – events that brought elites and trading contacts from far and wide. The region was an ideal hub for merchants and traders who specialised in exclusive wares.

The merchants of Champagne were then (and remain today) commercial opportunists, constantly on the lookout for new markets and new products they could sell to their wealthy clients. Prior to the rise of sparkling Champagne, the region was known as much for fabrics as anything, with a number of textile-trading families also dabbling in wine. In fact, in the 17th and 18th centuries, wine was rarely the primary income of Champagne's merchants. Clicquot, to give the most famous example, was a textile business first, before it turned to wine. It was the profits these merchants made from their trade in cloth, among other things, that funded much of the early development of sparkling Champagne.

Those merchants who did focus on wine cast their nets far and wide. They had no special allegiance to the local wines of their region. Merchants in Reims and Troyes were among the major buyers of Burgundy in the 17th century, selling the wines on to the wealthy in northern markets. One well-known merchant, Claude Möet, sold a wide range of wines from different regions at that time, including Porto from Portugal. It was, of course, the same merchants who dominated and controlled the sale of their local wines. This control was only further cemented by the rise of sparkling Champagne.

To profit from the burgeoning trade in bottled wine, and *mousseux* in particular, the merchants of Champagne were forced to hold large inventories and to master bottling and sparkling wine production. They were forced to shift from being simple middlemen or brokers to being négociants, controlling the production of the wines they sold, and selling the wines under their own names. Local growers, who had historically sold their wines in barrel immediately after the harvest and traditionally relied on merchants to sell and distribute most, if not all, of their wines, moved easily into the role of base wine suppliers. The raw commercialism of Champagne's négociants was reflected in the way they tailored their wine production to each market – adjusting the level of sweetness, for example – and in the way they blended wines from across Champagne and from other regions to create house styles, or brands. As we saw in the Prologue, this commercial expediency can be seen in the way the region markets its wines today.

Unlike in the Côte d'Or, in Burgundy, where monastic orders had established the practice of selling wines on the fame of the village or the individual vineyard, by the time sparkling wine production emerged in Champagne, its monasteries had been removed from the wine game by the French Revolution.[19] This was why, as one historian recently put it to me, 'in Champagne everything started with the négociants … from the very beginning, [sparkling] Champagne was a wine of brand'.[20]

Sweet, cold and bubbly, Champagne was to become the world's first mass-market party drug. It not only went down a treat; it went straight to your head. And it was rare in the early days, since the process by which the wine came to sparkle was so poorly understood. Its scarcity, and the high prices that resulted from the hit-and-miss methods of its production, only made the wine more appealing to the elite. 'Wealthy people are always looking for something new, something unique,' a historian working for a famous house recently told me bluntly. The négociants of today want us to believe that sparkling Champagne was always a fine wine, as opposed to simply a novelty wine. To this end, they are constantly evoking the famous names that have enjoyed their bubbles: kings and their mistresses, tsars and generals, politicians and movie stars. Of course, such examples tell us nothing about quality. Elvis loved deep-fried peanut butter and banana sandwiches; that doesn't make them haute cuisine.

Champagne's négociants have long understood that once famous people start to buy a product, the marketing becomes very straightforward. It was common knowledge in the wine trade from the 16th century that if you could only get a monarch or an emperor (or his wife or mistress) to buy or serve your wine at court, you would be well on the way to fame and fortune. Today, film stars, fashion models, singers and musicians are the new royals, and it is the large, aptly named 'royalties' that encourage such celebrities to endorse Champagne. When it comes to marketing Champagne, very little has changed.

MYTH I

In the name of the father: Dom Pérignon was the father of Champagne

There are so many myths about Dom Pérignon that it's hard to know where to begin. The typical story we are told is that he was a blind monk who discovered the 'recipe' for producing sparkling Champagne and that when he did so he uttered these immortal words to his fellow monks: 'Come quickly, I am drinking the stars!'

For a start, he wasn't blind. He could see perfectly well. It's also extremely unlikely that he ever said 'I am drinking the stars!' as these words first appeared in a print advertisement in the 19th century, well over a hundred years after Pérignon's death. He was certainly not the 'father of sparkling Champagne'.[21] More remarkably, it appears that he never even *made* sparkling Champagne (at least not deliberately).

The records of the Abbaye Saint-Pierre d'Hautvillers where Pérignon was the cellarmaster from 1668 to 1715, do not contain any evidence of sparkling wine being produced under Pérignon's reign. On the contrary, the records show that the abbey sold most of its wine during this period in barrel, so it could not have been *mousseux*. The limited number of bottled wines that were sold by the abbey at the time seem almost certainly to have been still, non-sparkling wines, as they were never described as sparkling in the correspondence between the abbey and its customers. Sparkling wines were still exceptionally rare during this era, and it would therefore have been remarkable for any orders and confirmation documents to not clearly describe the wine being sold as '*mousseux*'. But they do not, simply because it was for still wine that the Hautvillers abbey was in fact renowned under Dom Pérignon, and because, like all cellarmasters of the time, Pérignon worked hard to try to *prevent* the small amount of wine he bottled from becoming fizzy.[22] As mentioned in Part I, bubbles were widely considered a fault in Champagne during this era; sparkling Champagne became a commercially plausible wine style only well after Pérignon's death.

Let's not sell Pérignon short though. He does appear to have been involved in encouraging, and perhaps even developing, a number of practices in the vineyards and cellars that led to quality improvements. Under his management, the wines of the Hautvillers abbey were very highly regarded by buyers of Champagne and sold for high prices. But again, this renown was for still wines, not for wines that sparkled.

Another myth about Pérignon is that he was the first to use cork as a seal. Cork was used by the Greeks and Romans, to seal jugs and amphorae, and on bottled still wine and cider in England for a hundred years prior to Pérignon joining the Hautvillers abbey. When it came to French sparkling wines, the monks of Limoux, in the foothills of the French Pyrenees, were using cork to make their sparkling Blanquette de Limoux more than a century before Pérignon was born.[23]

It is also often claimed that Pérignon was the first to make blended Champagne. Again, this appears to be a myth. What he was actually credited with, in 1732, by the French priest and writer Noël-Antoine Pluche, was the mixing of *grapes* from different sources at the press. By 1778, this claim, which we have no way of verifying, had evolved from 'blending the grapes' in Pluche to 'blending of wines' in a biographical note on Pérignon.[24] And so, yet another myth was born.

Most of the myths associated with Dom Pérignon appear to have been started by Dom Grossard, the last treasurer at the Hautvillers abbey. Demoted to the level of parish priest after the French revolution, Grossard seems to have been determined to romanticise and glorify the abbey's work. Significantly, Grossard was not a contemporary of Pérignon and was writing a century after the latter's death. While there was no evidence to back up many of Grossard's claims (and in fact much evidence to contradict what he wrote), the legend of Dom Pérignon spread over the next century. Myth became 'reality' when, in 1889, the Syndicat du Commerce des Vins de Champagne, the négociants' official promotional body, began publishing material that declared Pérignon the 'father' of sparkling wine and reaffirmed many of the achievements falsely attributed to him.[25]

The story of Dom Pérignon ended up being indispensable to the propaganda of the region, as it romanticised what was ultimately a mass-produced and technological wine style. The brilliant marketeers of Champagne understood that no one thought about the large wine factories of the region's houses when they were being told the story of a blind monk who had 'tasted stars'. Moët & Chandon perhaps understood this best of all and legitimised the legend even further by naming their prestige cuvée 'Dom Pérignon'. At the time of writing, the Dom Pérignon web site makes the claim that the Hautvillers abbey (now owned by Moët's parent company, Louis Vuitton Moët Hennessy, or LVMH) was the 'birthplace of Champagne', a statement that is patently untrue.

PART II

In which we drive along a haunted racetrack in search of a singular grower and discover, not for the last time, that all is not what it seems in the world of Champagne

We could begin our travels anywhere in Champagne, but perhaps the most obvious place is in the north, in the wine country that surrounds the historic city of Reims, 140 kilometres east of Paris. From here, we can work our way through the region, travelling from north to south, dropping in on the greatest grower-producers as we go. In fact, we could have started even further north, in the Massif de Saint-Thierry area, where there is one grower, Chartogne-Taillet, based in the little town of Merfy, who has a fascinating story to tell and some excellent wines to taste. Saint-Thierry was famous for its wines in the Middle Ages, and Merfy was its finest cru, or vineyard area. Today, Alexandre Chartogne is helping us understand why the wines of this region were once renowned. But we cannot visit everyone, and so we are starting our journey further south, just west of Reims.

Around Reims, locals make the helpful distinction between those villages that sit directly on the slopes of the Montagne de Reims (more a large hill than a *montagne*, peaking at only 280 metres), south and southeast of Reims, and those of the Petite Montagne, a series of slopes at a slightly lower elevation (240 metres at the highest point), which sit off to the west and southwest. The Petite Montagne area is home to a range of villages (from Gueux to Sermiers), and the soils here have a more complex, sandy geology than the purer chalk and clay of the *montagne* itself, a reality that results in strikingly different wines. This is as good a place as any to begin our travels.

To make your way from Reims to Gueux (pronounced 'gerh', like 'girl' without the 'l'), you drive westwards for a short way along the N31, then take a left at the D27, and before long you are approaching your destination. Via this route, as you near the town, you pass between two ancient concrete grandstands that sit like sentinels on either side of the road – the road into Gueux was the finish line of the French Formula One Grand Prix between

The road to Gueux

1950 and 1966, when it was known as the Reims–Gueux circuit. An Australian, Jack Brabham, won the last Formula One race to be held here, in 1966. I'm no motor sports fan, but when you drive between these two ancient concrete grandstands, covered in faded automobile and petrol ads, the effect is strangely unnerving, especially at night. It feels like driving through an old black-and-white newsreel. Everything slows down, and there is an eerie resonance of the crowds that once sat and cheered here. Locals have preserved the stands in largely their original state, yet time has had its impact on the concrete surfaces and on anything painted. You know that what you're looking at is a monument of the past, that the stands are empty. And yet, you can almost hear the crowds. There have been times when I could have sworn I saw movement out of the corner of my eye, tempting me to turn my head and look – never a good idea when you are driving on the wrong side of the road (as an Australian always is in mainland Europe). Of course, there's never anyone there. The ghosts of history live only in the world of our peripheral vision.

Gueux is a postcard-perfect village situated on the northern edge of the Petite Montagne. It is a ridiculously attractive, doll's house kind of a place that can make you forget its tumultuous history. Like in all French wine regions, the vine louse phylloxera devastated Gueux's vineyards in the late 19th century, and the village and vineyards were badly bombed during World War I.

Although the damaged buildings of Gueux were rebuilt long ago, the vineyards never truly recovered. Pre-phylloxera Gueux had some 200 hectares of vines. Today, it has 30.

In recent years, Gueux has been inundated by tree-changers – city folk looking for a calmer, less hectic lifestyle. The proximity to Reims, the parks, the golf course, the picturesque church on the bank of one of several lakes all add to the appeal. It is easy to understand the attraction of living in such a pretty town of fewer than 2,000 inhabitants, surrounded by vineyards, and yet so close to the metropolis of Reims. But I am not visiting for a change of lifestyle. I am here to call on a tiny grower-producer of Champagne by the name of Jérôme Prévost.

Prévost is revered among lovers of great grower Champagne for the minute quantity of age-worthy Pinot Meunier he makes, mostly from a single 2-hectare plot of roughly forty-year-old vines in a vineyard called *Les Béguines*.[26] He calls the estate *La Closerie*.[27] Prévost's wines have garnered a global cult following and are sold strictly on allocation.

I like the way wine writer Peter Liem gives you an idea of the frenzy for Prévost's wines. He says, 'It's virtually impossible to be a hip wine bar or wine store in Paris, or indeed, anywhere in France, if you don't have champagne from Jérôme Prévost. Selling a Prévost wine, or ordering one at a wine bar or restaurant, has become almost a badge of honour, a secret sign that affirms your initiation into an exclusive club of those in the know. Unfortunately, with an annual production of only about 13,000 bottles, Prévost's wine is not always easy to obtain.'[28]

In 1987, when Jérôme Prévost was twenty-one years old, his mother inherited a 1.5-hectare parcel of *Les Béguines*. Prévost soon found himself with the opportunity to take over these vines in a *métayage* (rental) arrangement with his mother, an arrangement that continues to this day. He's now expanded these holdings to just over 2 hectares. At first, Prévost did not have a calling to be a winegrower – he was simply attracted to anything that could help him escape from the 'jail of school', as he describes it. Also, his mother told him that she doubted that he could make it as vigneron, and Prévost found this an irresistible challenge. 'I don't know why I found this a motivation,' he once told me. 'I'm not normally like that.'

Once he was in the vines, his father encouraged him to make his own wine, yet this was easier said than done. He did not have any cellars or any

A close up of the stands

winemaking experience. So he sold his grapes to the négociants for the first ten years as he built up his knowledge. After his compulsory year in the army, he completed one year of studies at the Lycée Viticole (Winegrowing College) in Avize but says he didn't learn anything there, as he was skipping classes and drinking Champagne the whole time. Rather, it was his experience as a member of Valoriser (a word that means 'to add value' or 'to develop' and the name used for a group of young vignerons we will encounter in detail in Part XIX) in the mid-1990s that led him to definitively decide to make wine. Finally, he was introduced to the renowned Avize grower Anselme Selosse, in many ways the father of the great grower movement, and a man who we will meet much later in our travels. The two men immediately connected, and it was this friendship that enabled Prévost to become a producer. Selosse invited Prévost to work with him and allowed Prévost to use his winery to make Les Béguines. The first vintage was 1998, and the wine was made at the Selosse cellars until 2003. Since then, Prévost has been making his wines in the garage at the rear of his home in Gueux.

When I arrive at Prévost's home, he greets me at the door in shorts, an old t-shirt and a pair of thick socks. He smiles warmly and ushers me into his living room while he goes looking for his boots. I take a seat and look around me.

Inside *Les Béguines*

On the walls are framed photographs, on the ceiling an original light fitting, while in the corner of the room sits an old wooden and glass cabinet (Prévost calls this his '*cabinet de curiosités*' – it's filled with odd objects he has collected and small sculptures in glass and metal and paper). Almost everything I can see was made by Prévost's own hand. He is an artist at heart. He was a painter as a young man and later turned to sculpting, photography and other passions. He is also handy with words, a poet of the Petite Montagne. His interest in art has led to a number of artists visiting his estate or even working with him in his vineyards. He has also organised wine and poetry celebrations with a number of French poets, such as Valérie Rouzeau, James Sacré, Bernard Bretonnière and the American poet John Giorno. He once told me, 'I like words, because they are like vines planted in the soil of culture.'

I wonder how Prévost's artistic background influences the way he grows his wine. He says, 'I do not think winegrowing is an art. It can be done with recipes, but this gives wine without spirit. Alternatively, you can work with nature to allow her to do what she wants. Of course, you have to decide when to do two or three things, and what is most important is to do these things at the right time and with the right intensity. You have to listen to nature, with the sensitivity of an artist, perhaps. But then, an artist seems to have mastery of their art. A good grower? No – as nature is ultimately the master.'

Still, I can't help but feel that there must be an advantage to having an artistic or creative temperament when it comes to being a vigneron or winegrower. It isn't a requirement: a number of great growers are clearly not creative types. But as Prévost indicates, having a certain intuition, a certain imagination, would seem to be an advantage. Also, the drive to produce greatness and the longing to be responsible for something beautiful: both have clear parallels with the artistic drive.

Maybe we're just talking about sensitivity. Maybe it's the more sensitive souls, the thin-skinned ones, that are driven to make the 'right' decisions more often. Perhaps such souls cannot rest easily knowing that there is something that requires action in their vineyards and so respond faster and with more urgency at critical times. Perhaps such personalities cannot bear the thought of shortcuts or of methods that might be expedient yet would limit potential quality or terroir expression. Perhaps these types are the ones who cannot help but take the more difficult, more labour-intensive road when they know in their hearts that this is the authentic path that will lead to the finest quality. Herbicides, for example, are easy to use and save a great deal of time and energy. For many a pragmatic vineyard owner, they are indispensable. Yet these same products kill much life in the soil and limit the interaction of plant and environment. For the hypersensitive grower emotionally attuned to the life and health of their vines and soils, herbicides are very hard to justify. They will almost certainly avoid their use, or abandon them altogether.

Sensitive, emotional, creative, artistic: however we'd like to categorise this element of a grower's personality, it naturally pushes these men and women towards a certain approach that, in my view, generates far more interesting and authentic wines. It does not guarantee quality in and of itself; a number of factors must come together to do this (factors that we will explore in these pages), but I am sure that we are touching upon an element that can contribute to this end.

Prévost reappears, now with his work boots on, and we leave his house and walk up the gentle incline of his small street – a street that leads directly to his vineyard on the edge of the town. When you spend time with a great grower in France, there is always a multitude of insights to be had, but you must be prepared to be challenged and sometimes even to have your preconceptions turned on their head. Prévost tells me he heard the manager of the local oil refinery being interviewed on radio earlier that day. The discussion centred on the process by which they refined crude oil into petrol, and Prévost was struck by how remarkably similar this process was to the conventional method of Champagne production. This will seem sensationalist to defenders of mainstream Champagne, yet there are obvious similarities. In both cases, something born of the earth is processed until it barely resembles its original form. Compare the base wines of a conventional Champagne producer with the final wine in the bottle, and the transformation is remarkable. The finished wine is as much a by-product of the winemaking process as it is of the searingly acidic, characterless base wine from which it was fashioned. By the way, nearly all pesticides and many fertilisers are made from oil – another connection between the petroleum industry and conventional Champagne, which relies heavily on such products.[29]

As I stand with Prévost in his vineyards, the discussion turns to his soils and his vines. To examine the soils in Gueux is to be reminded how much we wine people tend to generalise. Champagne's soils are predominantly chalk, right? A bit of shallow topsoil and then solid chalk all the way down? As always, the story is much more complex on the ground – and in the ground – than what we find in most wine books. Prévost's soils in Gueux, for example, are predominantly made up of layers of alluvial sand and clay mixed through with chalky fossils. Over millions of years, the oceans came and the oceans went across this landscape, leaving layers of sand and tiny crustaceans that eventually fossilised. The sands of Gueux are known as *'thanétian'* (in French), or Thanet sand in English, after the geological stage (Thanetian) during which they arose. There is an area in Kent, southern England, known as the Isle of Thanet, which shares the same soils.

Each time the seas retreated from Gueux, terrestrial soils (clay) built up over the sands until the oceans returned to deposit another layer of sand and fossils. This happened many times, and Gueux was left with a deep, stratified soil structure: a layer cake of calcareous sand over clay over calcareous sand and so on. Such soils signal the remarkable complexity of the vast and varied Champagne region. We are, after all, talking about a region that covers some 25,000 square kilometres. It also brings home why the work of producers

Prévost in the vineyards

such as Prévost, whose 'living soil' or terroir-driven approach (still a rarity in Champagne) is so important. Different soils (not to mention aspects and climates) means different terroirs (different places), a wide number of which can make fabulous, stand-alone wines. What a travesty it is to have so many of them blended away. A deep understanding of these different terroirs and the wines they produce, in turn, gives us a far deeper understanding of the Champagne region as a whole.

Prévost and I discuss the details of his work in the vines, all of which stem from his objective to extract the most authentic, terroir-rich wines from his soils. He speaks about the interaction of the vines and their soils at a molecular level and the way that enzymes and cultured yeasts, widely used throughout the wine world, 'cut' this connection by shearing through certain molecular chains 'like a pair of scissors'. He uses this analysis to underline why maximising biological life in the soils is the key to producing terroir-rich grapes, as well as pointing out that picking fruit when it is fully ripe is vital if the grower wishes to maximise this potential. Both points fly directly in the face of the typical practices utilised in the Champagne region, where early, low-ripeness harvesting is the norm and where the use of cultured yeasts and enzymes in winemaking is almost universal. (Only a tiny percentage of Champagne producers allow natural yeasts to drive their ferments.)

I do not want to give the impression that Prévost is an idealist. Like all of the great growers I know, his views are formed on the basis of his understanding of nature and science, and out of his desire for practical solutions to practical challenges. Conventional Champagne can be critiqued because something of the beauty and quality potential of the wine is lost via its methods, not for any empty ideological reasons.

Prévost's vines were planted in the 1960s, before the 'great industrial revolution in Champagne', as he puts it, before mechanisation, chemicals and clones became the norm. For this reason, his vines were planted with an old rootstock that was chosen for quality rather than for potential yield. It's a rootstock that descends deeply into the earth but takes far longer to grow above the ground – the opposite of what producers were looking for from the 1970s onwards. These vines naturally give lower vigour and lower yields, and Prévost is happy with this. Lower yields mean riper, more intense fruit, fruit that will more deeply reflect the place in which it was grown.

Prévost's vineyards and much of the Petite Montagne are planted with the variety Pinot Meunier. Pinot Meunier is a sprinter. It grows very rapidly. This is an area with a lot of frosts in spring, and the fast vegetative cycle of Meunier helps the grapes race ahead of the period of danger. 'Pinot Meunier was the most widely planted grape for a long time in Champagne,' Prévost tells me. 'But it is almost never vinified separately. This is because it is not overly perfumed when young, and if it isn't picked ripe, it gives you nothing.' As we shall see, very little of the fruit in Champagne is picked truly ripe, in the sense that Prévost uses this term. So Meunier does not have the reputation it deserves. Of course, for Prévost, the grape variety is secondary to the terroir. 'I don't want to make a wine of the grape variety. I don't want to make a wine of the fruit. This idea is crazy. If people want to drink something that tastes of fruit, they should buy a quality fruit juice. Wine is not fruit. It's a culture. It's born of fermentation. There are two main types of AOC in France: cheese and wine.[30] Then there is bread. All are products of fermentation. Milk is not cheese. Wheat is not bread. It's the starting point. It's the same with grapes.'

After quite some time in the vines discussing the above, and many other issues, we head back down the hill to Prévost's cellar (in fact, it's a *cellier*, a cellar on the same level as the street), simply the converted garage at the rear of his small cottage. It is a tiny space with a couple of settling tanks and maybe a dozen barrels. The soil underfoot is the same as that in Prévost's vineyards, something he believes is important, as he sees the maturation process as a continuation of what has happened in the vineyard. The juice will ferment and mature in the same natural habitat as the grapes, the same mineral and microbial world that helped produce the fruit on the vines. The wild yeasts that came from the vineyard will also remain connected to their natural environment and therefore will be able to thrive during the fermentation.

As we stand talking, it occurs to me that so much of Prévost's life is based around things that are as small and basic as possible. He lives in a small town and in a small cottage that he stocks with his tiny figurines and art works. Then there is his small vineyard, his tiny cellar, his minuscule production. He avoids any unnecessary gadgetry. His cellar is so basic that at first I wondered how he could possibly make wine in it. In the small world that Prévost has built, there is nowhere to get lost, nothing that can be missed. By keeping things compact and simple, he can control every element of his life and his work, without losing track of anything. This way he can achieve an engagement, a precision and a level of quality that larger producers or those with more clutter in their lives can only dream of.

When I gesture to the simplicity of his cellar, Prévost says, 'If you aim to work as simply as possible, you rely on very little. If you have a machine, you must use it. If you don't have one, you will find another way, and that way is usually better. The force of technology can turn us into idiots. When I was young, I used to visit all the great vignerons to try to discover their secrets. I thought if I could understand what they did that was different, what tools they used, I would understand the key to great wine. One day, I visited Nadi Foucault [of Clos Rougeard in Saumur]. I saw that he kept his barrels high off the ground. "Aha!" I thought. "This must be one of his secrets." So I asked Nadi why he did this, and he told me that it was simply because this made it easier to get his barrel jack under the barrels to move them. It was a major lesson for me. Everything is practical. There are no secrets, only practices for achieving higher quality and techniques for making this process more simple. Of course, there was a kind of secret, in that moving the barrels by jack meant that he didn't have to pump the wine. So, in his aim to be as gentle as possible, it was practical to have the barrels sitting high.'

We begin tasting. Prévost does not label his wines with a vintage, even though his wines are always the product of one year. This is because he does not want to be tied to ageing his wine for three years prior to release;

in Champagne, a vintage wine must be aged for at least this period of time (three years from the 1st January following harvest) before being offered for sale (non-vintage wines must be aged for at least fifteen months from the 1st January following harvest). 'I am totally against this idea,' he says. 'This reflects the logic that a wine should be ready to drink the moment that you sell it, that the wine is the product of the *chef de cave* [cellarmaster or winemaker]. The *chef* prepares it for you to drink today. Yesterday, it was too early. Tomorrow, it will be too late. I don't want to make a wine ready for drinking. Wine isn't whisky. My wines are not racked, not filtered, not stabilised, no additions apart from a small dosage. In the bottle, you have everything for ageing. All the potential.'

I think I see his point: the growers in other fine wine areas of France do not generally cellar their wines before release, so why should the Champenois? And yet, it is a shame that so much of his wine is consumed too young. Lately, Prévost's position on this may have softened, as he has started bottling a proportion of his wine in magnums in order to 'force me to keep them for longer before I release them'. Magnums are also more likely to be cellared for longer periods by wine buyers.

I ask Prévost at what age he believes his wines start to show their best. He tells me that wine maturation is *'une histoire de l'énergie'* (a history of energy) and that he thinks that it's at around six years of age when his wines start to open and begin to drink well. This aligns with my experience, and, as though to emphasise the point, Prévost opens a 2007 for us to try. This was a vintage that was super tight (or restrained) when released and even as late as 2012 looked quite closed, but it is now spectacular. I get intense, complex aromatics of cereal, hay and ripe nectarines rising from the glass. Prévost says he is reminded of a winter forest. There is a pillowy texture, yet a pithy, driven freshness and a finish that is all salty, iodiney and very long.

The 'ready to drink' logic that Prévost rails against is not simply to do with ageing. A typical Champagne is a vast, multi-commune blend, and everything about its production – conventional, high-yield viticulture, yeast and enzyme additions, fining, filtration, dosage and so on – is designed to produce a standardised wine or house style that is ready to drink on the day it is released. Prévost, like all the great growers across France, considers that his work is about maximising the potential of the vineyards with which he works and then transferring as much of this potential as possible into the bottle. Then it is ready to sell. One terroir, one season, one wine. Each release will of

A poet on a push bike

course reflect the vintage and will age accordingly. Yet, it will be the end user who decides when to drink his or her bottles. On this, Prévost is in sync with all the great still wine producers of the world but completely at odds with his region.

To bring home the beauty in the way that Prévost thinks, works and expresses himself, let me end with another quote. While discussing the reasons why his wines take a certain amount of time to open and why they transform so completely with age, Prévost says, 'The longer the wine rests after fermentation, the more it remembers its original sweetness.' A wine that 'remembers' its youthful succulence as it gets older is an image that I will not easily forget. It's the kind of poetic thinking that gives us an insight into the creative mind and artisanal wines of Jérôme Prévost.

As I prepare to leave, Prévost rides past me on a pushbike. He has a cigarette in one hand, and with the other he makes the 'call me' signal as a devilish grin breaks across his face. I watch him wobble up the hill towards his vines before getting back into my rental car and pointing it towards Ambonnay, our next destination.

The wines of La Closerie (Jérôme Prévost)

Jérôme Prévost's vision was originally to release only one wine per year under the Les Béguines label. One wine from one vineyard (*Les Béguines*), one grape variety (Pinot Meunier) and one vintage. He has largely stuck to this, although there have been some small batch exceptions. Une Fois Pour Tout in 2000, d'Ailleurs (2003) and Les Béguines Climax (2012) were barrel selections of the Les Béguines cuvée that were allowed to age for an additional twelve months in the cellar before undergoing secondary fermentation in the bottle. Prévost made these wines to give him a better idea of how the terroir of *Les Béguines* expressed itself via a longer *élevage* (maturation) in barrel. There has also been a fabulous Rosé called Fac Simile, again the same wine as Les Béguines, but with the addition of some red wine made from Pinot Meunier grown in the same vineyard. Fac Simile has now become a regular, albeit tiny, release – Prévost intends to make it whenever he can make a red wine, which, at the time of writing, he has done every year from 2007 to 2015, except 2010. He has now also planted a new vineyard parcel, right next door to *Les Béguines*, with some Chardonnay, Pinot Noir, Meunier and Pinot Gris. At the time of writing, the vines here are still young, and so this fruit is currently blended into Les Béguines. It may produce an individual wine in the future.

Prévost uses only a little dosage, subject to vintage (typically a nominal 2 grams per litre – 12 grams are permitted), and the wines are fermented and aged in 450–600-litre barrels called '*demi-muids*'.[31] He has also dropped his levels of *liqueur de tirage* (the liqueur added to start the second fermentation in the bottle and create the bubbles) from the 2007 vintage onwards, and this appears to have had a significant impact on quality. Today he adds no more than 23 grams, down from 24.5 grams in previous years, resulting in slightly less pressure, fewer bubbles and less alcohol. The wines are much finer as a result. Prévost picks ripe fruit, as discussed, and with traditional levels of *liqueur de tirage*, his wines were often achieving natural alcohols of around 13 degrees, which he found too heavy. From 2007, the wines are in the low 12s (2007 was 12.3 per cent), which is a level that Prévost much prefers. If you compare the 2006 with the 2007, the difference is clear.

The wines of Jérôme Prévost are as complex and as intriguing as the man himself. To give individual tasting notes is close to useless, as each vintage is unique and the wines shift and change as they evolve. Even when you open bottles of the same vintage at different points in time, the wines are often very different. What I can say in general terms is that they are dry, vinous (winey), aromatic, floral, spicy wines with salty minerality and huge energy, drive and longevity. They are textured yet very tightly wound and savoury, especially when young. They can be wildly complex, they are never boring, and they are great with food. I like them a lot, especially with age.

PART III

Where we meet the revolutionary parents of modern
Champagne – science and industry

Champagne is a child of revolution. First, it was the French Revolution, which took the vineyards from the clergy and ensured that it was the négociants, the traders, who controlled the production of and trade in *mousseux*. Then, the Scientific and Industrial revolutions that swept across Europe in the 18th and 19th centuries allowed the Champenois, over time, to develop the know-how and technology to begin mass-producing their new, novelty wine style.

The textile trade was at the heart of the Industrial Revolution, so it's worth repeating that the Champagne region has always been a significant centre for the production of and trade in textiles and that many wine merchants were originally textile traders. They naturally brought the same spirit of innovation, commercialism and technological investment that drove the textile trade to their production of sparkling wine. Like textiles, Champagne required a great deal of capital investment, in raw materials, the latest technology and labour. The textile traders had the funds and experience to pull these elements together.

And yet, right up until the late 19th century, sparkling Champagne remained a relatively rare and highly unreliable wine. Only after a range of key technological and scientific breakthroughs could its production be industrialised, enabling it to become a consistent, mass-market product. The work of the French chemist Pierre Macquer and the chemist and statesman Jean-Antoine Chaptal (after whom the process of chaptalisation is named[32]), in the 18th and 19th centuries, led to a much deeper understanding of the role of sugar in the fermentation process. In 1831, Jean-Baptiste François, a chemist who lived in Châlons-en-Champagne, developed the method that came to be known as *'réduction François'*, which enabled Champagne producers to precisely determine the quantity of sugar required for the secondary fermentation in the bottle (often called the *'prise de mousse'*). From that point, the Champenois could accurately control the gas pressure that developed in their bottles of sparkling wine. Before this, something like 50 per cent of sparkling Champagne bottles had broken due to excessive pressure. To help with the process, in 1836, François also invented the *sucre-oenomètre*, a device that allowed winemakers to measure the amount of sugar in their wine quickly and simply.

Prior to François' work, sparkling Champagne had nearly always been the product of continuous fermentation; that is, it had been made using the *méthode ancestrale* (ancestral method), or *pétillant naturel* (naturally sparkling, now often shortened to *'pét-nat'*). In these cases, the wine sparkled because it went into the bottle with some residual sugar and so would continue fermenting naturally. Only after François did the *méthode champenoise*, or *méthode traditionnelle*, start to establish itself as the typical method of production. The discoveries of Louis Pasteur and his institute from the 1850s onwards in the area of fermentation and the role of yeasts were also vital. Then there was the improvement in glass quality, which we have touched on already, that led to consistently stronger bottles capable of withstanding greater pressure from within.

Champagne producers themselves contributed a number of breakthroughs. Adolphe Jacquesson invented the muselet, the wire cage that holds the Champagne cork firmly in place and stops it being pushed out by the gas pressure in the bottle. Barbe-Nicole Clicquot-Ponsardin (better known as the Veuve, or Widow, Clicquot) and her cellarmaster Antoine de Müller developed the process of *remuage* (riddling) – the gentle shaking and turning of the bottles to encourage all of the sediment (or lees[33]) left over from the secondary fermentation to gather in the neck of the bottle. The sediment could then be removed via *dégorgement* (disgorgement or dispelling), which resulted in a clear, shimmering wine. Prior to the invention of *remuage*, Champagne had looked dull and cloudy.

In 1844, the invention of the first dosage machine streamlined the post-disgorgement addition of the *liqueur d'expédition*, or dosage (sugar added at the end of the maturation process in order to 'balance' the wine and prepare it for market), a previously slow and inexact process. Then, in 1884, a wonderfully named Belgian, Armand Walfart, invented *dégorgement à la glace* (disgorging by ice), a method of disgorgement that involved dipping the neck of the

The story of Champagne isn't only about the vineyards

bottle into a freezing brine solution, thus trapping the lees, post-*remuage*, in a slush of ice. The method was radically faster, simpler and more precise than the historical process of *dégorgement à volée* (disgorging by hand).

All of these breakthroughs enabled Champagne production to be far more prolific and efficient. Champagne became, as wine historian Rod Phillips has written, 'a mass produced wine, using methods that owed much to new industrial techniques' – and to the latest scientific know-how. 'Champagne was, in many respects, a product of the new industrial world.'[34]

From that time onwards, the merchants of Champagne were able to produce a consistent, standardised wine in far greater volumes. And because *mousseux* could be sold at significantly higher prices than still Champagne (not because it was necessarily better, but because it was rarer, more difficult to produce and in great demand), the négociants were motivated to continue investing in new technologies as they arose. By the middle of the 19th century, sales of sparkling Champagne had well and truly eclipsed those of the region's still wines, and by the fin de siècle, non-sparkling Champagne had all but disappeared. The region of Champagne would forevermore be associated with bubbles.

Taking their cue from Europe's elite, the middle classes also developed an insatiable thirst for sparkling Champagne. No significant celebration was complete without the popping of Champagne corks. Sales of sparkling Champagne boomed, growing from just under six million bottles in 1850 to twenty-eight million in 1900. As Kolleen M. Guy writes in *When Champagne Became French*, 'Champagne became a subject of mass culture, a centerpiece of bourgeois society.'[35]

The merchants of Champagne found themselves perfectly placed to dominate the new frenzy for sparkling wine. They were highly attuned to the market and enjoyed powerful contacts and trading structures across Europe. Thanks to the decline in still Champagne sales, they had a ready source of cheap grapes and aged, unsold wine stocks. For this same reason, they had the incentive to invest in the technological advances required to produce more and more *mousseux*. They now had cutting-edge knowledge regarding sparkling wine production, as well as the perfect climate and soils for growing and producing such wines – after all, this was a region in which the wines sparkled naturally. In short, they were in the right place at the right time to take advantage of the new fad for sweet, bubbly wine.

The extreme, northern climate of Champagne, its soils and its grape varieties gave it an enormous advantage when it came to producing superior sparkling wine. This terroir advantage was one of the reasons Champagne was able to see off so many of its challengers in the early days.[36] And yet, only very recently have we come to see such terroir (in the sense that the finest French vignerons use the term) being truly exploited, with a view to producing wines that intensely reflect the soils in which they are grown. It is the leaders of this new, terroir-driven approach that we are visiting in our travels.

MYTH 11

First place: Champagne was the original sparkling wine

It wasn't. In fact, Champagne was not even the first *French* sparkling wine. The oldest written records we have of sparkling French wine being made and sold are found among the papers of the Benedictine community at the Abbaye de Saint-Hilaire in the wine region of Limoux, in the south of France. They date to 1531, over 150 years before any sparkling wine was being deliberately made in Champagne.[37] The monks of Limoux made their sparkling Blanquette in glass flasks sealed with cork, using the *méthode ancestrale* (explained below), the original process for sparkling wine production. Limoux is close to the Spanish border in the vast, southern French area known as the Languedoc and benefited from its proximity to the Catalan cork forests. With access to quality cork, the monks of Saint-Hilaire were able to develop the savoir-faire regarding when to bottle their Blanquette with just enough residual sweetness to ensure the wine sparkled, but not so much that the bottles burst. What resulted was a fizzy, off-dry and cloudy wine that was celebrated for its bubbles.

Sparkling wine from Gaillac, just to the north of Limoux, developed (and was widely appreciated) not much later – again, long before it was commercially produced in the Champagne area. So popular was the sparkling wine of Gaillac that '*méthode gaillacoise*' became a widely used synonym for '*méthode ancestrale*'. So while it may indeed have been the French who first produced sparkling wine on a commercial scale, it was not the Champenois who achieved this milestone. Nor were the first sparkling wines made via the *méthode champenoise* (or *méthode traditionnelle*) that would become the norm in Champagne.

In the *méthode ancestrale*, a wine is put into a bottle and sealed *before* it has finished its first fermentation – that is, when it still contains some natural sugar from the grapes and when the wild yeasts are still active. The primary fermentation will then finish, to a greater or lesser extent, within the sealed bottle, trapping some gas and thus producing a gentle sparkle. The wine can be disgorged, a process to remove the lees left over from the fermentation, but traditionally it is not, and so it will often be slightly cloudy. Today, such wines are all the rage (though not in Champagne, where this method is strictly prohibited) and are often sold as '*pét-nat*'.

The *méthode ancestrale* is still commonly used today in many French regions, such as Limoux, Gaillac, Bugey-Cerdon and the Loire, as well as in countless regions across the globe. It was also the methodology that produced the first sparkling Champagnes, until the *méthode traditionnelle* progressively took over.

In the *méthode traditionnelle*, a sparkling wine is produced via two separate fermentations. The first fermentation, no different from the fermentation through which any still wine is made, occurs in barrel or tank and creates the 'base wine'. Once this base wine has fermented to dryness, it is ready to proceed to the second fermentation. At this stage the wine has no bubbles. It is put into bottles along with a small amount of sugar and yeast, and the bottles are sealed with either a crown seal or a cork. The yeast and sugar addition will trigger the second fermentation in the bottles, with the added yeast consuming the sugar and creating a little extra alcohol and plenty of carbonic gas (that is, bubbles). The bottles will then be disgorged, so that the finished wine is clear. Once it had been mastered, the *méthode traditionnelle* proved to be far more precise and produced a much stronger fizz and a clearer wine. For these reasons, it became the favoured method of production in Champagne.

It isn't only the invention of sparkling wine that the Champenois cannot claim as their own; the Champenois were not even the first producers of sparkling wines via the *méthode champenoise*! As we have seen, it was the English who achieved this honour, around the middle of the 17th century.[38] Sparkling cider was a well-known product in England in the 1600s, and author and cider historian James Crowden has shown that the English were experimenting with corks and bottles for cider as early as the 1620s.[39] It was the English who first learnt how to make fizzy alcoholic drinks by heavily sweetening their ciders at bottling, before they applied this methodology to wine. This helps to explain how and why sparkling Champagne became highly regarded in England in the 17th century, when it was still considered a fault in the Champagne region itself.

What is less clear is why it was Champagne, of all the wines that could be put through a secondary fermentation and made to sparkle, that ultimately became the favourite bubbly of the British upper class and the world in general. Was the rise of sparkling Champagne due to the qualities that drinkers found in the glass, or was it to do with historical, cultural or economic factors? Although this will never be a question that we can answer definitively (I have done my best in Part I of this book), Champagne's success was clearly a combination of all of these factors and possibly more.

PART IV

In which the author travels to the mountain to meet the rock of Ambonnay, tries to get blood from a stone and ends up leaving on better terms than when he arrived

The most picturesque route to travel between the Petite Montagne and the Montagne de Reims proper is southeast along the winding D26, which hugs the edge of the Parc Naturel Régional de la Montagne de Reims (the forest and national park that carpets much of the mountain). This road also passes through a number of the small villages of the Petite Montagne whose names themselves sound like exotic wine styles: Vrigny, Pargny, Sacy, Écueil, Chamery, Sermiers. This is fitting: the wines of Champagne were once often sold by the names of their villages; in the case of Vrigny, as we are about to see, some wines still proudly carry their village name on the label.

Once you pass the town of Villers-Allerand, you are in Montagne de Reims territory, with the road dividing the dense forest of the *parc naturel* to the south and rolling vineyards to the north. A forest of trees in one direction and a forest of vines in the other. One mostly the work of nature, one exclusively the work of culture, and both equally picturesque – except in winter, when the barren, leafless vines suffer by comparison.

The forest of Reims is some 12,000 hectares in size, full of game, birdlife and a wide variety of tree species, including the famous *faux de Verzy*, bizarrely twisted, dwarf beech trees, a plot of which is located near the village of Verzy. It's worth a visit if you have the time. Before you reach Verzy, on the outskirts of the great wine village of Verzenay, you will also come across one of the Champagne region's surprisingly few museums of wine and viticulture. If you want to visit, look out for the signs to Le Phare – Musée de la Vigne. You are unlikely to miss it, as Le Phare is built around an old lighthouse that towers over the local landscape.

Why a lighthouse in the middle of the countryside? There is no practical reason. It was built in 1909 by Joseph Goulet of the Champagne house Goulet-Turpin, to promote his Champagnes. The lighthouse was lit at night and could apparently be seen from Reims. Originally, it boasted a restaurant and bar. It's a classic tale of the kind of ambitious marketing that has always been a part of the Champagne story. But Goulet's dream was literally shattered during World War I when shells struck the site. Despite the damage, the lighthouse remained standing until the municipality of Verzenay took over the site in the 1980s, restored it throughout the 1990s and finally opened the Musée de la Vigne to the public in 1999.

To enter the Montagne de Reims is to enter the dress circle of Champagne's great Pinot Noir villages. In Ambonnay, Bouzy and Verzenay we have three of the very greatest places for growing Pinot Noir in the area. These villages, along with nearby Aÿ, are capable of producing the most powerful, mineral, long-lived and profound Pinot-based wines of the region and have been famous for doing so for centuries. When history speaks, it is often worth listening, and history tells us that these villages (Bouzy, Ambonnay and Aÿ in particular) were well known for their still, Pinot-based wines long before the rise of sparkling Champagne. It is to the village of Ambonnay that we are heading, to meet with the *montagne*'s most renowned grower, Francis Egly.

The boundaries of Ambonnay take in part of the heavily wooded forest of the *parc naturel*. The rest is all vineyard, apart from the town itself (although even here there are some vineyards, as we shall later discover). Although the village has half the population of Gueux, it is far more famous. On its very edge, tucked in among the vineyards in the direction of Trépail, are the cellars of Egly-Ouriet.[40]

Francis Egly is a rock, a man who prefers his actions to do the talking. He clearly doesn't like to talk about himself. He also does not much like interviews. He doesn't tell me this directly, but his eyes betray him with their unmistakable look of impatience. So do his answers, which are short and often take aim at the questions themselves.

Before we even start, Egly spends a good ten minutes berating me for visiting him in May. Organising a rendezvous with Francis Egly can be difficult at the best of times (even for his importers), but he has a strict 'no visits' policy between April and June, as he has so much work to do in the vines and the cellars. He has made an exception for our meeting, yet he obviously did so reluctantly, and he wants me to know it. He explains that he can either put his efforts into growing great fruit and making great wines or he can spend his time conducting visits. 'I now get requests for three visits a day,' he tells me.

'So what am I to do?' He points out that neither of his children (yet) work in the domaine, and he is the only one who can host such visits.

As you can probably tell, Francis Egly is something of a straight shooter. Of course, I fully understand the point he is making. The man is a perfectionist and refuses to let his standards drop simply because he is now so popular. I respect that. We encountered the sensitive, creative type of grower when we visited Jérôme Prévost. Egly does not fit into this category. The quality of his work is driven by an obsessive personality that simply cannot stomach mediocrity. His dedication to his vines and wines is well known. As French wine writer Michel Bettane claims, 'Few producers can equal Francis Egly in skill and experience, and larger houses cannot hope to emulate the cultivation norms.'[41]

Little surprise, then, that Egly always strikes me as a man in a rush to get back to his vines and his work – without doubt, a good sign in a grower. But I don't want to give the impression that he is rude. In fact, he is typically very welcoming and generous. But he talks plainly and never leaves you in any doubt of what he is thinking. You always get the feeling that he has a lot on his mind and that, no matter how pleasant the visit, there will be much for him to do once you have gone.

Other growers usually speak of Egly with admiration and often mention in hushed tones that they have never had a chance to meet him, or, if they have, that they could hardly get a word out of him. He is something of a loner, a man who understands that he needs space and time and silence to think deeply about what he is doing if he is to achieve the unparalleled standards he sets for himself and his wines. But I digress. Egly has only one hour to spare, and the clock is ticking.

We are sitting in Egly's multilevel, concrete cellars, which were completed in 2006. These are the cellars of an uncompromising personality: spacious, solid concrete, gravity-fed, temperature-controlled, with every element of the winemaking and *élevage* taken into account. The density of the walls and the cool temperatures make the cellars ideal for wine storage, which means Egly can clarify and stabilise his wines without any additions, just as the ancients once did, (by putting the barrels outside in winter). Cooler temperatures also enable him to use less sulphur and ensure a slow, even maturation of wine in both barrel and bottle. The multiple levels allow for the use of gravity rather than pumps, and the amount of room, far more than Egly needs, means that there is never any pressure to move wine around unnecessarily.

The rock of Ambonnay, Francis Egly

These deep, dark cellars also reflect the introspective personality of the man. When you taste in the barrel room, it is like tasting in a bunker or an austere cathedral. Concrete walls, no noise from the outside world, total darkness when no lights are on, no visible clocks, no mobile phone reception: it's a contemplative, silent place, cut off from the outside world.

Finally, I am able to ask my first question. I am here to try to get to the bottom of the Egly phenomenon: I want to know how he came to be one of the icons of the grower movement. How was it that, so early in the piece (relative to most other important growers), his practices and wines made a radical divergence from the regional norms? So I start with a question to do with the differences between his approach and that of conventional producers. 'When you consider your approach to viticulture and winemaking, and how it differs from the traditional approach –'

Egly interjects, 'But I am traditional. It's those who follow different methods that are not traditional.'

Ambonnay vineyards at the base of the slope

'So let's talk about how your methods differ from the norm, then. And how you arrived at your way of working.'

'I've invented nothing. My path has simply been to search for ripe fruit from the vineyards I work with. Regarding the evolution of my work, nothing happens suddenly. Everything happens step by step, little by little.'

Egly's 'search for ripe fruit' cannot be separated from the quality of his vineyards. Only first-rate vineyards can produce truly ripe fruit in the marginal climate of Champagne, and this reality points us to a universal law of wine: to truly understand a great producer, the wine traveller must first understand the vineyards with which the producer works. It is the strength of the sites themselves, their ability to produce quality, that defines the limits of the greatness that can be achieved and therefore the reputation of the producer. The vineyards also explain a great deal about the style of wine that a producer offers. A producer, then, is only as good as his vineyards.

And Francis Egly has a remarkable set of vineyards. He produces wine from vines planted to 70 per cent Pinot Noir and 30 per cent Chardonnay on 12 hectares, most of which are in Ambonnay, with the rest in Bouzy and

Verzenay; there are also a few plots in Vrigny, which he inherited through his wife, Annick's, side of the family. Apart from the Premier cru, Pinot Meunier plots in Vrigny, all of Egly's wines come from exceptionally positioned Grand cru vineyards.[42] They are, for the most part, hillside terroirs facing south-southeast, with light, chalky clay soils over deep, deep solid chalk. Sandstone also plays a part in the terroir here. Mature vines in such Montagne de Reims vineyards (the average age of Egly's vines is forty years) naturally give wines of enormous power and richness – wines that remember their still wine heritage, if you like.

Vineyards are the starting point, but only when Egly's remarkable vineyards are married with his meticulous vineyard work and his search for truly ripe and expressive fruit do we begin to find a valid explanation for the quality and uniqueness of his wines. Regular ploughing (to avoid the use of herbicides), no pesticides, only organic compost, shoot thinning, leaf and fruit thinning when required to guarantee full ripeness and harvesting at exactly the right moment (far later than the norm) summarise the vineyard practices. Then, in the cellars, long lees ageing in barrel, very long lees ageing in bottle (with a usual duration of over four years and often more than ten), high levels of 'reserve' wines in each blend (40–50 per cent of older wines from previous vintages are included in the non-vintage wines) and very low dosage levels (always under 3 grams) are just some of the atypical practices that are followed here.[43] The results are wines that deeply reflect their place and express unparalleled fruit intensity and power and yet somehow manage to juggle that power with remarkable precision, mineral drive and finesse.

When people talk about an Egly 'style', they are really talking about the ability of his terroir to produce ripe fruit, plus the uncompromising practices mentioned above. Every single step introduced by Egly in the vineyard is there because he is convinced it enables his vines to produce more expressive, higher quality, perfectly ripe fruit. Every step in the winery is there because it allows the wines to better express their quality and their terroir. And that is all. What we are talking about here, as with all of the great growers, is not a house style but a terroir style.

A little history. Egly was an only child expected to take over his family's domaine once he reached adulthood. He returned home in the early 1980s after completing his studies and compulsory year in the army. He was only twenty at the time and initially worked with his father, Michel.

Egly's parents and their generation had lived in Champagne during a very different era from the one we know today, an era that was far less commercially successful and far more isolated. This was before the rise of a global wine media, before the internet and before importers like me went looking for interesting artisans. Small growers usually didn't travel, they didn't taste wines from outside their own region, and they lived in a culture so dominated by the big commercial houses that it was almost impossible to think beyond this paradigm. So nobody did. Egly's father sold most of his fruit to négociants.

It was only several years after Francis Egly became involved, in the early 1980s, that the estate began to bottle all of its production. Even in that era, being a Champagne winegrower was hardly a sexy profession. Yet, today, the best grower-producers are more revered in certain circles than the most famous houses. The generation of Egly's parents must be bewildered when they look around their region now and see the international success of the best growers.

But I want to know what got Egly started, what inspired him to break with the norms of his region. He tells me he could name many small, rather than large, influences. But after pondering this for a few moments, he says, 'Well, I should mention Michel Bettane. He certainly had an influence.'

This is no surprise: Michel Bettane, the renowned French wine writer, encouraged many of the finest growers and was certainly a key promoter in the early days of both Egly and Anselme Selosse (the renowned Avize grower who has played such a pivotal role in the great grower movement). Bettane began visiting Egly in the 1980s, not long after the latter had returned home. He not only influenced Egly by visiting and tasting at the domaine; he also introduced many people to the wines of Egly-Ouriet, and to those of Selosse (among others), through his writings and his trade contacts. Thanks to Bettane, many people became aware of what Selosse and Egly were up to in Champagne and of what might actually be possible in this region if a different path was taken: the path of the great grower.

'He encouraged us to seek more ripeness and also encouraged us to consider bottling our terroirs separately,' Egly says of Bettane. 'On one occasion, he visited and tasted wine from *Les Crayères* [one of Egly's greatest vineyards that is today bottled as Blanc de Noirs] in the barrel. He was amazed and told me I should bottle this wine separately. But I explained to him that it was only Pinot Noir – at the time, straight bottlings of Pinot Noir were almost unheard of. He said, "And? So you bottle a Blanc de Noirs. There is no problem with that." So we did it, first in 1989, as an experiment, then from 1992 onwards. It was a wine that got a lot of attention, and so we have done it ever since. From then, I have always sought to find ways in which I can improve quality.'

The Egly-Ouriet Blanc de Noirs was the wine that established Egly-Ouriet's fame and set it on the path to greatness. This was also the period during which Egly began to take full control of the domaine, as his father stepped back. For Egly, 1990 was the watershed year, as this was the vintage when he started to pick all of his fruit fully ripe (in the sense that he would use the term today). Then in 1995 he stopped filtration and the next year fining. This was also the period when he began to progressively introduce more and more oak maturation – not for flavour, but rather for the gentle exchange that barrels offer, as well as the ability to keep all of his parcels separate.

I have often heard comparisons made in France between Anselme Selosse and Francis Egly. These two are certainly the most iconic grower-producers in their respective areas and grape varieties: Egly in the Montagne de Reims and with Pinot Noir–dominant wines, and Selosse in the Côte des Blancs with Chardonnay-dominant wines (for the most part). In many ways, they are the foundation stones of the great grower movement and as such they share much common ground. Both blazed trails that others could follow. Both were heavily influenced by Burgundy. Both aim for fully ripe fruit and harvest significantly later than their colleagues. And both use 228 litre Burgundian barrels as their maturation vessel of choice. Undoubtedly, Selosse, as a more outspoken, open and charismatic figure, has been far more influential on the grower movement in general, yet the Egly legacy is also significant.

Despite their similarities – in truth, similarities that most vinous pioneers share – the two men are very different, and their differences are perhaps more important than what they have in common when it comes to understanding their wines. The difference that I find most striking is also the most challenging to put into words. A colleague who knows both men well described it this way: 'With Anselme it is always questions, while with Francis it is answers.' Although both men are deeply inquisitive, Selosse leaves many of his questions open. He will provide possible answers, but, unlike Egly, he isn't the kind of man that typically arrives at final, rock-solid conclusions. Selosse once definitively answered a question I put to him, paused, and then said, 'But, of course, if you ask me tomorrow my answer might be different.' While Selosse seems never to stop questioning his own answers, Egly appears to arrive at clear and self-evident conclusions and then moves on.

On practical matters, both men will weigh up all the information, conduct whatever trials are required and then make a decision on how to progress, yet Selosse never really seems to close off the possibility that there may be another path, and that this other path may in fact be the one he chooses the next time he has a 'gesture', as he calls it, to make. On the other hand, once Egly has established that a practice will aid him in his quest for greater quality, greater terroir expression or better fruit, he seems to apply the 'gesture' confidently and continues onwards.

Another way of saying this is to state that Selosse is of a more volatile, creative type – a more macro, imaginative thinker – than Egly, who is a brilliant artisan, deeply rational and able to focus clearly and precisely on whatever practical challenges are before him, ponder his options lucidly and proceed once the choice is made. I dream of having such a personality! We will meet Selosse again later. For now, it is enough to say that he and Egly respect each other's work and enjoy good relations; they are part of the same tasting group, Trait-d-Union, and Selosse buys Egly's Pinot Noir in order to produce his Rosé.

I am, of course, making assumptions about Egly. He is not the kind of man to discuss openly the questions he asks himself or the responses he arrives at. Yet, the proof appears to be in the wines themselves. There is always a temptation to look for similarities between the personalities of growers and those of their wines – like we do with dog-owners and their dogs – and in the case of Selosse and Egly, this temptation is well justified, as both men's wines do reflect something of them. Both are powerful figures deeply connected to their terroirs, and both make powerful wines that speak loudly of where they are grown. Equally, in the wines of Anselme Selosse, there has always been something of the wild, creative, inspired persona, from which you are never quite sure what you are going to get, while there is remarkable precision and consistency in the wines of Francis Egly. There may be fewer surprises with Egly than with Selosse, but chances are you will encounter something equally profound.

As we have seen, Egly is very clear about the connection between genuinely ripe fruit and the quality of Champagne. He tells me, 'If you do not start with perfectly ripe fruit, then you will not make a great wine. That is for sure.' In order to understand the provocative nature of such a statement, you need to recall that he is talking about a region where early picking of green fruit is standard practice. Egly often *begins* picking in Ambonnay when the rest of his village has already finished harvesting. Picking this late, in a region that is located so far north, where the cold and rain can hit so suddenly, is considered wildly risky, and this is one of the main reasons why other producers in the area have been unwilling to follow Egly's lead, despite his obvious success. There are other reasons. Egly's far lower yields, long ageing and minimalist winemaking seem too costly for other grower-producers to contemplate, even though they see the speed at which his wines sell and the prices he is able to command. Then again, in order for such an approach to make sense, they would need the same standard of vineyards, the same experience and skills, and so on.

One of Egly's passions is show jumping. He still competes, and sometimes when I talk with him it is easy to imagine him on horseback – sometimes trotting, sometimes stationary, sometimes galloping at a ferocious pace. His conversation ebbs and flows like this. When I ask him questions about the large houses, for example, at times he simply shrugs his shoulders. At other times, he is calm and entirely positive about their role in the region, saying things like, 'It is clear that they do a very good job [in terms of wine quality] when you consider the volumes with which they work. They are very important for the region. I have nothing bad to say about them.'

Then, when I mention again the difference between his terroir-driven approach and the approach of those who seek a house style, he gets the whip out. 'House style doesn't exist any more. What exists is the industrial style. Once, house style did exist, and then you could clearly taste the difference between the houses. Today, the wines are more and more neutral. This is because so much of the wine is sold too young, and young wine shows so much yeasty characters. The transition of the wine away from this yeasty stage takes time. It's somewhere between the third and fourth year in the bottle that a Champagne starts to lose its fermentation and yeast notes, and during that time the yeast feeds the wine. Only after this time is the terroir truly able to express itself, and this is the same for the house style. But now, the taster has been conditioned to think that these characters of yeast and fermentation are the real characters of Champagne.' This is a powerful point for the trade and for wine critics to take on board. The characters that many look for and praise in Champagne are often simply fermentation, yeast and dosage characters. It is time for us to start expecting more from Champagne.

When my time is up, Egly sees me to the door and makes me promise to be more thoughtful when making my future appointments. I promise I will, and we shake hands warmly. His mood has lightened considerably from when I arrived. Extracting words from Francis Egly has been a challenge, as I expected. But then, what is there to say when the answers are so self-evident?

The wines of Egly-Ouriet

Egly's wines can be imposing, especially when encountered for the first time or without context. These are contemplative wines – often monumentally powerful and intense, with such clarity of fruit and mineral intensity that they can stop you in your tracks. Yet, somewhat paradoxically, they also offer tremendous finesse. They have no equivalents in the entire region. The house equivalent would be Krug, or Bollinger RD, in terms of weight and power, yet the wines from these négociants have far more make-up and a more austere acid profile, which you often feel in your gums after the second glass. In short, they come from fruit that is less physiologically ripe. The wines of Egly also show clearer, purer, fruit-driven expressions (and are therefore more seductive) than those of any conventional producer.

The Egly-Ouriet range begins with a deep, intense and fruit-rich Pinot Meunier called Vignes de Vrigny. It comes from 2 hectares of old vines in the Premier cru village of Vrigny, the village we drove through as we left Gueux, on our way to Ambonnay. It has 2–3 grams of dosage.

After this wine, it's top-notch, Grand cru vineyards all the way, starting with the Brut Tradition (70 per cent Pinot Noir, 30 per cent Chardonnay), one of my favourite Egly Champagnes. Although this is Egly's 'entry-level' Grand cru, it is a wine that would embarrass many a so-called prestige cuvée from the famous brands. After all, how many prestige cuvées are 100 per cent Grand cru from only great sites and from vines at least forty years old? How many include 50 per cent reserve wines (if non-vintage) and are of low dosage (3–4 grams)? And that's without taking into account the viticultural and winemaking standards, which far exceed the norm. It is a revealing exercise to line this wine up in a blind tasting against large house prestige cuvées. It lacks for nothing. In fact, it has a purity of fruit (you can actually taste the Pinot!) that contrasts deeply with the more expensive wines' reliance on dosage and winemaking artifice. Its intensity and length will also surprise by comparison.

Then we move up a register, with the Blanc de Noirs Vieilles Vignes, a single-site wine chiselled out of the chalk of Ambonnay. It comes from Pinot Noir vines that are approaching seventy years of age and are rooted in the vineyard called *Les Crayères*. This is the emblematic Egly wine: remarkable depth and power of fruit yet with a pillowy, layered texture and an electric intensity of chalky freshness that keeps the wine dancing across the palate. This was a single-vintage wine up to the 2006 release. Since the 2007 base release, it has contained 40 per cent reserve wine and is all the better for it. It has only 2 grams of dosage. It is one of the great wines of the region and in my experience the greatest Blanc de Noirs. If I had to choose two wines to highlight the work of Egly, it would be this wine and the Brut Tradition.

Then there's the Extra Brut VP, so named for the long period that it spends on its lees.[44] Here, we return to Egly's typical blend of 70 per cent Pinot Noir and 30 per cent Chardonnay, with 40 per cent reserve wine and six or seven years on lees prior to disgorgement. Despite the length of time spent ageing, the wine remains pure, bright and downright youthful, an ode to the irrepressible energy of Egly's fruit. It contains 1–2 grams of dosage.

Then there are the monumental vintage releases: again, wines that spend very long periods on lees (usually ten or more years). These are made from 100 per cent Ambonnay fruit and are among the region's most powerful wines. Finally, as far as the sparkling wines goes, there's Egly's beautiful Brut Rosé. If you value purity and finesse, then this wine is well worth seeking out.

Egly also makes a Coteaux Rouge Pinot Noir that has no rival in the region for depth and power and very few rivals for sheer quality. It is a remarkable wine (as reflected by the demand and the admittedly very high price tag) that helps remind us that this area was famous for its still wines before sparkling Champagne became the norm. It completes a range of wines that are without parallel in the entire Montagne de Reims area.

MYTH III

The good and the great: Grand cru vineyards produce the best wines

Out of 319 villages in Champagne, 44 are classified as Premier cru and 17 as Grand cru. This leaves 258 villages that don't get either classification, a somewhat bewildering reality. The rating system was historically known as the '*échelle des crus*' (ladder of growths) and evolved as a structure to determine the payment per kilogram of fruit that each village would receive. While the *échelle* was officially abandoned, in 2007, the rating of those villages with a Grand or Premier cru has been maintained.

Sadly, the system is deeply flawed. First, it applies only to villages in the Marne department, and, second, it rates entire villages, or communes, rather than individual vineyards. In any village of Champagne you can find both outstanding and mediocre vineyards (and everything in between), so to group all of the vineyards of a given village under one classification is obviously problematic. It may be true that, in general, the best sites of a Grand cru village will consistently produce better wines than the best sites of a Premier cru village, subject to the grower and the vintage. Yet, it is also true that the best sites in a Premier cru village are often superior to the worst sites in a Grand cru village. And there is no reason to believe that the best sites of certain non-classified villages are not superior to many lesser sites in Premier or Grand cru villages. As always, it is the location of a site within a village that determines the quality that is possible. Having Premier and Grand cru vineyards is one thing; having them in the best sites in the village is quite another.

Then, the age and standard of the vines and the way they are managed are just as important, as a well-managed vineyard that is harvested ripe in a less famous village will invariably produce better fruit and better wine than a conventionally managed, high-cropping, early-harvested site in the most famous village. For these reasons, the classification system in Champagne is a poor guide to quality.

PART V

Where we head to 'Rahnse' to visit the cathedral and then travel south to Épernay, for a stroll down the legendary Avenue de Disney

While you're this far north, you should visit the ancient city of Reims and its 12th-century Gothic cathedral, Notre-Dame de Reims. Reims was one of the most important cities of Roman Gaul and is today the largest city in Champagne. Before you arrive, it's handy to know that 'Reims' is one of those tricky French words whose pronunciation seems to have little to do with the way it looks on the page. In French, it's pronounced 'Rahnse' with a rolling 'r' at the back of the throat: 'Rrrahnse'. You could practise your pronunciation while standing under the heavily sculpted portals of the cathedral's façade, packed as they are with statues of bishops and kings and biblical figures. You may also want to ponder the French monarchs who were crowned here by the archbishops of Reims, twenty-five of them in total, starting with Louis VIII, in 1223. The last was the Bourbon Charles X, in 1825.

Ponder also all the elites from across Europe who travelled to Reims to be a part of the coronations and to pay tribute to each new monarch. Naturally, predominantly local wines were served at the accompanying court festivities, and many of the visiting dignitaries would have tried the wines of Champagne here for the first time. Until the 18th century, all of the Champagne served would have been still wine, but this nonetheless helped set the stage for sparkling Champagne's success, by establishing a strong connection between the region's wines and Europe's elite. Such a promotional opportunity would not have been lost on the local traders – Reims was, after all, one of the great trading cities of Europe at the time, and the local wine merchants knew a sales opportunity when they saw one.

You may also want to stop by one or two of the big Champagne houses while you're here. Taittinger and Veuve Clicquot are based in Reims, as are Lanson, Charles Heidsieck, Piper-Heidsieck, Mumm, Louis Roederer, Pommery and Krug, among others. Some of these houses offer tours, and each will charge you accordingly. Usually, you'll watch a short film, hear a sugar-coated history of the house and of the region in general, visit the ancient part of the cellars – where very little (if any) of the real wine production goes on these days – and, to finish, taste one or two basic wines. It is a fascinating experience for the wine traveller, both from a pop cultural perspective and because you get to visit the ancient cellars, carved out of the chalk bedrock. Tourist buses pile into town for the experience, as they do in Épernay, for the famous houses that occupy its Avenue de Champagne.

To get from Reims to Épernay you head towards the southern edge of the city and get onto the D951. Once you arrive, if you follow the signs to the Avenue de Champagne, you will soon find yourself on perhaps the most famous street in the world of wine.

You only have to walk down the cobblestoned Avenue de Champagne to understand how much money has flowed through this region over the years. The mansions that line both sides of the street reek of 18th- and 19th-century decadence. These buildings often carry famous names like Pol Roger, Perrier-Jouët and, of course, Moët & Chandon, but there are also some buildings occupied by a few lesser known wannabes of the négociant world. Nevertheless, the avenue remains a shrine to the glory days of Champagne, a theme park where wine lovers can indulge in the fairytales that the Champenois like to present to the world. The avenue was designed to help foster the prestige of the négociants based here, and it has been maintained impeccably for this reason. Everything here is carefully constructed, with not a brick out of place. Like the marketing of the region in general, it is a work of genius and puts Disneyland Paris, only one hour away on the train, to shame. The only things missing are some actors playing the roles of historic figures.

I think this is a missed opportunity. Imagine a real-life Dom Pérignon, the supposedly blind monk who so many people around the world believe to have invented Champagne, pouring frothy liquid excitedly for any interested passer-by while shouting those famous words 'Come quickly, I am drinking the stars!' Imagine Madame Clicquot or her cellarmaster Antoine de Müller cutting holes in the kitchen table to invent the first riddling rack. Or Chaptal and Pasteur conducting the experiments that ultimately led to the mastery of bottle fermentation and dosage addition, practices so integral to the Champagne tradition. Surely such re-enactments are not far away? They could really take

Underground cellars at Laurent-Perrier in Reims

the experience of strolling down the Avenue de Champagne to another level for the countless wine tourists that travel to Épernay each year.

Even without any actors, you can already meet Dom Pérignon on the Avenue de Champagne. Just enter the courtyard of Champagne's largest house, Moët & Chandon, and there he stands, cast in bronze, atop a plinth. He is surprisingly tall, yet also stout, and wears the traditional habit of Benedictine monks. He must be seventy, by the look of the wrinkles on his face and the sagging skin under his chin, although he has the presence, the energy and the posture of a much younger man. His face is kindly yet also serious and knowledgeable. There is something sad, too. His pose is that of a great teacher. Imagine a much-loved grandfather who also happens to be a Nobel laureate, and you'll be getting close. In his left hand, he holds a perfectly formed bottle of a kind that I doubt was available in his day. The bottle has been freshly opened, and sparkling wine is foaming from its top. Pérignon's right hand is raised in a pedagogical gesture; he could be standing alongside Plato and Aristotle in Raphael's *The School of Athens*. It seems as though Pérignon is about to tell us something important regarding the bottle of wine he is holding up. Perhaps he is going to say that in this bottle is the greatest vinous discovery of all time. Or, perhaps, that it is an abomination that we must work tirelessly to eradicate. I have discussed in Myth I (page 30) which of these views Dom Pérignon is more likely to have held, but for the moment, frustratingly, his lips are sealed. This Pérignon is destined to stand silent before us, forever rendered mute by the bronze in which he is cast, fated to have other, more modern folk do the talking for him.

No Champagne company is more famous than Moët & Chandon, and I have come here today to take a tour of the cellars. Moët occupies two grandiose 18th-century buildings that sit opposite each other on the Avenue de Champagne, towards the centre of the town. On the eastern side of the street is the large building that hosts the public tours and the extensive Moët gift shop, fronted by the bronze of Dom Pérignon. On the other side is what is known today as Hôtel Moët, the mansion built by Jean-Rémy Moët in the 19th century. It is not open to the public, although it is available for hire as a function venue, and Moët uses it to host VIP guests. When I last visited, my tour guide (on the other side of the street) delighted in telling me that Kenzo Takada had recently been a guest there.

Moët, as the biggest brand in Champagne, naturally receives the most visitors per year, some 90,000 people. Each of these guests pays to be put through a painstakingly orchestrated tour of the cellars. Moët is by far the largest producer and landholder in the region, releasing, as mentioned, around thirty million bottles a year and owning over 1,000 hectares of land. It also buys fruit from an additional surface of 2,000-plus hectares. In fact, it has been the largest producer for a long time – since 1762.[45] One of the first things my group learns on today's tour is that 'a bottle of Moët is opened somewhere in the world every two seconds of every day, of every year'. This figure might even be on the conservative side – remarkable, when you consider the price of these wines.[46]

The tour begins with a five-minute film that offers little meaningful information and is more in the style of a long television commercial. Then, our tour guide takes us down to the cellars, or the '*caves*', as they are called here. These are not any old Moët cellars. These are meticulously organised and sanitised sections of the cellars, designed to present the idea of the Grande Maison as an artisanal producer. They have been prepared like a stage set in order to play their part in the illusion. Here, everything appears to be done by hand. We see bottles ready for riddling by hand, and we see ancient cellars that have been chiselled out of the cool, moist chalk, the score marks on the walls reminding us of the manual labour involved in creating these tunnels all those centuries ago. We see no vehicles, no machinery, no warehouses and, in fact, no workers. All the modern means of production are completely hidden from view.

We make stops along the way with our guide explaining the stages of the winemaking process and peppering her lecture with anecdotes about the history of the house and region. She manages to include many of the clichés and myths that we will tackle in this book and avoids any uncomfortable questions by pointing out that some things are too complicated to explain in the brief time we have together. Such tour guides in Champagne tend to be impressively trained, although their rote-learnt stories could be lifted straight out the PR brochures of the region.

As we come to the end of our walk through the cellars, we are ushered into a tasting room and served an ice-cold glass of Moët & Chandon Brut Reserve, the entry-level Champagne of the Moët range and the biggest selling Champagne of the region. It is remarkable only for the surprising quality that has been achieved for such a massive volume wine – a testament to the terroir of the Champagne region and the centuries of winemaking and technological know-how that have been built up by the best houses. Of course, in the context of the kinds of Champagne producers covered in this book, the wine is a caricature. It is a simple, yeasty, tangy sparkling that relies on significant sugar additions. It nonetheless remains considerably more palatable than many lesser grower and négociant wines. I ask for a spittoon, as I am driving and, well, to be blunt, this is not my sort of wine. My hosts seem very surprised, and several staff head off on the hunt until, finally, a small *crachoir* is found. Clearly, this is not a common request.

Within minutes, I am approached by two staff members who seem rather agitated. 'Are you a professional?' they ask.

Deciding to spit has apparently blown my cover. I acknowledge that I am indeed a wine professional, and they immediately seem concerned. I have been using a dictaphone, and now Team Moët want my assurance that I won't be using the audio for any public presentation and that I won't be putting it on the internet. I give them my word and tell them that it is only for my research, but they don't seem particularly reassured.

In the cellars at Moët

One of the staff, a young man who speaks perfect English, informs me that it was unprofessional not to have informed the tour guide that I was a member of the wine trade. I counter that, as far as I knew, the tour was open to anyone willing to pay, and nowhere have I seen it stated that members of the trade are not welcome or that they should announce their arrival to the Moët staff.

I make my way to the exit, half-wondering if a security guard will appear and demand to inspect my dictaphone. But I am being paranoid, and no such encounter occurs.

In the front courtyard, there is now a line of fellow tourists waiting to take a photo of Dom Pérignon. He continues to stare benevolently at the visitors, who flash their cameras at him. Of course, like almost everything we hear about the monk Pierre Pérignon, the statue is pure mythology. We do not know what Pérignon looked like, as there are no photographs of him (he died in 1715) or any drawings or paintings of his likeness that have survived, if they ever existed.

Like Moët's impressive statue of Dom Pérignon, we should not confuse what we find on the Avenue de Champagne with the real world of big-brand Champagne. The real world of Champagne is not open to the public. In fact, the large-scale, mechanised world of mass production that is the reality behind

Statue of Dom Pérignon in the courtyard at Moët

the region's global Champagne brands is deliberately hidden, even to most people in the wine trade. Still, as I have said, it is well worth a visit to one or two of these big houses, to see the historical cellars firsthand and to hear the entertaining stories they have to tell.

A very short walk away is one of the smaller, lesser known négociants of the Avenue de Champagne. I will not name it, for reasons that will soon become obvious. This producer offers us a typical example of how a small, mediocre house can use an address on the avenue in an attempt to raise the prestige of its brand and to sell more wines. You will not find the wines of this producer listed in any decent Champagne guide – the wines do not merit it. They are searingly tart concoctions of battery acid plus sugar, with no trace of fruit. And yet, there is a regular stream of visitors through the producer's tasting rooms on the avenue who walk out with bottles, all congratulating themselves on their purchases. Whether or not these sales justify the cost of the property I cannot say. Perhaps not, as the producer also rents out several serviced apartments that it has established on the site – apartments that I regularly stay in as I travel through the region.

MYTH IV

Silver spoon: Placing a spoon in the top of a Champagne bottle helps preserve the bubbles for longer

Although it is a widely held belief that putting a teaspoon handle (silver or otherwise) into the neck of an open bottle of Champagne can help keep the bubbles in the wine for longer, my own testing has shown that this is not the case. This conclusion has been supported by a study put together by a group of Stanford University researchers in collaboration with food science writer Harold McGee, which remarkably showed that 'leaving the bottle open and untreated worked better than hanging a spoon inside'. Whether this simply reflects a variation in gas pressure between bottles or whether, indeed, hanging a spoon in a bottle of Champagne actually accelerates the loss of gas is an open question. The science to explain this remains a mystery, as far as I am aware. A study by the Comité Interprofessionnel du Vin de Champagne (CIVC) also confirmed the ineffectiveness of the spoon method. French science writer Hervé This, who observed the study, writes, 'I think we can affirm now that a spoon, made of silver or stainless steel or of aluminium, has no effect on what the French term "éventage," or the loss of gas.'[47]

Not surprisingly, the simplest way to preserve both the bubbles and the freshness in a bottle of Champagne over the course of several days is to use a traditional Champagne stopper. Even better is the Perlage preservation system, which works so effectively in keeping Champagne fresh and sparkling for weeks on end that I have started importing it to Australia. My tests comparing bubble preservation in an open bottle with that in a bottle using a traditional stopper often show very little difference between the two wines for the first two days or so. Over longer periods, there is progressively a greater difference between the two wines, especially in regards to oxidation characters in both the flavour and aromatics of the wines. The bubbles however persist for a surprisingly long period of time, even in an opened, unsealed bottle of Champagne.

PART VI

In which the wine traveller drives south from Épernay to Avize and discovers that all that glitters is not gold

It's a short trip from Épernay to the Côte des Blancs, a largely continuous strip of mostly east-facing slopes that runs south of Épernay, and you have two clear choices of how to get there. The first is to head out of town on the D40 in the direction of Pierry and then take the D10 towards Cramant or Avize. This route takes you towards the vineyard slopes to the south and southwest of Épernay. The vineyards are today referred to as the Coteaux Sud d'Épernay, or simply Coteaux d'Épernay.

The Coteaux Sud d'Épernay area sits at the crossroads of the Côte des Blancs and the Vallée de la Marne (the latter an important region that we will not have the chance to visit on these travels), and its complex soils include the classic clay over chalk, as well as sandstone, flint and schist. Pinot Meunier can do very well here, and distinctive Chardonnay and Pinot Noir can also be grown.

Heading in this direction, you will pass by the town of Chavot-Courcourt, famous for its 12th-century Romanesque church and also the home of the only grower of genuine interest that I have stumbled across in these parts: Aurélien Laherte of Laherte Frères (a young grower making delicious and unique wines that are getting better and better). The village of Chavot gives us a clear insight into how much we tend to oversimplify the soils of Champagne. Most writing on the region talks only of the famous chalk soils; however the CIVC (the regional association that represents the producers and growers) notes that there are at least thirty soil types in the region, and fifteen of those exist in Chavot alone!

Stay on the D10 and you will travel directly through the vineyards and wine villages of the Côte des Blancs: Cuis, Cramant, Avize, Oger and Le Mesnil-sur-Oger. The road then joins up with the D9 heading to Vertus.

The other, faster way to travel through the Côte des Blancs is to head out

The Romanesque church in Chavot-Courcourt

of Épernay on the D3, past Chouilly, the Grand cru village just to the east of Épernay, until you hit a major roundabout, from where you take the D9 in the direction of Avize. It's impossible to get lost on this route – each wine village is carefully signposted on the right until you arrive in Vertus, at the bottom of the Côte des Blancs. As you enter the D9 you cannot miss the substantial local glassworks to your left, a dilapidated industrial complex that looks like a set from the *Mad Max* films. A major wine region like this needs to produce wine bottles, but why build an enormous and ugly factory at a major crossroads on the edge of the vineyards? Keep your eyes to the right and you'll enjoy a prettier scene: a wonderful view of the hillside towns of the Côte des Blancs and the vineyards that made them famous.

If you drive past any Champagne vineyard on one of those dazzlingly bright northern spring or summer days, you may notice something quite remarkable: the soil seems to sparkle, as if glitter has been sprinkled between the vines. Pull over and take a closer look.

The first thing that will become obvious is that the ground is flat, hard, unploughed and grassless. This is a bad sign in viticulture. It means the soil has been compacted and that the vigneron prefers to use chemicals prescriptively to treat the grass and weeds in his vineyard rather than cultivating the earth.

The road to Chavot-Courcourt

Cultivation (a gentle turning of the topsoil, as opposed to a deep ripping that blends the different soil levels) is considered by all of the best French vignerons that I have encountered to be an essential practice if the aim is to have a healthy vineyard that can produce superior fruit, rich in personality. Careful and well-timed cultivation de-compacts and oxygenates the soil and drives the vines' roots deeper into the subsoil by tearing the rootlings near the surface. This in turn encourages more interaction between the roots and the rocky subsoil, thereby increasing the potential terroir intensity of the fruit produced. As the vines' roots descend, they are also able to draw on deep, subterraneous reserves of moisture and are therefore more resilient during dry spells. A 'broken', cultivated soil assists in this process by allowing rainfall to easily penetrate the surface and move through the profile. Cultivation can also, somewhat counter-intuitively, minimise erosion by preventing run-off. Rainfall running down hard, flat, herbicide-treated slopes will build up speed and power, taking precious topsoil and stones with it. The broken, uneven surface of worked soil, on the other hand, tends to limit this occurring, as the water does not build up momentum but enters the soil more easily and more evenly.

Conventionally managed soil in Champagne

Perhaps most importantly, cultivation allows the grower to avoid using herbicides, since it works the grass and weeds back into the soil, in turn providing the soil with its own natural fertiliser. Chemical herbicides and pesticides not only kill grass, weeds and insect pests; they also destroy bacterial life, fungi, worms, beetles and other beneficial insects that play key roles in the interaction of the vines and their terroir. Vine roots naturally form symbioses with delicate fungi (called 'mycorrhizae') and with specialised bacteria that deliver nutrients and assist the vines to fix nitrogen.[48] By breaking down elements in the soil on behalf of the vines, the microbes form a direct link between the plants and their terroir. Chemical herbicides and pesticides sever this connection by destroying much of the life in the soil. Vignerons who use chemical herbicides and pesticides will also typically use industrial fertilisers to artificially feed their vines. This in turn encourages vine roots to stay near the surface, as that is where the food and water are to be found.

Non-cultivation, and the use of herbicides, therefore encourages vines to develop superficial roots that do not extract much from the soil and results in soils in which there is limited life, soils that are not oxygenated: soils that are

Woodchips being prepared for the vineyards

effectively dead. It is argued, again, by every first-rate French vigneron I know, that uncultivated vineyards produce fruit of lower quality and with less terroir intensity. This is a difficult hypothesis to prove beyond doubt, and yet the fact that all great French winegrowers seem to agree on it (even the iconoclasts and those sceptics who have tested it) speaks volumes.[49]

If there is any truth or value to the concept of terroir, maximising the life of the soil simply makes sense. Microbial life is required to break down elements in the soil in order for them to be taken up by vines. Not only are microbes and fungi part of the terroir, but they perform a vital range of tasks in allowing vines to interact fully with their environment and to produce fruit that can, in turn, express the place in which it was grown – that is, to produce aromas, flavours and structural elements that speak of the terroir. Inhibit life in the soil, therefore, and you inhibit terroir. A soil rich in microbial life can occur only with viticulture that minimises or avoids the use of synthetic chemicals, especially herbicides and pesticides, and careful and timely cultivation is nearly always the foundation stone of such an approach in France.[50]

French vignerons with any interest in history are aware of the shift away from cultivation after World War II and the move towards prescriptive usage of chemical herbicides, pesticides and fertilisers; they are also aware of the impact this change had on their vineyards and their wines. The lifeless soils, along with higher yields from overzealous fertiliser use, resulted in a flood of poor-quality, short-lived wines from the 1960s onwards – even from France's most famous terroirs. It was this crisis that led to soil scientist Claude Bourguignon's now famous observation, made in the late 1980s, that 'there will soon be no more life in [the soils of Burgundy] than there is in those of the Sahara'. And it was this crisis that spawned the radical shift back to cultivation and organic viticulture undertaken by so many top producers over the past twenty years.

But let's get back to the vineyards of Champagne and their sparkling soils. Walk through these vineyards and, again, take a closer look at the soil under your feet. You'll find that it is something quite surprising causing the glittering effect: crushed glass. Glass was an ingredient in the ground-up city rubbish, or *boues de ville* (also called '*gadoues*'), the dominant form of fertiliser that was used for decades in the vineyards of Champagne, from the 1960s until it was finally outlawed, in 1998. The legacy of this practice is that, today, many of the vineyards are full of powdered glass and other rubbish scraps. Visit a vineyard being grubbed up for replanting, something which occurs far too frequently and far too early in Champagne, even in some of the most famous vineyards (because younger vines produce higher yields), and you will see all kinds of junk in the soil: bits of shampoo bottles, Tetra Paks, dolls' heads, batteries, scraps of metal, bottle tops, crushed cans and so on. But there is no need to dig; on the surface of most vineyards, including the most famous, you will easily find specks of glass and shreds of blue plastic littered across the soil. Blue was the colour of the rubbish bags in which the *boues de ville* arrived.

Today, wood chips have replaced rubbish as the dominant 'soil addition'. This is also an industrial, low-cost and potentially destructive choice. Heaping wood chips on the vineyards smothers the soil, changes the nitrogen balance, negatively impacts life in the soil (pine wood is full of terpenes that inhibit insect and microbial life), and possibly brings a range of new fungi to the vineyards that are not indigenous but derive from the plantation forests. Vignerons remain unsure of the implications of these fungi, but one thing is certain: they have nothing to do with the previous terroir of the vineyards. The major advantage of the wood chips is that they give the soils more structure, minimising erosion and allowing vineyard workers to drive tractors across the vineyards in wet weather. Ironically, such artificial 'strengthening' is required because the soils have been weakened through prescriptive use of chemicals – soils high in organic matter and microbiological life tend to be much 'stickier' and resistant to erosion.

The Champagne region has been remarkably good at hiding any viticultural shortcomings from the rest of the world. This is why many still haven't heard of *boues de ville*. Andrew Jefford's superb work *The New France* is the only book I knew of, until the recent publication of the updated *Christie's World Encyclopedia of Champagne & Sparkling Wine*, that mentioned '*gadoues*' and openly analysed the problems with the viticulture of the Champagne area.[51]

On a positive note, vineyard management in Champagne is slowly changing. Apart from the lead being taken by the finest grower-producers, most of whom abandoned prescriptive chemical use years ago, the CIVC has been gently encouraging growers across the region to implement more 'sustainable' viticulture. Although much of this is simply lip service, it is a start. There have also been initiatives like the AMPELOS and Viticulture Durable en Champagne (VDC) certifications that encourage a move away from chemical usage and a number of houses are running 'trials' or implementing positive changes to many of their vineyard practices. To give only a few examples, Moët has planted crops between the rows in some of its vineyards while Roederer and Veuve Clicquot have begun trialling low-input – and even organic and biodynamic – viticulture in a few sites. Of these larger houses, Roederer appears to have taken things furthest, although it has not sought certification.[52] Clicquot and now Philipponnat also pay bonuses to growers for improved vineyard practices.

Regardless, to have any genuine impact on the style of wine emanating from the region – that is, to have any chance of resulting in wines with the interest and quality of those made by the producers we are focusing on in this book – these vineyard trials would need to be vastly expanded, as, for the moment, they are occurring across a relatively small area of land. They would also need to be matched with a significant drop in crop levels and a revolutionary shift in cellar work. So while these initiatives offer clear benefits for the environment, when it comes to the impact on wine quality I admit that I am skeptical. If the changes are not occurring to produce quite different, more authentic wines – and none of the major houses nor the CIVC are claiming that this is the case – it would seem that the motivation for such trials lies elsewhere.

The glassworks at the edge of the Côte des Blancs

All of this is not to say that a house cannot begin to work in a way that comes closer to the practices of the best growers outlined in this book, although size and market expectation are obviously barriers. Jacquesson, a much smaller, quality-focused house, is rightly held up as an example of what is possible. Owners and brothers Jean-Hervé and Laurent Chiquet have spent recent years ridding themselves of many grape contracts and deliberately shrinking in size, in order to achieve higher standards in the vineyards and the cellars – in an era when most famous houses have been aggressively expanding. Today, Jacquesson owns 28 hectares and buys fruit from only another 8 hectares. Jacquesson's current vineyard practices and yields are very similar to those of the growers we visit in these pages. There is a clear and simple logic behind this reality: Jacquesson wants to produce high quality, expressive fruit in order to make high quality wines that also speak of their terroirs.

Jacquesson is the exception. In fact, it isn't really fair to compare Jacquesson with larger, more conventional houses. Technically, Jacquesson remains a négociant, but in practical terms, when you consider how little it purchases (and then only from growers in the villages where it already has vines) and how it operates in the vines and the cellars, it is really closer to being a grower-producer. Actually, it works at a far higher level and with far lower yields than 99 per cent of Champagne growers!

When I asked Jean-Hervé Chiquet about the changes he and his brother have made to the estate – why they now buy so little fruit and work as naturally as possible in the vines – he answered, 'Our aim is quality, and if your aim is quality then you want to control as much as you can.' Getting such a clear answer from the larger houses is not so simple, although this does not mean there is no rationale behind their actions. Moët and Roederer are international brands that need a strategy for their environmental image. They also would be very keen to emphasise to their market how 'natural' their products are. Such image requirements should be important for a company that sells something we ingest – and even more so for one selling its wares at luxury prices. To this end, it makes sense for Moët and Roederer to be looking for ways to move away from the typical industrial viticulture of the region, so they can argue that their methods are sustainable and more in tune with nature. The ability to show journalists some organic or biodynamic vineyards is also a major marketing advantage. While this message can work very well in the superficial world of wine PR, it becomes more garbled when you look at things in a little more detail.

Nonetheless, it is all part of a (still limited, yet growing) movement away from chemicals that is obviously positive for the environment, regardless of the motivations.

Outside the houses, there is also an increasing number of growers who are cultivating their soils, avoiding the use of herbicides and moving towards a viticultural approach that works with nature as much as possible. The group that calls itself Terres et Vins de Champagne, for example, contains a number of producers who are taking this 'terroir first' approach. One well-known member of the group, Vincent Laval (of Georges Laval), heads up the Association Interprofessionnelle des Vins de l'Agriculture Biologique de Champagne (the Organic Association of Champagne) and told me that there are now over 60 certified biodynamic or organic growers in Champagne and over 1 million bottles of Champagne produced each year from organic vineyards. This needs to be put into context: there are around 15,800 growers in Champagne today, and the region churns out at least 300 million bottles a year. So we are talking about a tiny fraction of the region's output. Yes, there is progress, but it is painfully slow.

Of course, organic or biodynamic certification is no guarantee of wine quality. For great wines to be produced, three factors need to be present. First and foremost, you need great terroir. It's a truism that only great vineyards can produce great wine, but it is not often acknowledged publicly that there are plenty of lesser terroirs in Champagne. (The same goes for every other wine region, no matter how famous.) Second, you need an intuitive, skilful winegrower who understands what great wine is and what it should taste like, and the viticultural and winemaking practices that are most likely to bring about terroir-rich, authentic wine of the highest standard from their vineyards. Finally, you need the commercial structure, the capital and the demand to allow the winegrower to do all that is required to achieve the highest standards.

Certainly, working closely with nature in order to have a living, dynamic soil is a critical ingredient in producing great wines of terroir. But certification is not required to achieve this end. In fact, a number of important grower-producers in Champagne have avoided certification. They are not interested in paying money to be told what to do. They work as closely as possible with nature in order to make the finest, most authentic, most terroir-rich wines possible. Their wines speak well enough of how successful they have been. Certification is largely a waste of time for them. Many growers also prefer to have the option to use a chemical fungicide if the mildew pressure gets out of control. They would rather do this than risk losing their crop or being forced to use too much copper. Further, some of these producers are disillusioned with the certification bodies, as they have historically had nothing to say about high yields, under-ripe fruit and what happens in the winery in Champagne.[53] If your vineyards are certified organic but you crop high, pick early, inoculate with cultured yeasts, fine, filter aggressively, use enzymes and heavily dose your wine with sugar, then you are missing the point. Of course, you may have less of an environmental impact, but your wine will not hit any great heights. In this context, certification is meaningless.

Back to that glittering soil. The reality of the *boues de ville* is usually a jaw-dropping shock to Champagne lovers who have never heard of the practice. It certainly was for me. How could such a practice come about in such a famous and prosperous wine region? How could French vineyard owners, living in a culture that loudly and proudly espouses an ideology of terroir and stewardship of vineyards, let rubbish be dumped on famous vines for decades? How can they now let pine chips suffocate their soils and distort their terroir?

To begin to answer these questions, we need to recall one of the historical forces that has shaped the Champagne region.

It is important to understand that the size of most individual vineyard holdings in Champagne is minuscule. The Champenois have long been tiny landholders, with the average vineyard sitting at around the 1 hectare mark in 1929. Today, despite a lot of consolidation, vineyards remain small, with the average grower holding just 1.8 hectares (when the holdings of the négociants are removed). Thanks to French inheritance laws, a number of these parcels are owned by a group of relatives, some of whom do not even live in the region. Such landholders may have little, if any, cultural connection with Champagne and may have the land managed on their behalf. Their instructions will therefore be to maximise the financial return of their shareholding. While the majority of vineyard owners *do* live in the region, they also typically view their vineyard as an investment first – and extracting your sole income from 2 hectares (or less) of vines can't be easy. Many vineyard owners also manage or rent parcels owned by relatives who no longer wish to work the vines but still want a return. Again, as you might expect, the pressure will be to keep costs as low as possible and to maximise profits. This means using the cheapest available inputs and generating the highest achievable yields. This is only one of the factors that can help explain why Champagne has the highest yields and some of the most industrial vineyard practices of any French fine wine region.

PART VII

Where we encounter more threats to Champagne's 'Great Wine' pretensions and find out what conventional Champagne has in common with baked bread, roasted nuts and seared steak

In the Prologue to this book, I raised some challenges to Champagne's claim to 'Great Wine' status. Part VI addressed the typical viticultural standards across the region as one challenge. Now I'd like to address some others that are often raised by critics of Champagne both within and outside the region.

Let's begin with crop size. The vineyards of Champagne are the highest yielding of any fine wine area in France apart from Alsace; yet Alsace produces a lot of bulk wine – Champagne does not. This was not always a problem: Champagne's yields have increased tenfold since the 1950s and by 40 per cent in the last twenty years alone, and these figures take into account only what is legally harvested, not what is left on the ground or on the vines. It is a common viticultural practice in Champagne for growers to crop at 20–40 per cent above the (already high) legal levels and then harvest only what is permitted. This over-cropping is justified as 'insurance' against potential bad weather and loss to mildew late in the season.

The CIVC further encourages this logic by allowing producers to ferment some of their over-production (up to 8,000 kilograms per hectare) as *réserve individuelle* – still wine held in tank that can be drawn upon should they suffer poor yields in future years. So although yields may be usually set at somewhere between 10 and 13 tonnes per hectare – already significant numbers – the vineyards of Champagne are in fact characteristically cropped at far higher levels. To give this some perspective, the maximum yield permitted under the regional laws in Champagne in any given year is 98.4 hectolitres per hectare, or 15.7 tonnes of fruit.[54] This is higher than the maximum permitted for France's lowly Vin de Pays appellation (a classification typically used for basic regional wines) and more than twice what you find in quality Burgundy vineyards.

High yields and early harvesting have long been justified by many Champagne producers, growers and négociants alike, as well as by many outside the region, with the following logic. The *méthode traditionnelle* (the process by which Champagne is made) adds a great deal of richness and complexity to the final wine, so you need to start off with austere, relatively neutral base wines. High crops and early harvesting are said to produce exactly the type of base wine required to create a balanced and fine Champagne. On the other hand, according to this argument, if you crop vines at yields that are too low or pick grapes that are too ripe, the result will be base wines that are too rich and Champagnes that are heavy and lacking in elegance. Of course, this can be true if taken to the extreme: yields that are too low *may* result in heaviness in any wine style. But yields that are too low are very rarely a problem in Champagne. What is a problem is that people use this specious reasoning to justify yields that are far too high, even by Champagne standards, and to pick their fruit too early, before it is ripe (9 per cent potential alcohol being typical).

High yields in Champagne are also frequently justified by the claim that many of the region's greatest vintages have been the highest cropping years. Vintages often cited include 1982, 1990 and 2004. The problem with this argument is that in order to understand the role that high crops have played in the quality and style of a given vintage, we would need to have wines from the same vintage and sites but made from lower yields in order to make comparative tastings. From this we could deduce whether higher crops had aided or diminished quality. But of course such wines are not available, so our question becomes purely theoretical. Could better wines have been made in high-cropping vintages if the yields had been more reasonable? To my mind, based on my experience in comparing the wines of the finest growers (at lower, more balanced yields) with the prestige cuvées of the larger houses, the answer is a resounding yes.

Whether or not you acknowledge that high yields in Champagne are a problem – and many Champenois do – the notion that excellent Champagne should be made from austere, characterless base wines that derive from early--picked, high-yielding vineyards seems to radically distance conventional Champagne from other fine French wines.[55] French growers in other quality wine regions aim to pick truly ripe fruit with maximum flavour expression, in order to maximise the quality and personality of their wines and to produce wines that taste of where they were grown. The best growers of Champagne do the same, but they are in a tiny minority. If the initial wine lacks depth and character, and most of its final personality derives from the process by which it is made, we are closer to a commodity beverage than we are to an authentic, high-quality wine.

Which leads us neatly to another apparent challenge to Champagne's aspirations to be considered a 'Great Wine' by serious wine travellers: the way in which it is made. Rightly or wrongly, many wine buyers (both trade and public) associate authenticity today with a minimal approach in the cellars. Most top winegrowers, including those in Champagne, reinforce this logic by questioning every intervention they make and limiting their work in the cellar to only those actions that they are certain will help them to produce the best possible wines. The term 'minimal intervention winemaking' has entered the lexicon thanks to the approach of such growers. These same growers will also repeatedly emphasise that the quality of their wines derives primarily from the work they do in the vineyards.

On the contrary, many conventional Champagnes, even so-called prestige cuvées, are nearly always heavily manipulated, and this clashes with most of our preconceptions about fine wine production. Manipulations such as cultured yeasts and enzyme additions, strong filtration, chaptalisation and so on are all unnecessary interventions, and yet they remain standard practice among most Champagne producers. There is no need to analyse all these processes here, or to further debate whether they are good or bad in and of themselves. Let's just agree that they are not the kinds of practices that wine travellers have come to associate with Europe's finest wines.

Apart from those in the list above, there are two interventions that are pretty much unique to sparkling wines like Champagne: the secondary fermentation in bottle and the *liqueur d'expédition*, or dosage. The secondary fermentation is obviously a key element of the *méthode traditionnelle* and one that I believe helps illuminate, rather than diminish, Champagne's terroir as well as generally improving the quality of the wine. Any rudimentary comparison of a Champagne grower's still and sparkling wines will almost always establish this to be the case. In short, it is very, very rare to encounter benchmark still wines in Champagne, yet there are obviously many examples of benchmark sparkling wines. The *méthode traditionnelle* certainly brings something very positive to the wines of the region.

The *liqueur d'expédition*, the addition of sugar at the end of the maturation process, is a more complex area. It is, in fact, legal to add sugar at three stages during the winemaking process in Champagne. First, a producer can add

A Champagne vine laden with grapes

sugar in order to chaptalise the primary fermentation – that of the base wine. Chaptalisation is of course optional, but it is very widely practised, as it helps give the early-picked juice more body and texture and enables the producer to legally add up to 2 per cent to the volume of the wine. As sugar is cheaper than Champagne grapes, chaptalising is a cost-effective and legal method of increasing your wine volumes – a fact that sadly goes a long way to explain the popularity of this practice in the region. The second time that a producer can, and in fact must, add sugar is for the *liqueur de tirage* – a necessary addition of sugar, yeast and often other secret bits and bobs that creates the secondary fermentation in the bottle. Finally, there is the addition that we are most interested in here, the *liqueur d'expédition*, a shot of sugar and wine that is added after the Champagne is disgorged and before it is sent out to market.

This final dosage can vary enormously, from zero to a maximum of 12 grams of sugar per litre for wines labelled as Brut, the most common category. Until recently, the maximum that could be added for wines labelled as Brut was 15 grams per litre. Typically, most Champagne, even prestige cuvées, has between 8 and 12 grams of added *liqueur*, while the best growers tend to add between zero and 4 grams. There are any number of zero-dosage wines on the market these days, some of the finest of which are covered in this book. As outlined previously, most Champagne starts life as austere-tasting grape juice, and while the second fermentation in the bottle and the subsequent ageing on lees lend richness and complexity to the base wine, such wine will usually remain tart and hard without a significant dosage. The reason that the best growers can, and do, use far less dosage is that their fruit is harvested ripe and therefore does not require the same level of 'balancing'.

Let's be clear on two points. First, the absence of *liqueur d'expédition* does not necessarily result in better wine. In fact, many zero-dosage wines, especially those produced by négociants and co-ops, who are often simply trying to fill a gap in the market, are far less attractive than those with dosage additions from the same producers. Second, many wines from the growers we will meet on our travels contain small additions of *liqueur d'expédition* and appear to be better for it. Wines can sometimes even taste drier with a small addition of *liqueur d'expédition* than without: a strange phenomenon that I cannot explain. Champagne has an extreme, northern climate with an alkaline soil that can have around 40 per cent active lime content. This produces grapes that are normally rich in acidity, with a low pH, and it gives intense energy and a certain electricity to the wines. Very often, though not always, a small dose of sugar works to 'ground' the wine and make it more expressive. For the best growers, the idea of such an addition is not to mask but rather to 'open' and 'lift' the wine. Of course, we are talking about small amounts added carefully and based on trials – an approach that is taken by only a tiny percentage of Champagne producers. By contrast, the role of dosage in most Champagnes is to mask imbalances in the wine, to give the wine much-needed texture, sweetness and character and to simply make it more appealing to a mass audience.

Indeed, many of Champagne's famed flavours of toast, baked bread, biscuits, pastries and grilled nuts derive not from the fermented grapes but from the Maillard reaction, a process involving the interaction of amino acids with the added sugar in the wine. In other words, the characteristics have little to do with terroir and everything to do with generous sugar additions. The Maillard reaction also gives bread its brown crust, and it is implicated in many cooked foods: seared steak, caramel (when made from milk and sugar), chocolate, roasted nuts, maple syrup, coffee beans and so on. You can therefore see the connection between the aromas of many of these 'browned' foodstuffs and the characteristics that we often find in conventional Champagne. It is often claimed that the latter are the results of yeast autolysis, and, while this is indirectly true (amino acids that are required for the Maillard reaction are liberated as yeast cells break down), my experience is that the vast majority of low-dosage wines that have also had extensive lees ageing lack these characteristics. I have therefore come to believe that these aromatic notes are in fact the by-products of the Maillard reaction only and that they depend on generous dosage additions. The exception to this rule is wine from warm, sunny vineyards, especially in warm, sunny years. Such wine can have a touch of caramelisation from the sun's impact on the grapes themselves. Whether this is a type of Maillard reaction occurring in the grape itself I do not know.

A French friend whom we met in the Prologue and whom we will meet again soon enough, Dominique Denis, recently said to me, 'Sugar is like the fourth musketeer of Champagne: there's only supposed to be three: Pinot Noir, Chardonnay and Meunier.[56] Then you read the book and find out, to your surprise, that there is in fact a fourth musketeer and, even more surprisingly, that he plays a major role in the story!'

To get to our point, for most commercial Champagne, much of the wine's aroma, flavour and texture comes from the winemaking process rather than from the grapes themselves. This inverts just about every cliché of French fine wine, most significantly the idea that great wine is 'made in the vineyard', that the winemaker is merely a caretaker whose role, via gentle and minimalist handling, is to produce a wine that maximises the personality and quality already inherent in the grapes at the time of harvesting. This may be an ideal, yet it is an ideal that, when striven towards, produces the greatest wines of Europe. And it is an ideal that is followed by only a very small band of Champagne producers.

MYTH V

Holy Trilogy: Only three grape varieties are used to make Champagne

In fact, there are at least seven varieties used to produce Champagne today. Like almost all wine regions across Europe, Champagne was ravaged by phylloxera at the end of the 19th century. Phylloxera is a nasty vine louse that was imported to France on vine cuttings from America. At one stage in its life cycle, the phylloxera feeds off the roots of a vine, puncturing them and creating wounds that encourage the growth of infections and galls (scar tissue) that eventually block the flow of nutrients and kill the plant. While native American vines evolved with the louse and therefore developed defences against its attack, European vines were without such protection and quickly succumbed. Thankfully, it was discovered that grafting European vines onto American rootstock combated the effects of phylloxera. This both saved European viticulture and meant that all existing vineyards needed to be replanted. Today, the overwhelming majority of European vineyards are grafted.

Before phylloxera, a far greater number of grape varieties were cultivated across Europe than we find today. In some French regions, there are records for over a hundred varieties where now there are merely a handful. Historically, vinegrowers always preferred to keep their vineyards as diverse as possible. This tended to protect their harvests from total catastrophe: if one variety failed to ripen or was attacked by a blight, at least some of the other varieties would produce crops, and the grower would still make some income or some wine to drink. When growers were forced to replant due to phylloxera however, they focused on those varieties known to work best in their region: the easiest to grow, the most abundant, the most disease resistant and those that produced fruit and wine that was the easiest to sell. This is why Pinot Noir (roughly 38 per cent of today's plantings in Champagne), Pinot Meunier (roughly 32 per cent) and Chardonnay (roughly 30 per cent) came to dominate plantings across the Champagne region.

However, a handful of growers maintained small patches of other, lesser known varieties, and some of these have therefore had a continuous history in the region. Four of them are approved for use in Champagne: Arbane (or Arbanne), Pinot Gris (historically known in Champagne as Fromenteau), Pinot Blanc and

Petit Meslier. All are white varieties. The vines make up less than 0.3 per cent of the total vineyard area of Champagne, but the grapes are found in a number of today's wines.

Add Pinot Noir, Pinot Meunier and Chardonnay to the mix, and you get seven *permitted* varieties in Champagne, not three. I have also come across three other varieties, or cultivars, on my travels: Pinot de Julliet, Pinot Rosé and Chardonnay Muscaté (which may be the same as Chardonnay Musqué), the last being a natural hybrid of Chardonnay and Muscat. I believe there is still the odd Gamay vine kicking around, as well.

I import two cuvées to Australia that make use of all or most of the seven officially recognised varieties: Pascal Agrapart's Complantée uses six (missing only Pinot Gris), while Aurélien Laherte's Les 7 uses of all of them. A number of other producers also offer wines with these almost extinct varieties. Cédric Bouchard makes a 100 per cent Pinot Blanc from his parcel in *La Bolorée*; Bertrand Gautherot does the same from the *Fonnet* vineyard with Textures; Pierre and Philippe Aubry produce a wine called Le Nombre d'Or from all seven varieties; and Jean-Mary and Benoît Tarlant make a blend of Pinot Blanc, Arbane and Petit Meslier. Also, the Drappier family produces a cuvée from all of the four white varieties permitted; the Moutard family makes a straight Arbane; and the Duval-Leroy family makes a 100 per cent Petit Meslier. There are no doubt others that I have not come across. The wines point to a historic, more savoury and complex style of Champagne very different from the wine we typically consume today.

PART VIII

In which we pay a visit to Pascal Agrapart, and the
author acknowledges that he can sometimes miss what is
right under his nose by playing the man and not the ball

In recent years, Anselme and Corinne Selosse did something that baffled many followers of their famous estate. Already internationally renowned as icons of the great grower movement, the Selosses decided to open a boutique hotel-restaurant in a restored château in their hometown of Avize. They gave their establishment the name Les Avisés, which means The Wise Ones or The Ones in the Know and clearly plays on the name of the famous village in which they are based while suggesting that it will be mostly folk with their fingers on the pulse who end up at the place. While many friends initially questioned why the couple would make so much extra work for themselves (exactly the kind of bemusement that Anselme Selosse revels in, by the way), there is no doubting the results. Les Avisés is a very fine boutique hotel and is, by some margin, my favourite restaurant-hotel in the Champagne region (and I am not alone).

The kitchen is run by the talented Stephane Rossillon, while his wife, Natalie, coordinates the front of house. Don't expect three-star fluffery; this is a totally unpretentious, perfectly executed affair (much like the hotel) in a tiny dining room that can serve a maximum of twenty guests. Seasonal produce of the highest quality is cooked to perfection and presented via a set menu that changes daily. I tell you all this partly because I don't want you to miss out on a meal here the next time you are in Champagne but mostly because I was booked in for lunch following my tasting with Pascal Agrapart, and I was already fantasising about the meal that lay ahead. But first, I had some work to do at what is today one of the very finest addresses in Champagne.

Avize, where Pascal Agrapart is also based, is a small village in the heart of the Côte des Blancs, the strip of mostly east-facing hillsides that we have been driving along. This is the area of Champagne famous for its Chardonnay, hence the name Côte des Blancs, and several great growers are based here. In Avize alone are two of the greatest modern names in Champagne: Anselme Selosse and Pascal Agrapart. Agrapart certainly is a far later entry into the annals of the great grower hall of fame, as the story below will indicate, but there are few in the know who do not consider him one of the greats today. Agrapart's style of wine is very different from that of his pioneering neighbour, Selosse. In short, Agrapart harvests earlier and produces, on the whole, a more primary, less oxygenated style of wine than Selosse. I like both styles very much.

We wine people like our stereotypes. They help us make sense of the complex world of wine we encounter every day. This vineyard makes wines in this style; that one in that style. This vintage was terrible; that one was great. This year was good for reds; that one was good for whites. This vineyard is of Premier cru standard; that one is definitely Grand cru. This region has this type of soil (as though a vast area of land could be reduced to one type); this grape variety makes wines with these aromas and flavours; this wine style goes with that type of cuisine. And so on. No matter how many exceptions we come across, wine travellers tend to stubbornly stick to these rules, as they help us navigate through the often blurry, sediment-rich oceans of the wine world. The exceptions, we tell ourselves, must surely be the ones that prove the rule (until the rule changes, of course).[57]

In keeping with this world of generalisations, it seems natural that wine travellers might develop a stereotype for what makes a great wine producer. No, great growers are not all carbon copies of each other; but they nearly always share many common practices and philosophies. This is logical: many of the great growers learnt or were inspired by other great growers or by the same traditional practices. It makes sense that their practices would converge to a significant extent. Experienced wine buyers know this and will often 'scan' a new producer when they first visit, looking for signs that might suggest greatness (signs learnt, like a language, by observing other great growers). This is especially the case if it is a young grower or, let's say, a grower on the rise, not yet acknowledged as one of the greats but possibly heading in the right direction.

As we have touched on above, any grower with aspirations of greatness needs to be the holder of great terroir (vineyards that have the potential to produce great wines) and will manage these sites in such a way as to maximise the quality and the terroir expression in the grapes harvested. So a quick visit to the vineyards can tell you plenty. Talking to other great growers in the same region helps as well. They will certainly know the standard of their colleague's work in the vineyards. Tasting back vintages from bottle and upcoming releases from barrel is also an effective way of exercising due diligence.

But there are other, less tangible details that can be just as reassuring for the wine hunter. It's always nice if the personality and philosophies of the grower are of the kinds likely to drive them to ever greater heights, traits that will naturally lead them to feel obliged to honour the vineyards with which they work. If they are perfectionists, never satisfied, highly self-critical, these are often good signs. Such personality traits will send the right messages, as will a sharp intellect. They might drop the names of the great growers, or great artists or thinkers, who inspired them. The uttering of counter-intuitive and insightful statements is also somehow encouraging, reminiscent of other great growers and indicative of a deep thinker. Of course, all of this needs to be backed up by what is presented in the glass, yet these aspects of a grower's personality, along with many, many other details, help the wine traveller contextualise the quality of the wines they are tasting and hint at the long-term prospects of the producer. The wines may be good on a first visit, but will they always be so? Will they improve further? Great growers who produce great wines rich in personality often have personalities of the kind described here. But things are not always so simple.

In keeping with the above, when I visit a producer for the first time, I am always looking for signs of greatness. Or, to put it negatively, for signs of mediocrity, signs that might suggest that this is a producer who may not succeed in extracting the full potential from their vineyards. To this end, I have to admit, I was a bit slow on the uptake with Pascal Agrapart. In fact, the first time I visited Agrapart (in the early 2000s), I was immediately thrown.

First, the wine labels at that time were poorly done. Perhaps this seems superficial, and on one level it is. Yet a professional wine buyer is, by definition, a critical observer. They enter the domaine of the wine producer and ask, 'Am I moved by what I find here?' To this end, every aesthetic element is to be considered, including packaging. There is no question that bad labels make wines much harder to sell, no matter how good the wines are. Anyone in the wine trade will tell you this. And poor labels may tell you something about the producer's eye for detail or suggest that they are not fully across all areas of their production. Agrapart's labels weren't just bad; they were *really* bad. They looked shoddy and cheaply done. So I was instantly worried. Then, the range

Vineyards in Avize

as a whole was inconsistent. There were certainly some stunning wines, yet there were also some wines that failed to excite me or in which one element of the winemaking did not seem to have worked.

Pascal Agrapart himself clearly knew his stuff but was modest, reserved and down to earth. No mixed metaphors, complex allusions or word games. Here was a practical man who answered questions simply and humbly and without pretension. He was open and very likeable, but there were no grandiose visions, simply a clear discussion on the quality and terroir expression of each wine. He suggested no mystery or magic in how he approached things, only logic and experience – his own, and those of the people who had come before him. He didn't seem to be in any great rush to get where he was going. And he gave no hints of the changes that were to come.

I realise now that I missed the signs I was offered. This was, in fact, a producer in transition and heading to greatness. I could see the potential and taste the remarkable standard of the top wines, but the packaging and the inconsistencies in the range raised questions in my mind and dulled my intuition. And Agrapart's down-to-earth personality let me underestimate him, when all the while it was the clue to his future greatness.

Pascal Agrapart in the vines

Of course, the best of Agrapart's wines kept me visiting. With each visit, the wines seemed stronger; there were fewer inconsistencies, more highlights; and one wine, the Rosé, had even been abandoned, because Agrapart was not convinced by it. The packaging remained mediocre for a few more years, but the wines were too good to ignore. I finally shipped a few cases of selected cuvées, and for the wine that I bought in the largest quantities (Terroirs) I convinced Agrapart to use an alternative label that I had spied on display in his tasting room. It turned out that this label had been originally designed by Agrapart's US importer as a special one-off for the 2000 vintage and included an abstract painting of a nude woman. Agrapart explained to me that it had been rejected by US customs, because it depicted, no matter how vaguely, a pair of female breasts. So, it was available for us to use if we wanted. Thank you, US customs.

I did not buy the number of bottles that were made available to me (something that now I regret) but shipped a conservative amount, to be sure I would not get stuck with stock. Those old apprehensions were still there. Still, I did bring some wine to Australia, and the cuvée with the boobs sold well. The two cuvées I bought under the old labels (Minéral and Avizoise) were brilliant wines but sold very slowly, presumably because of the packaging. I kept visiting and kept shipping small quantities.

Then, very rapidly, everything seemed to change. In the space of a few years, Agrapart trimmed the range, completely upgraded his packaging and introduced two new, potentially revolutionary cuvées, called Expérience and Complantée. This gave the estate five outstanding *vin de terroir* cuvées. It all happened over the course of a few vintages, but it seemed to be in the blink of an eye. The top wines got even better, the press wrote glowing articles, and a star was born.

Clearly, this evolution was what Agrapart was always working towards, but I was slow to pick up on it, and he certainly did not try to sell it to me – to his credit – selling is not his thing. Agrapart's personality is that of a true farmer, a man of the soil. He is no marketeer, which is why he was so unwilling to proclaim the bright future he was guarding in his imagination. I initially assumed that the range would remain inconsistent, but now every wine is exceptional, tastes remarkable, and the whole world seemingly wants an allocation. I have regularly tried to significantly increase the size of my order, but there is no longer enough wine to go around.

Of course, it could be worse. I could have missed out altogether! In fact, I get an allocation of every cuvée, and I am grateful for every bottle.

This experience has taught me an important lesson: when a producer has wonderful vineyards, is an exceptional grower, is managing the vines along the lines of the great addresses and already makes some first-rate wines, everything else can be worked through. Buy the best wines, discuss the others, encourage a label change, and get moving. It seems so obvious in hindsight.

Pascal Agrapart came to grapegrowing as easily as any farmer follows in the footsteps of their parents. It was always planned that he would return to the domaine after his schooling, so he studied oenology at the Avize Lycée Viticole before returning to the 'farm' in 1981, at twenty years of age. He was in charge by 1985. His parents and grandparents had been farmers, not simply vignerons. They raised chickens, rabbits and cows and grew various agricultural crops apart from vines. Agrapart believes that this diverse farming background has been crucial in developing his outlook. When I ask him about his vineyard practices and how he has managed to avoid ending up on the chemical path of so many of his peers, he says, 'My model is the pyramid. If the foundation is not solid, then nothing works. I viewed the practices of previous generations of my family as my base. If I had used herbicides, if I had not worked the soils, then I would have been undermining the foundation of the estate.'

He also had the good fortune to be able to compare, at the very start of his career, base wines made from chemical farming with wines made from his family's cultivated soils. Before he left college, Agrapart acquired a small parcel of vines in Avize that had been managed conventionally with herbicides and chemical fertilisers. The soil of the site was densely compacted, thanks to the use of a heavy tractor and because the soil had never been cultivated. When Agrapart returned to the domaine, he decided to make the wine from this new vineyard separately, in order to understand its personality and to see what impact such vineyard practices had on the style of wine produced. When he tasted his *vins clairs* (still wines, which have not yet gone through the second fermentation in bottle) each year with his friends, he often found that the wine from the new vineyard lacked freshness, that it was less precise and less fine than the wines from the domaine's historic vineyards.

After three years of evaluation, he decided to convert the new vineyard to his family's typical practices and found that the standard of the wine improved quickly, until it was soon at the same level as that of the other cuvées. For Agrapart, here was undeniable evidence that cultivation of the soil (or mechanical weeding) had a marked, positive impact on wine quality, and that the use of herbicides and soil compaction had a detrimental impact. This gave him a great deal of confidence that his vineyards were being managed correctly, and it has guided his thinking ever since.

Through his regular *vins clairs* tastings, Agrapart naturally came to understand which of his parcels make the most interesting wines. He also arrived at a conclusion regarding blending that was quite radical at the time (even though it was a conclusion that has been independently arrived at by a number of the great growers). Like many domaines of any size, the 12-hectare Agrapart estate is made up of many small parcels of vines – over seventy, in fact. So blending is a necessity. As a rule in Champagne, the wines of different villages are pressed separately and then kept separately in tank, in order to be used as blending components down the line. Agrapart took this a step further, by organising his pressings and tanks according to soil type ('clay-rich' or 'very chalky'). Through regular tastings of the tanks, he came to realise that the blending components were sometimes already complete wines and, further, that their completeness was diminished when they were blended with wines that derived from different soils. He discovered also that wines from similar soils often blended together comfortably, and he hit upon the idea of producing what he now calls 'geological blends': finished Champagnes that come from vineyards with the same geology, as opposed to those made with the more usual practice of blending disparate terroirs to arrive at a house style.

After our tasting, we walk uphill to the top of the village, where Hôtel Les Avisés is based. As always, we eat and drink well. I remember a bottle of 2004 Minéral, a bottle of Selosse Millésimé 2003 and a bottle of Jacques Lassaigne Le Cotet. I also remember Selosse bringing out some of his sweet oloroso-style fortified wine, Il Était une Fois, at the end of the meal. This is a wine, he says, made to 'show my friends in Jerez that they should be making sparkling wine'.[58]

I ask Agrapart a question that I have asked all the growers that we visit in this book – that is, is he optimistic about where the region is heading?

'Yes, I am,' he says. 'Things are changing slowly.'

'Is this change too slow?'

'Yes, the change is slow, but it should be slow. What slows it most is that things are too easy today. When things are easy, it's hard to change. But still, I am for the most part an optimist. Since 2000 there have been a lot of changes.'

Despite his optimism, he is also ready to talk about what has been lost.

'Before the 1970s the region was full of true vignerons who made true wines. Then you had the chemical revolution in the 1970s. Before 1975 you could find great bottles in practically all the houses. Different in style, but nonetheless great.' The increase in yields, the technical approach, the chemical viticulture that came to dominate through the 1970s did the damage. Many of the large houses have also grown enormously since that time, and with that growth has come a sacrifice in quality.

I think Agrapart has a point regarding the pace of change. Sometimes, it is better if change doesn't occur too quickly. After all, it was rapid change that encouraged the explosion in chemical usage and aggressive mechanisation in the 1960s and 1970s. I also agree that success and wealth can act like a handbrake. Growers are currently paid very well for their fruit, so the more they grow, the better. When the culture is dominated by dollars and everyone is making money, why change?

Underpinning this logic is, again, the spectre of the Grandes Marques. The strength and success of the large négociants of the region created the logic of commercialism that dominates today. As the true concept of terroir came late to Champagne and was born into a market dominated by megabrands, it has been much more challenging for the artisanal approach to carve itself a significant niche. It is coming, but it has taken a longer time than it otherwise might have. Many of the growers in this book believe that they owe at least some of their success to the Grandes Marques, which they rightly credit with creating the global market for Champagne.

While I understand this argument, there are other ways that one can tell the same story. On the one hand, the success of the Grandes Marques created a global market of wine buyers who now also buy the wines of the great growers. On the other hand, the immense success of the Grandes Marques repressed the logic of terroir in Champagne for centuries and made it very hard for the best growers to rise above the marketing noise of their region's mass market brands.

The wines of Champagne Agrapart

As we have seen, Pascal Agrapart's original idea was not to produce single-site wines, although he has ended up producing some of these, but rather blends of wines that share the same geology, the same terroir and the same vintage. From 1983, he contemplated this seriously and began trials. In 1989, he produced the first release of Avizoise, a powerful Blanc de Blancs (100 per cent Chardonnay) from two clay-rich vineyards (*Les Robards* and *La Voie d'Épernay*) that sit next to each other on the slopes of Avize. Later came Minéral, another Blanc de Blancs and another blend of two sites, one in Avize and one in Cramant, both very close to the border between those two villages and both on similar, very poor, chalky soils.[59] The vines are over fifty years of age, and Minéral (like Vénus, discussed below) is aged for between seventy-two and eighty-four months on lees. The dosage is always less than 5 grams per litre.

Over time, a series of single-site wines followed: firstly Vénus, from a specific Chardonnay parcel in *La Fosse* vineyard in Avize that was originally kept separate in order to demonstrate the benefits of working the soil by horse (which does not compact the soil as much as a tractor). The horse's name was Vénus, and although Vénus has since died, the site is still worked by horse, and the wine still carries the original worker's name. (A picture of Vénus is mounted on a post in the vineyard.) There is no dosage added, and, for me, this is Agrapart's greatest wine. It is also one of the greatest wines of the region.

Then came Complantée, another individual-site wine that again derives from a plot in *La Fosse* terroir, which in 2002 and 2003 Agrapart co-planted with six of the historical Champagne varieties: Chardonnay, Pinot Noir, Pinot Meunier, Pinot Blanc, Arbane and Petit Meslier (see Myth V, on page 98). This is a tiny production, as the vineyard area is only 0.3 hectares. The wine spends from twenty-four to thirty-six months on lees, and again the dosage is around 5 grams per litre.

And then there is Expérience, Agrapart's most experimental wine but also the one that perhaps gives the best insight into his personality and approach. The Expérience cuvée is a 100 per cent Chardonnay vintage wine made without the addition of any sugar whatsoever. Although a number of Champagnes do without the *liqueur d'expédition* (added after disgorging), all require sugar for the *liqueur de tirage* (to start the second fermentation). At least, they have done, until now. In the early 2000s, Pascal Agrapart started experiments to produce a wine that included nothing but the juice of the grapes of Champagne. By 2007 he was in a position to commercialise a small quantity of bottles. He succeeded in making the wine again in 2012, 2014 and 2015. How does he do it? In simple terms, the base wine ferments and ages for twelve months, and then Agrapart blends in a proportion of the next vintage's unfermented juice from the same vineyard, *La Fosse*, and puts this blend into bottle. This juice addition is carefully proportioned so that it brings enough sugar and wild yeast to ensure a secondary fermentation in the bottle. In short, the juice replaces the typical tirage addition of sugar and yeast. By the time the secondary fermentation in bottle is over, the added juice has fermented dry. No *liqueur d'expédition* is added, and hence this is a Champagne with absolutely no additions. No sugar, no yeast, no enzymes – nothing. Only the wine, made from the fruit of a specific site – *La Fosse* in Avize. The wine spends two to three years on lees, and only 600 bottles are made in certain vintages. It is a fascinating wine, extremely pure and primary, with a completely different personality from that of Agrapart's other wines. To my palate, it is not one of his best wines, but it is certainly one of his most thought-provoking. It is important to note that Agrapart is not 'anti-sugar'; he uses it to dose the other wines in his range.

Agrapart also produces two more accessibly priced cuvées. The first is Terroirs Extra Brut, an outstanding Grand cru, Blanc de Blancs, 100 per cent Chardonnay blend from the villages of Avize, Cramant, Oger and Oiry. It has 60 per cent reserve wine in the blend, is aged for three to four years on lees and has a maximum 5-gram dosage. The other is 7 Crus Brut, from the fruit of seven villages (90 per cent Chardonnay and 10 per cent Pinot Noir), which again ages for three years on lees and is dosed with no more than 7 grams. The Pinot Noir for this wine comes from the village of Avenay-val-d'Or, in the Montagne de Reims area, where Agrapart has a hectare of vines.

Agrapart has also started releasing a Millésimé after ten or more years of ageing (four or five on cork, post-disgorgement). In fact, this is simply the Minéral cuvée with an extra period of aging in the Agrapart cellars.

If we wanted to discuss a style that runs through all of Agrapart's wines, we could talk of pillowy textures from ripe Chardonnay that has been aged on its lees and has gone through malolactic fermentation married to a saline, mineral freshness that all the wines share. Because of these two features, they are mouth-filling and relatively full-bodied wines, yet they are never heavy; rather, they are always refreshing, energetic and racy. They are without doubt some of the very finest wines being produced today in Champagne.

PART IX

Where we unearth even more image problems for Champagne (by comparing the 'approach Champenois' with best practice in Burgundy) and learn that the English are the necrophiliacs of the wine world

The key role that blending plays in most Champagne may also, rightly or wrongly, reinforce the view of Champagne as a heavily manipulated product. Champagne is nearly always a blended wine made from grapes sourced from many disparate vineyards and villages. All the grapes must come from within the Champagne region of course, but the Champagne AOC is a vast and wildly diverse area of land. The region has over 80,000 vineyards and 280,000 individual plots of vines that add up to an area of almost 34,000 hectares. These vineyards are then spread over 25,000 square kilometres of land – an area almost the size of Belgium, larger than Israel and around ten times the size of Luxembourg.

Naturally, such a vast area has many soil types, aspects and climates. Champagne houses typically blend many wines from different parts of the region in order to achieve a consistent house style and to achieve a quality that is 'greater than the sum of its parts', a phrase that is widely used by the region's négociants. A large house may draw on hundreds of vineyards for their largest blends.[60] There is no desire to directly reflect the personality or terroir of any particular parcel of vines, as the wines of single sites are said to lack the balance, complexity and harmony of a multi-vineyard blend.

The 'art of the blender' story is in many ways a convenient myth that diverts our attention from the historical factors that led to blending becoming the norm in Champagne. As I make clear in Myth VI (page 119), I am not at all against blending; many great wines are blends of some sort or another. Yet, the type of large-scale, multi-vineyard and region-wide blending that is the norm in Champagne is reserved only for basic wines in other French fine wine areas.

Even when the wine of a traditional Champagne producer (large or small) *is* made from a single site, it is often farmed conventionally from young vines, cropped high, picked early, dosed with a reasonable whack of sugar and made

Henri Krug blending the cuvées at Champagne Krug

more with a view to house style than to terroir. In other words, the wine still has more to do with winemaking than winegrowing, and the personality of the vineyard is usually suppressed, even if the marketing spin claims the contrary.

If the blending described here sounds familiar, it is. Most large, industrial--scale wine producers from across the globe follow this multi-region or multi-terroir blending model. Yet, the fact remains that this logic is highly unusual when it comes to other top-quality French wines. When wine travellers think about the greatest wines of France, they nearly always think of wines that derive from a single vineyard, estate or commune (that is, a small geographic area) and of wines that reflect their place of origin. Such wines are normally made by winemakers who know, thanks to decades or centuries of local experience, how best to grow the wine of a given site in order to bring out the personality of its terroir and to maximise its best attributes. In this desirable stereotype, the makers of great wines seek to harvest reasonable, balanced yields and utilise 'living soil' viticulture and minimal intervention winemaking in order to produce wines that intensely reflect where they were grown. This is the winegrowing ideal that excites the wine traveller. Until the relatively recent rise of the finest grower-producers, this terroir-driven approach simply did not exist in Champagne.

This is why the wine I encountered at the start of this book was such a surprise. The Terre de Vertus I had in my glass was the product of a specific area, mid-slope, in the commune of Vertus (a village at the very southern end of the Côte des Blancs). It was 100 per cent Chardonnay from a single harvest and from vines that averaged over forty years of age, with some over fifty (extremely old for Champagne, where vines are widely considered to be due for replanting once they reach over thirty years and their productivity starts to drop). The vines were managed biodynamically and were cropped at something like 60 hectolitres per hectare, well below the regional average. The wine was made slowly and naturally, with no yeast addition for the first fermentation, no fining, no filtration and no dosage. Single variety, single terroir, single year. Everything about the viticulture was designed to maximise the quality and intensity of the grapes. Everything about the winemaking was designed to minimise the influence of the winegrower and maximise the expression of the vineyard. Hence the name: Terre de Vertus (Earth of Vertus). Pierre Larmandier wanted us to taste the best possible expression of the place in which the wine was grown, so he worked as hard as possible in the vineyard and interfered as little as possible in the winery to achieve this end.

If I was describing a great wine from Burgundy, I would be saying nothing new. All the producers you meet in Burgundy will get busy telling you about how much their wine reflects the terroir of the vineyard or village in which it was grown and how little influence the winemaking has had on the wine in the glass. This is the context in which Burgundy has always been discussed. But to talk about Champagne in this way was something radically new only a decade ago.

The wine laws and labelling in Burgundy reflect this culture of terroir. All of Burgundy's finest wines are labelled according to the specific vineyard or village from which they derive. They are not Burgundy as such, or even Côte d'Or, but Gevrey-Chambertin, Chambolle-Musigny or Puligny-Montrachet (villages) or Clos Saint-Jacques, Les Amoureuses or Chevalier-Montrachet (vineyards). They are all wines of very specific places, and they are revered because the places in which they are grown are held to consistently produce wines of outstanding quality, each with its own distinctive personality.

This link between site and potential greatness is not unique to Burgundy, of course. As mentioned above, most revered French – and European – wines are the products of specific vineyards or villages. The concept merely reaches its greatest level of complexity in Burgundy, since so many individual plots are separately vinified and labelled and because this practice has occurred continuously here for many centuries.

The widely acknowledged association between greatness in wines and wines that reflect their specific terroir presents problems for Champagne. While Burgundy, with its fragmented patchwork of vineyards and micro-cuvées, has become the apogee for the terroir-focused wine lover, Champagne nearly always speaks in the foreign tongue of the mass-market blend. Only the cheapest wines of Burgundy, such as Passetoutgrains and Bourgogne, are (sometimes) blends of vineyards in different communes. On the other hand, it is extremely rare for Champagne to be the product of a single terroir or a single vineyard, and even when it is, such wine is rarely a *vin de terroir* in the Burgundian sense. The wines of the best growers are the exceptions.

There are still other reasons why Champagne struggles to achieve the gravitas accorded to esteemed wines such as those grown in Burgundy. Great wines are nearly always food wines, to be matched with suitable cuisine at the table. Yet, Champagne is widely held – incorrectly, I should add – to be best drunk on its own or with finger foods. This may be because of Champagne's bubbles, possibly because of its history as a sweetened wine and certainly because it has been so commonly marketed as a party drink. The UK is the exception here. There is, in fact, a tradition in the UK, from the earliest days, of drinking Champagne with a meal. This was probably why the UK was the first market to demand drier styles of *mousseux*. Yet, in most markets, including France, Champagne was, and is, more commonly drunk as an aperitif, with nibbles, with dessert or alone; hence, sweetness may have been favoured.

Champagne is still quite commonly suggested as a good match for dessert. It isn't. This tradition originated in the days when Champagne was a very sweet wine and typically had at least 30–60 grams of added sugar, and often quite a lot more. It was undoubtedly these higher levels of sweetness that made it possible to match Champagne with dessert. Today, with generally no more than 12 grams of sugar added per litre (the maximum permitted for Brut Champagne) – and often quite a lot less – your average Champagne is simply too dry to match with anything sweet. On the other hand, there are sweeter categories of Champagne: Sec (17–32 grams per litre), Demi Sec (32–50 grams per litre) and Doux (over 50 grams per litre). These sweeter Champagne styles are rare these days, but if you can get hold of one, especially at the Doux level, it can work with a suitably matched dessert. As a general rule, however, Champagne is very much a wine for matching with savoury dishes.

The best way to dismiss the claim that Champagne doesn't belong at the table is to point out something quite heretical to most Champagne lovers and producers: great Champagne can be a wonderful drink without bubbles. This is because great Champagne is, first and foremost, great wine; and great wine is more than comfortable being served without gas. Yes, I am talking about only a select few Champagnes, although it is quite easy to test if your favourite Champagne is one of these. Open the wine an hour or two before service, decant it, keep it at the temperature you wish to serve it but let the gas dissipate as much as possible. You can also drink what is left of a bottle the next day, or even two or three days later, with the same effect (the residual gas will help preserve it). After all, if you can't drink and enjoy it without persistent bubbles, how good a wine can it be? Doing this, along with serving it at a reasonable temperature (say, 8–12 degrees Celsius) in a tulip-shaped wine glass and with a savoury dish or two, will tell you everything you need to know about the quality of the wine.

Champagne is also generally not considered to have cellaring potential, in contrast to most 'Great Wines', which are famed for their ageing ability. Here, I am talking about a wine's ability to age on cork (that is, after it has been purchased) and to continue improving with bottle age. I am not talking about recently disgorged Champagne that has been kept on lees, in the producer's cellars, only to be released many years later, soon after being disgorged. Again, only in the UK does there seem to have developed a genuine tradition of cellaring Champagne on cork, and some English wine writers have promoted the practice. The tradition may, once more, be a by-product of the English tradition of serving Champagne with food. But it remains the exception. Many Champenois disagree with the practice. A producer once told me, 'The English are the necrophiliacs of the wine world. They prefer to wait for a wine to be dead before they will touch it.' To be clear, I do not agree at all with the two stereotypes above (I both cellar Champagne and regularly drink it at the table), yet they are nonetheless widely held beliefs.

The final image problem that we'll touch on here is the sheer volume that is produced of the best known Champagnes. Wine collectors are not fools; they know that a wine made in massive volumes from predominantly purchased fruit or juice and marketed as a luxury item is unlikely to be as fine or as interesting as the best small production wine made exclusively from a grower's own grapes.

MYTH VI

Blending is better: Champagne is blended in order to produce a better balanced, better quality wine

No one who knows anything about wine could be against blending. Many outstanding wines are blends; in fact, almost every wine is a blend of sorts. Even single-vineyard wines are technically blends – of different grape varieties grown in the same vineyard, perhaps, or of different clones, different parcels within the vineyard or different soil types and aspects. At the very least, wines are nearly always blends of tanks and barrels (each ferment is at least slightly different, as is every barrel). So, this is not a criticism of blending per se. Rather, my aim is simply to challenge the long-held view that blending of the kind we see in Champagne – across a vast number of geographically diverse vineyards and communes spread over 25,000 square kilometres of land – *necessarily* produces better wines than those that derive from a single site or a single terroir.

In Champagne, the logic of blending has been taken to the extreme. The region's wines are typically blends not only of grapes from many different places, but also of several grape varieties and, usually, multiple vintages. This practice has long been justified by the claim that Champagne is nearly always a better wine when made this way. The wine is said to be more complete, more balanced, more consistent.

The reasoning runs something like this. In such a northerly, marginal climate, having blending options is essential. In some vintages, the growers will struggle to achieve genuinely ripe fruit, so it's better to have other vintages (some of those from warmer, riper years) to be able to 'balance' the lesser vintages. Some communes will also perform better than others in some vintages, and each commune will offer wines with different personalities that the experienced blender can bring together into 'a sum that is greater than its parts' (a term I have heard used many times in Champagne and that appears in a great deal of literature on the region). Blend a richer, riper wine from one vineyard or commune with one that is leaner and crunchier, and you will end up with the best of both worlds. Or so the story goes. This argument has been repeated so often that many in the wine trade have accepted it as fact.

And yet, this is not at all why blending first arose in Champagne. The real reasons were commercial and pragmatic. We should recall that Champagne's original still wines were often sold for low prices, so the efficiencies gained by blending made sense. Also, there was no premium paid for the wines of individual terroirs (with very few exceptions), so blending wines of different places together was never taboo. This allowed the region's first sparkling wine producers (who were merchants rather than growers) to prioritise house style over place (often not even listing Champagne on their labels in the early days) and to prioritise market demand over any desire to make wines that reflected their individual *climats* (specific terroirs or sites).

Large-scale blending came about in Champagne primarily as a solution to what was (and is) a commercial challenge: how to create a consistent product as inexpensively as possible and in enough volume to satisfy a fast-growing, mass-market audience. The solution was (and is) to source from far and wide and to aim to blend to a house style. The story that relates blending to quality came *after* the practice was well established.

Multi-vintage and multi-commune blending is also a wonderful solution to the problem of what to do with a lot of excess inventory, which Champagne has had many times during its history. It is no coincidence that in Europe this type of blending (region wide and multi-vintage) tends to be exclusively practised by large négociants, and that we find this approach dominating only in regions and wine styles in which négociants dominate production and export — that is, Cognac, Port, Sherry and Champagne.

Another problem with the argument that blending makes better Champagnes is the simple fact that some of the region's most famous, expensive and sought-after wines are produced from single vineyards or communes. Even within the portfolios of the négociants, the very folk who constantly talk of the 'art of the blender', the most prestigious wines are often single-vineyard or single-commune wines: Salon, Krug's Clos du Mesnil and Clos d'Ambonnay, Philipponnat's Clos des Goisses and so on. Traditionalists may argue that such wines are exceptions born of incomparable, unique terroirs that enable balanced wines of greatness to be produced via a single site or, in the case of Salon, from a single village. But, as we will soon see, Clos d'Ambonnay comes from a site that was not at all historically famous and yet has ended up producing one of the region's most expensive and revered wines. Why wouldn't there be many other vineyards in the vast region of Champagne capable of generating such reverence? As the great growers are demonstrating, there are indeed many such vineyards.

Champagne today is infinitely more interesting than it once was, because there are more wines of place, more wines of specific vineyards or communes, more wines of terroir. Are these wines better than region-wide blends? Not necessarily. But they do, if we are being honest, have an edge over their blended counterparts in terms of intellectual interest for experienced wine travellers. The best examples tend to be grown more than made, and they have the added allure of reflecting a specific place and, often, a specific season. Coming from a defined area of land and being made in smaller volumes also offer the advantage of greater attention to detail in both the growing and the making. Blending has a role in Champagne, an important role, but it is simply inaccurate to claim that it necessarily makes better wines.

PART X

In which the author tries to comprehend Anselme Selosse via a blend of pop psychology and historical minutiae and then plays word games with the man himself

While we are in Avize, we must of course visit the most revered grower of them all, Anselme Selosse. His wines (still labelled under his father's name, Jacques Selosse) are some of the most sought after in the entire region and fetch crazy prices on the secondary market. Selosse himself is celebrated for having been the most significant figure in the great grower movement. Wine lovers travel from all corners of the globe to visit Selosse and to taste in his cellars. From this perspective he is remarkably generous and welcoming, conducting countless tastings that appear to have no benefit, commercially speaking. He could sell his wine many times over without ever doing a tasting. I have always had the impression that Selosse gets a great deal of pleasure from these interactions and that he relishes the chance to discuss his philosophies with those people who are willing to visit. This speaks directly to his passion and talent for teaching, a passion that we will touch on again below.

Selosse was not always so popular, however, and endured a challenging and often unpleasant childhood. He remembers feeling like an outsider from a very early age, primarily because he was an overweight child and also suffered from a visible skin disorder. As you can imagine, in a small country town like Avize, Selosse found himself ostracised by many of his peers. This rejection marked him deeply and fostered in him a strong drive to achieve something significant. It gave him something to prove. Being an outsider taught him to play and work alone and, later, to feel comfortable innovating without the need to seek consensus. It also taught him that what is different is sometimes worth celebrating, even when it challenges us – a key pillar to his understanding of terroir.

Two other factors were vital to Selosse becoming the man he is today. First, for as long as he can remember, he has been obsessed with understanding how things work. As a teenager, he was constantly pulling apart machines

It's the vines first with Selosse

and reconstructing them in different ways to see if he could improve on the originals. Throughout these formative years, he developed a strong desire to look beyond the superficial, to deeply understand his world and to never accept anything as a given. This is a key to comprehending his approach to winegrowing. He broke with biodynamics because he found that there was an element of 'auto-suggestion' in the thinking of many biodynamics practitioners; that is, many elements were accepted as working without any true understanding of how or why. He was not, and is not, satisfied with such an approach. For Selosse, a practice becomes valid only with a deep knowledge of why and how it works.

Second, Selosse had a very strict mother. This is significant, as it was her domineering nature, along with his sense of disconnection from his peers, that encouraged him to leave Avize as soon as he had an excuse to do so. He went to boarding school from the age of twelve, and by fifteen he was studying in Beaune, in the heart of Burgundy's Côte d'Or. Most children of Avize growers, if they studied winegrowing at all, would have done so at the Lycée Viticole in Avize. There, they would have been indoctrinated in the 'traditional', or

Selosse vines in Avize

conventional, winegrowing and winemaking methodologies that still dominate today in Champagne. Selosse studied at the Lycée Viticole in Beaune.

No one who spends time in Burgundy can miss the fact that the structure of the region and its AOC laws are designed to celebrate the terroir of individual vineyards and communes. This was a radical departure from what Selosse had known. More significant were some of the teachings that he encountered at the *lycée*. Like courses at any wine school at the start of the 1970s, many of those taken by Selosse were conventional. However, some were not. At the time, the Beaune *lycée* was a pilot school for a new course in ecology, which ran for five hours a week. It explored areas that had not previously been studied systematically in wine schools: ecosystems, biotopes, the interaction between geology, climate and plant life, and the idea of observing nature in order to learn from it. The course was radical for its time and had a major influence on Selosse.

Up to that point, Selosse had not been particularly passionate about wine. He went to a wine school because he was the son of a vigneron, and he would need to take over the family domaine at some point. Yet, winegrowing was not a calling. It was the ecology course that opened Selosse's eyes and sparked a fire that has blazed ever since. He had discovered that there was a much bigger picture available when it came to the management of vineyards, that there was a great deal not yet understood about how vines interact with their environment, and that it was highly likely that many conventional practices were built on false premises. These were not necessarily the objectives of the course, but they were the conclusions that Selosse took away.

After finishing his studies, Selosse headed to the Rioja region, in Spain, to gain some additional experience. This was, again, an unconventional move for the son of a Champagne grower. In Spain, he encountered two winemaking techniques that strongly influenced his approach when he returned to Champagne. The first of these was *reserva* ageing, in which wines are held for extended periods in barrel prior to bottling, thus fundamentally changing the structure and the aromatic and flavour profiles of the wine. The second was the *solera* system, something we discuss in more detail below, in which many vintages are blended together to create the final wine. Such a practice results, in theory, in a more complete wine than could be produced from a single harvest. Selosse realised that both of these methods had parallels with the Champagne tradition of blending and its use of older, reserve wines. Making this connection gave him fresh insight into the history of his region and fundamentally influenced the way he ended up producing his wines.

When Selosse returned home in 1974, he was 'given the keys' to the domaine, and by 1980, his parents had stopped working altogether. His father died in 1984. Initially, Selosse was relatively conventional in his approach. He abandoned the use of herbicides, but he remained, as he puts it, 'a technician'. As he says, the 1970s were 'the worst decade for viticulture. This was a time when science still pretended it could fully dominate and control nature.'

Selosse may not have been able to immediately break free from the dominant paradigm of his métier, but nor was he comfortable functioning within its rules, as the move away from herbicides makes clear. He had grasped that the relationship between the vines and their terroir was deeply complex, and that many common viticultural practices were based not on quality or genuine knowledge but on commercial expediency. Little by little, he began to change things. He questioned every process, every rule. When he asked 'Do we need to do this?' or 'Does this make better wine?' the answer was often 'No.' And so, he began to eliminate those practices (or 'gestures', as he calls them) that were not necessary.

The first gesture to go in the cellars was filtration, a modern technology introduced to facilitate a faster clarification and enable producers to get their base wines to bottle more quickly. Traditionally, wines made via the *méthode champenoise* did not require filtration, as the processes of settling, riddling and disgorging resulted in a clear wine anyway. Selosse realised that something was being lost through filtration: wines were spending less time in contact with their lees, were being stripped of their natural character and often picked up unpleasant aromas and flavours from the asbestos, then cellulose, filtration technology of the time. So he abandoned this practice. It was a daring step in an era when oenologists routinely advised their clients that filtration was required to ensure 'stable', 'clean' wines. And yet, it had a positive effect on Selosse's bottlings. This in turn gave him the confidence to question other conventional practices.

Over time, he abandoned or altered his approach in many areas of viticulture and winemaking. Most significantly, his work in the vineyard – where he came to focus on working with nature in order to maximise the health, quality and terroir expression of his vines and the fruit they produced – radically broke with the accepted practices of his region and put many of his colleagues offside. To Selosse, this only seemed to validate his approach. He had started down a path on which he would deeply explore every element of the viticulture and viniculture of his region, an exploration that would profoundly influence the future of Champagne.

At first, Selosse's work caused barely a ripple. Most of the growers who knew what he was up to thought he was mad. Then, as his wines started to receive some acclaim, there were many who openly called him a charlatan or accused him of producing wines that were not 'true' Champagnes, because their depth and style differed so much from the norm. Others seemed obsessed by the fact that Selosse was using oak barrels for the maturation of his wines and criticised the style for being too 'oaky' or too 'oxidative'. These are criticisms that can still be heard today. The focus on the style of wine produced by Selosse misses the significance of what he brought back to Champagne: the philosophy that authentic wines are unique wines that reflect their unique terroir and that the only way to make such wines is to encourage a living soil and balanced yields, to harvest fully ripe fruit and to make use of winemaking that allows the terroir to speak as clearly as possible.

Selosse realised that the finest terroirs of Champagne were every bit as

Tasting at the cellars

interesting as those of the Côte d'Or and, even more significantly, that they could produce unique vineyard, or commune-specific wines of a standard and interest that were every bit as valid as the other great wines of the world. He saw beyond the dominant ideology of his region, and there was no going back. His work became the engine that powered all those who followed in his footsteps.

One key factor in the great grower movement that cannot be overstated is Selosse's generosity and talent as a teacher. He has played a key role in helping many young vignerons gain a deeper knowledge of their work. A number of the growers mentioned in this book – Jérôme Prévost, Olivier Collin and Alexandre Chartogne – have benefited from working directly with Selosse; others have profited from his advice and encouragement; almost all have been inspired by the path he blazed.

Selosse's iconic status in the wine world has seen him held up as a poster boy for everything from biodynamics (he prefers his work not to be restricted by a label and long ago rejected biodynamics' faith-based approach) to any position regarding Champagne that is anti-establishment (he isn't). Perhaps the most misleading of these associations has been with so-called natural wine, a slippery, ideology-laden term that is most commonly associated with low- or no-sulphur wines. In fact, Selosse is no fan of the term or the movement. He once told me, 'This idea makes no sense. The vineyard is not natural. The vineyard is a monoculture. Nature is the forest.'

He is right, of course. The vineyard and the wines that result from it are far from 'natural' in any meaningful sense. In the vineyard, a single plant dominates in a way that could not occur in a natural setting, and this creates a quite *unnatural* imbalance. Nature – whose logic is to introduce biodiversity to compete with and feed on any imbalance or abundance (in this case the vines and their fruit) – must be kept at bay, at least to some extent, if quality wine is to be produced. In many ways, the work of the vigneron (even a vigneron who works as closely with nature as possible) is in direct opposition to the forces of nature. Many crucial decisions revolve around when to intervene in order to help the vineyard resist the threats that nature will inevitably throw at it.

The great growers never kid themselves. They do their best to work as closely as possible *with* nature, yet they know what they do is not *natural*. 'Natural' means 'of nature', and it literally points to the work of the natural world – specifically, without the influence of humankind. That is the root of the word. For a vineyard to be planted, the land has to be cleared and the vines selected: in the case of *Vitis vinifera*, the European vines we use today, this selection process occurred over thousands of years, so that they are quite removed from their wild ancestors. These vines must then be propagated, (often) grafted and artificially protected from competition, rot, insect pests and animals (even if no synthetic chemicals are used). And that's before we get to the winemaking. No, the vineyard and the wines that result from it are the products of thousands of years of *culture*, not *nature*, a reality that we should both marvel at and celebrate.

Speaking of culture, a number of Selosse's wines are produced via what we could call a 'perpetual blend' methodology. I've seen it described as a *'solera'* many times, but I am not sure that's a completely accurate term, as Selosse's process doesn't have the various *criaderas* (age levels) of the typical *solera* system as practised in Spain to produce sherry. Rather, Selosse blends together all the vintages of each single terroir in one vessel, topping it up each year with the new harvest before bottling a portion of the blend as his next release. Such a system, I believe, is more accurately described as a 'perpetual blend', or perhaps a 'historic blend'. Yes, I am being a stickler, but I think it's important to be accurate here, as it helps us to understand precisely what Selosse is trying to achieve.

In a *solera* system, the various *criaderas* plus the *solera* (the oldest level) are all kept separate. This allows the producer the possibility to selectively blend wines of various ages in order to produce a consistent house style or *solera* style. Certain *criaderas*, or the *solera* itself – and even certain barrels – may play a greater or lesser role in the blend. They may also be left out of the blend altogether, if they interfere with the style of wine being sought. Selosse, by contrast, has everything blended together. His idea is to use this multi-vintage blend to minimise the impact of a single year and to present the drinker with a bottle of wine that represents a more complete vision of each terroir – warts and all. Whether it is a more complete picture or simply a different picture I am not sure. It is certainly an approach that makes us think more deeply about the concept of terroir.

The wines of Champagne Jacques Selosse

In general, Anselme Selosse produces rich, intense wines of extraordinary depth and vinosity; they are very textural and 'winey'. This reflects the fact that he harvests only fully ripe, expressive fruit (far riper than what is typically considered ripe in the region, and even riper than what some other quality growers consider to be ripe) and also that he then ages the wines slowly in barrel, on their lees, with minimal sulphur. The wines are definitely not for everyone (as the reviews of certain wine critics make clear), and that's okay. The English wine writer Tom Stevenson has been the most vocal critic, but I have also heard a number of other wine professionals proclaim that 'they are not my style'. Of course, many others love the wines, and I am one of these. You need to try a few bottles and make up your own mind. Be sure to try them in a decent wine glass and with food – and with friends willing to share the cost.

As he makes so many wines these days, I asked Selosse to play a word-association game with me – I read out the name of each of his wines, and he said the first thing that came into his mind. Until we get to the single-site Lieux-Dits wines and with the exception of the Rosé, each wine discussed below is a Blanc de Blancs, 100 per cent Chardonnay.

Me: Initial.
Selosse: My honour.
Initial is a blend of three successive vintages from Avize, Cramant and Oger. Most sites are low on the slopes (less than 15 per cent gradient), with deep, clay-rich soils. It spends five to six years on lees. The dosage is 3.5–5 grams.

Me: Version Originale.

Selosse: The Londoner as I imagine him, with his bowler hat and umbrella. Very dignified – serious and dignified.

Version Originale (VO) Extra Brut is again a blend of three successive vintages from Avize, Cramant and Oger, but there is more Avize fruit, and the vineyards are mostly on the higher slopes (greater than 15 per cent gradient). The soils, therefore, have less clay, and the vines tap more directly into the chalk. It spends six or seven years on lees and has a tiny dosage of between 0 and 1.3 grams.

Me: Exquise.

Selosse: Bénédictin (as opposed to Cistercian – that is, something hedonistic, joyous, for pleasure).

Exquise Sec is an off-dry wine sourced from four south-facing parcels in the foothills of Oger. It spends a minimum of five years on lees. The dosage is between 20 and 24 grams.

Me: Millésimé [vintage].

Selosse: The scars of the year, the imperfections that it gifts ... In life, we get knocked around. Each blow we receive helps to shape us. They give us our character, forge our personality. The Millésimé reveals the character of experience.

Millésimé is sourced from two sites in Avize: Les Chantereines (east-facing) and Les Maladries du Midi (south-facing). As the name suggests, it is the wine of a single year. It spends nine to ten years on lees. The dosage is between 0 and 2.4 grams.

Me: Substance.

Selosse: Something that annoys me. The repetition irritates. It's a process, by which I mean that there is something about it that becomes systematic.

Substance is drawn from a 'perpetual blend' that began in 1986. The juice comes from two sites in Avize, one facing south, Le Mont de Cramant, and one facing east, Les Chantereines. Each release spends between five and six years on lees and is bottled with a dosage of 1.3–2.4 grams.

Me: Rosé.

Selosse: Elusive.

The Selosse Rosé is a blend of two successive vintages of Avize Chardonnay grown on the slopes, with 6 per cent Ambonnay Pinot Noir Rouge from Francis Egly. It spends five years minimum on lees and has a dosage of 2.4–5.5 grams.

Then we have the six single-terroir Lieux-Dits wines. Some of these can be purchased individually, although Les Chantereines and Chemin des Châlons can be bought only as part of a mixed case containing one bottle of each of the wines in the series. Selosse's idea is to offer the taster the chance to compare the variations of expressions offered by the wines of six single sites in six different villages. All of these wines are made via the perpetual blend methodology described above, and the year that the vineyard was purchased or the wine is first bottled separately, lets us know when each perpetual blend commenced. After bottling, all of the Lieux-Dits wines spend six years on lees and have between 0 and 3 grams per litre of dosage. All are labelled according to the historic name of the vineyard – that is, the *lieu-dit*. The wines from Avize, Cramant and Le Mesnil-sur-Oger are Chardonnay based, while those from the villages of Aÿ, Ambonnay and Mareuil-sur-Aÿ are Pinot Noir dominant.

Me: La Côte Faron.
Selosse: The contrast.
This wine was formerly known as Contrast, so named because Selosse has always found a contrast between the nose and the palate. It is a Blanc de Noirs from a single, steep, south-facing plot of Pinot Noir in Aÿ that Selosse purchased in 1994. The blend was started in the same year.

Me: Les Chantereines.
Selosse: Serious serenity.
Les Chantereines is a historic, east-facing Avize parcel of the domaine on a gentle slope. The fractured chalk of the Côte des Blancs allows for the vines here to plunge deeply into the bedrock. The vines are very old and were planted in 1922, 1928, 1935 and 1945. This wine has been made separately since 2003. It is always a wine of great elegance and harmony – in short, classic Avize.

Me: Chemin de Châlons.
Selosse: Presence and depth. Powerful to a point.
The vineyard is on another historic parcel of the domaine, in Cramant, once again east-facing on a gentle slope with deep, deep roots embedded in the chalky soil. This terroir delivers a very ripe, expansive wine of great depth, which has been made separately since 2003.

Me: Sous le Mont.
Selosse: And why not a Rosé?
This parcel, in Mareuil–sur-Aÿ, was acquired in 2003. It is east-facing and in the middle of the hillside. There is magnesium in the chalk here, to which Selosse attributes the gentle bitterness often found in the wine.

Me: Le Bout de Clos.

Selosse: The power of deep roots.

The wine is from a plot in Ambonnay acquired in 2001. There is a lot of clay in the soil, which gives a wine of richness and power. It is mostly Pinot Noir, with 20 per cent Chardonnay.

Me: Les Carelles.

Selosse: *Les perrières*. We are reminded of what they call '*les perrières*' in Burgundy [that is to say, a very rocky, mineral site].

This wine comes from a rocky site acquired in 2002 in Le Mesnil-sur-Oger that faces south and southeast. It is quite steep, with fractured chalk bedrock and very deep roots. These characteristics give a wine that is seductively textured yet with great complexity, rocky minerality and length.

And finally, without warning, I threw in the name of Anselme and Corinne's son, Guillaume Selosse, who will at some stage take over the estate.

Me: Guillaume.

Selosse: Humble. Reserved. As if he were saying, 'I'll only start speaking when I have something to say.'

PART XI

Where we blend a few things together in order to produce a *histoire vraie* of Champagne and then explore the extent to which brand has come to dominate land in this famous region

The fragmented nature of landholdings in Champagne is far from unique in Europe, yet when it is considered alongside the style of wine produced, it becomes one of the keys to understanding the region. Before the world shrunk to a size that enabled wine travellers to scour the globe for the wines of great artisanal producers, it was difficult for small landholders to make and market their wines directly. When the wine style was as complicated and expensive to produce as sparkling Champagne, it was almost impossible. This is why most of the fruit grown in Champagne has always been either sold directly to négociants or delivered to the local co-operative of which the grower was a member.[61]

The separation of grower and producer has had a significant impact on the culture of the Champagne region. A quick look at the way the relationship between the two currently functions makes this obvious. The co-ops and Champagne houses pay their growers by the kilogram, with only basic quality checks and no incentives to keep yields at reasonable levels – that is, below the permitted maximums. In a region where demand outstrips supply, no one wants yields to drop; and with grape prices so high, growers are not interested in discussing potential bonuses or incentives for higher quality juice that may derive from lower yields. Yield related bonuses have been put forward on a number of occasions in regional meetings, and each time they have been rejected by both the growers and the négociants. As a result, payment for grapes is still made purely on weight.

The majority of the fruit that the co-ops receive from their member growers will be pressed and then blended together before being on-sold to négociants, either as juice, still wine or sparkling wine. Co-ops may also produce some 'own branded' wines for supermarkets and the like, or they may make wines that they market under their own brand names, on behalf of their members. In both cases, the wines will carry the *coopérative-manipulant* (CM) designation on the label. The largest co-op brand is Nicolas Feuillatte, a product of the massive Centre Viticole de la Champagne (CVC – in fact, a collection of co-ops), which produces 7 per cent of Champagne's total production. Co-ops also often distribute finished Champagne back to their member growers, who then sell it under their own labels, even though the wine will be a commune-wide blend from the fruit of many growers. These wines should be marked *récoltant-coopérative* (RC), although some producers utilise a quirk in the law to have them labelled as *récoltant-manipulant* (RM): if you disgorge the wines yourself, even when they are made by the co-op, you are able to sell them under the RM classification. This practice is misleading, as RM is widely believed to denote a grower-producer wine that has been made at the estate, by the estate and exclusively from the fruit of that single estate's vineyards. This is the same part of the law that allows négociants to buy wine that has been made and bottled by co-ops, disgorge the wine themselves, slap their own labels on the bottles and sell the wine under the *négociant-manipulant* (NM) designation, as though it was actually made by the négociant – another misleading practice.

Most growers have only rudimentary contact, if any, with the négociants who make wine from their fruit. There are simply too many growers supplying each house for the major négociants to have regular interaction with each of them or to examine their vineyards or the fruit that is coming in to the local presses or co-ops. This is not how the system works. Co-ops, which provide a significant proportion of the requirements of the négociants, do not sell or deliver the wines of individual vineyards. Rather, they make communal and varietal blends from the grapes they receive from many parcels and many growers. So growers who deliver their fruit to the co-ops know three things: that their fruit will receive only a rudimentary inspection – as long as it is clean and cropped within the legal limits, there will be no problem; that the juice of each communal parcel will be blended together with the juice of other parcels; and that the village blends being shipped to the Champagne houses will then be blended with the wines of other communes from across the vast Champagne appellation in order to produce a house style. This will be the case even when the négociant has a direct relationship with the grower.

This all means that vineyard-specific terroir is largely irrelevant and that any personality the fruit may have had will disappear in the name of the blender's art. In short, most of Champagne's 15,000-plus growers have no connection with the wines that result from their labours. It's important to acknowledge that almost all growers are totally satisfied with this system; it serves them well commercially. My point is simply this: when the labour of the grapegrower has become completely alienated from the wine that results, there are bound to be issues for quality.

The separation of grower and producer is another radical shift from the ideals of fine wine regions across Europe and, in fact, the rest of the world. Although we might justifiably liken the structure of the Champagne region to that of the Australian wine industry, this comparison is unfair to Australia. Yes, in Australia, production is also dominated by large producers who buy much of the fruit they need and then typically create multi-vineyard or multi-regional blends. Those blends are also designed to reflect a house style and are marketed under brands that aim for consistency rather than vineyard and vintage expression. The vineyard management of Australia's Grandes Marques will also generally be 'conventional' and the winemaking necessarily interventionist. So, there is a lot that mainstream Australian wine – mainstream wine from anywhere, in fact – has in common with that of Champagne. Yet, many Australian mass-market producers differ markedly from their Champagne counterparts, in that they usually take an active interest in the vineyards from which they source their fruit. They generally work directly with their growers, tend to purchase fruit only (not juice or wine) and either harvest the grapes themselves or have them delivered directly to their wineries for processing on site. Large Australian producers also often incentivise their growers with bonuses to produce quality, ripe fruit from reasonable yields. No such framework exists in Champagne.

How did Champagne get here? How and why did the region develop a structure in which large companies receive much of their production requirements as juice or wine from regional press houses and co-ops, which they then blend to a house style for a global market that buys on the basis of brand recognition? Why didn't Champagne evolve like Burgundy, to become a region whose producers label their wines according to the village or specific vineyard from which they were sourced, and whose most revered producers are the smaller growers, those who typically make wine from vineyards that they either own or manage directly? Let's try to answer these questions by making a Champagne blend of our own.

We have seen that Champagne has always been a region with average vineyard holdings of between 1 and 2 hectares, so let's first add tiny vineyard holdings to our *assemblage*. Now let's add export sales to the vat, as Champagne is a region that has always relied heavily on exports. As early as 1844, Champagne exports were double the volume of what was consumed in France. Exporting wine requires significant capital outlay, administrative and sales resources, expertise in shipping and strong contacts in foreign markets. The last of these is the reason that many of Champagne's famous names are not French in origin: Bollinger, Krug, Deutz, Heidsieck and Roederer are German names. This roll call of many of the region's most hallowed brands is not surprising when you consider that the largest markets for Champagne throughout the 19th century were the German-speaking states. Well-financed, native German speakers were therefore perfectly positioned to acquire jobs within the Champagne trade and then to start their own firms; they had both the contacts and the required language skills.

Now let's add perhaps the most important component: winemaking costs and expertise. Quality sparkling wine is much more complicated and expensive to produce than still wine. It requires a great deal more labour, capital and technical expertise; the holding of large wine inventories for far longer periods; significant investment in technology; more workers; and sophisticated machinery. In short, the huge capital, labour, technology and expertise needed to produce sparkling Champagne have historically ruled out all but the largest landholders and those with the capital (that is, the region's négociants) to purchase grapes, juice or still wine from many growers and to process it into sparkling wine.

Finally, our blend will not be complete without a healthy dose of raw commercialism. The négociants of Champagne were originally traders first and foremost and were understandably driven by profits. The Church – so important in defining and promoting the concept of terroir in Burgundy – was booted off the land during the French Revolution, prior to sparkling wine becoming a genuine force in Champagne. This left the way open for private capital to completely control the production and marketing of Champagne, and profit has been the number one motivation ever since.

A small grower in the 19th and early 20th century could not hope to pull together the elements required to take a serious shot at being a sparkling Champagne producer. In the same way, a large négociant could not hope to find enough land to purchase in order to supply all of their grape needs (nor would it have been financially prudent to go down this path). For these reasons, Champagne became a region whose viticulture and viniculture were radically separated in a way that is unique across the French fine wine landscape. Cognac is the only other prestigious French region with a similar structure, yet here we are talking about a distilled spirit or brandy – not a 'table wine'. Nothing has changed. Today, the growers still control nearly 90 per cent of the grape supply, while the négociants dominate production, sales and marketing.

Our historical blend explains some of the puzzling structural features of Champagne. For example, as the large négociants of the region are buying from a wide variety of sources, located over a vast area, in order to satisfy significant export orders, it makes far more economic sense to create megablends conforming to a house style than to produce a plethora of small batch wines from individual terroirs (unless it is for a limited-production prestige cuvée that can be sold at far higher prices). Our blend also shows why, from the very beginning, the marketing of Champagne has been all about brand names as opposed to terroir. Prior to the 20th century and the foundation of the appellation laws, the term Champagne rarely appeared on wine labels; instead, the wines of Champagne were almost exclusively marketed according to the brand name of the house that produced them. By the time the appellation laws came into being, in the early 20th century, the structure of the region demanded that there be only one appellation name, Champagne, to cover the vast, complex and varied terroirs from which the négociants sourced their fruit. Anything else would have contradicted the history of sparkling wine in the area and would have been a major imposition to the commercial imperatives of both large houses and growers. This is why the 'art of the blender' story has become so central to the narrative of Champagne. It's a story that takes the emphasis away from the land and gives it to the *chef de cave*, or cellarmaster. In this tale, the terroir provides only the raw material for the producers to work their magic upon, and it is this work that is paramount.

To understand just how effectively brand dominates land in Champagne, you need only consider the story of the region's most expensive fine wine, Krug's Clos d'Ambonnay. It may surprise you to learn that this wine comes from a vineyard that was never highly regarded before Krug released the aforementioned wine. It is easy to see why when you visit the site, located as it is on the edge of the village, as opposed to on the slopes above (where the finest terroirs are typically found). Many locals did not even know the site existed prior to the wine being released. This is largely because the vines on the site have a very short history. Originally, the walls of the property enclosed the winery and gardens of the négociant Henri Petitjean. There were no vines there at all until the 1970s; the walls were built around a garden, not a vineyard. So it is not a true *clos* (an enclosed or walled vineyard) in any historic sense. Even when the Petitjean family decided to plant some vines there, only part of the area could be planted, as the rest of the garden fell outside the boundaries of the AOC. The vines were therefore not known as the '*clos*'; nor was the fruit considered to be any better than that of the other vineyards in the area. It was never bottled separately but was blended away into the basic cuvées of the Petitjean négociant business. The Petitjean family planted the site only because they realised that part of their garden was within the AOC and grape prices were going up – so why not plant some vines?

In the late 1980s, the continuing hike in grape prices caused the Petitjean business to run into trouble. The decision was taken to close it down and to rent out the winery building and land to Charles Heidsieck, then owned by Rémy Cointreau, which also owned the Piper-Heidsieck and Krug brands at the time. As Krug had always processed a lot of fruit from Ambonnay, Rémy Cointreau decided to convert the property into a processing centre for Krug. A lot of repairs were required, including a new roof, and, as the Petitjean family did not have the funds to renovate the facility, Rémy was able to purchase the property outright in 1994. Louis Vuitton Moët Hennessy (LVMH), owner of the Moët & Chandon and Veuve Clicquot brands, among many other wine, cosmetics, perfume and fashion businesses, bought Krug from Rémy in 1999.[62]

How, then, does one of the region's most expensive wines come to be fashioned from a site with such an unglamorous history? We can arrive at only two possible conclusions. First, it took the Krug team to recognise the inherent quality in the *clos*, an inherent quality that had somehow been missed by centuries of growers in Ambonnay. This is essentially the story put forward by Krug, that it 'discovered' the *clos*. The second conclusion that could be reached is that it was the genius of the Krug winemaking team that enabled such a great wine to somehow be coaxed from the site.

While either explanation could be rationally argued, one thing we can say with certainty about the Clos d'Ambonnay is that it is not a historically great terroir in the sense that a Grand cru in Burgundy is a historically great terroir. In a Burgundy Grand cru, the elevated pricing is premised on the ability of

Only Krug has a Krugmobile

the land to produce wine superior to that of the rest of the commune, as borne out by centuries of experience and as reaffirmed by the general consensus of local vignerons and the marketplace and, finally, the appellation laws. I doubt you could find a vigneron in Gevrey-Chambertin, for example, who does not believe that the Grand cru vineyards of that commune, as a general rule, consistently produce the finest wines of the village when managed appropriately. Ask vignerons in Ambonnay about Clos d'Ambonnay and you will likely get a very different response. They may be delighted with the attention that the wine has brought to their village. But as to the quality of the terroir itself in comparison to the best sites of the village? That is quite another discussion.

In short, Clos d'Ambonnay is, like Krug itself, a brand first and a wine of a particular terroir second. Many of the qualities that the wine has, including its remarkable price (the first vintage, 1995, was released at a staggering US$3,500 a bottle), have more to do with production methods and marketing than with terroir. Only in a region where brand dominates land could the most expensive fine wine be marketed from a vineyard that was never, historically, considered to be the finest in the commune, let alone in the region as a whole. The fact that this wine is priced so highly makes a clear statement that is in some ways the key to understanding the history of Champagne: anyone with access to the right grapes can produce an Ambonnay, but only Krug can produce a Clos d'Ambonnay.

MYTH VII

Simple fizzics: Where bubbles come from

For years we were told that the bubbles we found in our glasses of Champagne had formed on the imperfections that existed on the surface of the glass – indentations, scratches and so on. Thanks to the work of French physicist Gérard Liger-Belair, we now know this is not the case. It turns out that such imperfections are too small to be bubble 'nucleation sites', but they *are* places where microscopic strands of dust (cellulose fibres) can accumulate, and, as remarkable as it might seem at first, it is these dust strands that allow the bubbles in Champagne to form.

These tiny dust filaments are everywhere. The air we breathe is full of them. They are tubular in shape, and they have tiny pockets of air trapped inside their partially hollow frames. Champagne is supersaturated with carbon dioxide from the secondary fermentation – it has around 6 atmospheres of gas under pressure, which is considerably more pressure than a car tyre – and that gas desperately wants to escape the liquid.

Once poured, most of the carbon dioxide in a glass of Champagne escapes from the surface of the liquid without forming any bubbles. Yet, as we know, many bubbles do form – roughly two million per glass. This is where the dust filaments come in. As the carbon dioxide rises up the glass towards the surface of the liquid, it encounters the dust fibres and, as they are not solid and have pockets of air trapped within them, the pressurised carbon dioxide forces its way through them, in turn forcing the trapped air out of the other end, releasing a bubble and setting in motion a 'bubble train' – a continuous stream of bubbles. The rising carbon dioxide is drawn to the pockets of air within the filaments for the same reason that it is drawn to the surface of the liquid: the trapped air pockets have the same (lower) pressure as the atmosphere. Each filament can cause a stream of up to thirty bubbles per second, a process that gradually slows down and eventually stops as the gas pressure in the liquid equalises to the same level as that of the surrounding air.

So the physics of how supersaturated gas in a liquid behaves, along with our dusty planet, explains why bubbles form in a glass of Champagne (or any fizzy drink, for that matter). Liger-Belair and his colleagues at Reims University spent close to two decades assembling an impressive body of evidence that includes countless photos and videos taken of bubbles forming from the ends of dust strands, which are too small to see with the naked eye, using high-speed cameras fitted with microscopes. They further tested their results by pouring Champagne in a vacuum, from which all the dust particles had been removed – the Champagne poured flat. The experiments have been repeated and the results published in a number of scientific journals.

This also helps to explain why you shouldn't wash Champagne glasses with detergent (or, if you do, why you should thoroughly rinse them with fresh water afterwards). The detergent forms a sticky residue that traps and clogs the dust filaments, thus hindering the amount of gas that can work its way through them and limiting the number of bubbles that can form.

The cellulose filaments at the heart of this story are some of the oldest particles on earth. In fact, they are intergalactic in origin. They are part of the greater galaxy; they are stardust, if you will. This adds another dimension of romance to Dom Pérignon's mythical cry of 'Come quickly, I am drinking the stars!' What a shame he never actually uttered those words. They would have come far closer to the truth than he could have known.

PART XII

In which we head south to Vertus and visit a great grower
making 'crazy wine' in order to remind ourselves, once again,
that Champagne is a wine, first and foremost

The drive between Avize and Vertus is simple, short and unremarkable. You leave the town of Avize by the route you came in and turn south onto the D9. You soon pass through Le Mesnil-sur-Oger and then, after only a few minutes, arrive at the edge of Vertus, the southernmost village of the Côte des Blancs (if we discount the small hamlet of Bergères-lès-Vertus). It may not be an eventful voyage, but it is one well worth taking, for Vertus is the home of one of the truly great growers, Larmandier-Bernier.

Sophie Larmandier and I jokingly call Pierre Larmandier *'le moine de Vertus'* (the monk of Vertus), and not only for his devotion to great wine, cheese and charcuterie. It is also for a certain ascetic, almost puritanical element of his personality that reminds us of the monastery. He is not a talkative man; if you didn't know him, you might even think he was a little introverted. This isn't the case; he simply prefers to speak only when he has something meaningful to say. Then there is his love of working alone and of making decisions based on his own conclusions (of course, with some influence from Sophie, his wife, as we shall see below). There is also his strong, seemingly unwavering sense of purpose and conviction – he never seems to doubt that he is heading in the right direction. And there are the wines that he produces (again, with some help from Sophie): wines of great purity, monuments of restraint that once more nod towards the monastic. It is all of these traits combined, along with his imposing physique – tall, with square shoulders – that allows us to imagine him so clearly in a brown habit and with only a perfect circle of hair. But if I am being honest, it's mostly for his pious devotion to cheese, wine and charcuterie that we call him *'le moine'*.

Pierre Larmandier once took me to visit his favourite supplier of smallgoods at the local markets. The stall was a white caravan with a glass window crammed full of terrines, bacons, stuffed pigs' heads, *jambons crus*, pâtés, confit, sausages, galantines and ballotines, all glistening with fatty, aspic-coated succulence. To stare at this offering was to be reminded of the greatness of French culinary history and to wonder at the remarkable evolution that led a culture to produce such works of art from a humble pig. Pierre was clearly a very good client, because the proprietor smiled broadly as we approached and immediately moved from one side of the caravan to the other, squeezing past several of his staff in order to greet us. Such was his size that there was a discernible groaning from the caravan's supports as he moved towards us. His pale pink face and the rolls of fat around his neck suggested that he had been eating too much of his own fare and I couldn't help but be reminded of how closely we are related to our curly-tailed cousins. We are what we eat, after all. Pierre, to his credit, has thus far avoided too much of this piggy devolution by training for, and regularly running in, marathons with Sophie.

Pierre's father, Philippe Larmandier, died when his son was eighteen years old. It was 1982, and at first he thought he would have to abandon his studies and immediately return to the estate. Yet, his mother, Elisabeth (née Bernier – hence the estate's name), a strong, principled woman, whose resolute personality Pierre has inherited, insisted that her son should be allowed to continue his studies if he wanted, despite the outcries from other family members. 'You have a son, he is eighteen, so he must come back and help you,' they said. 'A woman cannot manage this alone.' His mother did not waver, however, and Pierre kept studying, helping out in his summer holidays and at harvest time, until his education was complete, five years later. Then there was one year of compulsory army duty before he returned to take over the estate, in 1988.

He was twenty-four years old. He had not always been sure he would return. The passing of his father had made the choice clearer. His sister's decision not to return also helped. If he was to do this, it was to be on his own terms. He had no fear of taking over from his mother. He had grown up in Vertus. He had been raised on the estate and had always helped his parents. He knew what was required. The domaine had a good team of experienced workers and consultants, so he would have help when he needed it. And there was another person who would help and influence him.

'I grew up in Avize,' says Sophie. 'And I always said that I would never marry a winegrower, because they were forever talking about the chemicals that they used on their land.' Sophie is a slender, athletic woman with an infectious smile. She likes to eat very simple, healthy and often raw foods – she is whip thin and extremely fit. Perhaps this abstemious element of her personality is why they have made such a successful couple and why she has been able to have a significant impact both on Pierre and on the direction of the estate.

As her statement above suggests, Sophie has long had an aversion to agricultural chemicals, and it was her abhorrence of the quantity of these products being spread across her region's soils that provided a major impetus for change on the Larmandier-Bernier estate. When Pierre returned, in the late 1980s, it was being farmed conventionally, with herbicides, pesticides and chemical fungicides. The wines were inoculated with cultured yeast and filtered, and the dosage was at standard levels. When I ask him what prompted the move away from such practices and towards the biodynamic viticulture we see across the estate today (where no synthetic chemicals are used at all), he answers simply with a shrug of his shoulders. 'My wife.'

Sophie, he explains, was 'a little obsessed' in her struggle against chemical usage, sometimes losing her cool when hearing her husband comparing chemical practices with other growers. Yet, her anti-chemical stance somehow rang true to him, and, once he understood that the quality and terroir expression of his wines could also improve as a result of abandoning chemical herbicides and pesticides, he began to consider what alternative systems there might be. Together, they started on a journey away from the conventional.

The move away from chemicals is not the only area in which Sophie has had an impact. She has long been her husband's 'right arm', in fact. 'For me it is difficult to be totally without her,' he says. 'The great thing about Sophie was that she was not just interested in the administrative side of things; she has always helped me in all areas of the business. She has been involved in all the decisions for a long time: the tastings and so on. This was important, as it was risky, what we did. So we had to take these decisions together. It's true that I manage the workers and she is more on the commercial and administrative side, but we don't have truly defined roles. We share everything.'

Of course, there were other influences. 'Anselme [Selosse] was the first grower to have a certain image and to have a different approach,' says Pierre. The couple didn't know him personally in the early days, but for them it was enough to see that a grower could take an alternative path, a terroir-first path, and that this approach could lead to success. By breaking the mould, Selosse touched everyone. He revealed the cracks in the paradigm of conventional Champagne practice. He successfully challenged an orthodoxy previously

Le moine de Vertus, Pierre Larmandier

Photo: James Broadway

Large cask and amphora in the cellars of Larmandier-Bernier

thought to be immutable. He shone a light into a space where there had been nothing but darkness.

'And also, our experience at Groupe des Jeunes was important,' says Pierre. The Groupe des Jeunes Vignerons de Champagne (Young Growers of Champagne Group, or GJVC) is a chapter within the CIVC that was established in the 1950s. Pierre Larmandier was the president from 1992 to 1996. Under his leadership, the GJVC established the subgroup Valoriser, whose purpose was to educate and influence the young growers who got involved, through tastings, travel and contact with the growers of other regions. Valoriser went on to have a marked influence on a number of important growers, as we shall see later.

'What we realised through our experiences was that we were here, in some of the best areas of Champagne, but we were only producing a nice wine,' says Pierre, 'a reasonable wine. We wanted to do more than that. But then the question was what to do. You can make changes in the winery, decide to use wood and so on, but what we chose to do was to search for riper, more concentrated grapes, to search for more expression and better quality from our vineyards. This was the path we chose.'

Of course, it is one thing to know where you want to go, but quite another to know how to get there. It has never been simple to convert an estate from conventional viticulture to the traditional practices that we now call 'organics'.[63] In Champagne in the 1990s, it was even more challenging. First of all, there was a completely different set of tools to discover and buy. There was also a completely different savoir-faire to learn and apply. And there was almost no local knowledge. Organic practices had been pretty much lost to the Champagne area by the time Pierre Larmandier took over his family domaine, and there were many lessons that had to be learnt the hard way.

To give one example: when the Larmandiers bought their first plough from Burgundy, in order to cultivate the soils rather than use herbicides, they had their tractor mechanic in Vertus assemble it. This was a man very experienced in vineyard equipment, yet he put the plough together upside down, with the tines facing upwards. He had never dealt with such a contraption. Once this was sorted out, they started cultivating and ploughed too quickly, too early, and wiped out 20 per cent of their vines. 'The older vines that had been worked before [in the distant past] had fewer problems adapting to being worked again, but the young vines did not cope well at all,' says Sophie. This taught them to go more slowly.

They also lost control of the weeds in some sites, and the locals thought they were mad. Even the local priest complained to Sophie's mother about the state of their vineyards. Imagine, a priest complaining about a monk! Yet this was (and is still predominantly) a region where a 'well-managed' vineyard is considered one devoid of any living greenery on the ground, in which herbicides have killed everything. Imagine how much the Larmandiers' vineyard – full of grass and herbs and weeds – would have stood out. Things progressed slowly from this point on. There were no major leaps forward but, rather, many small ones.

'Every year, we tried to improve things,' says Pierre.

'Things were not always easy, but there are moments that give you the courage to continue,' Sophie adds.

There were many positive influences along the way. Consultants such as Thierry Blaise were a big help, and renowned producers from other regions (in particular, Burgundy and Alsace) provided the inspiration. 'What you learn from visiting other important growers is that it isn't necessary to do the same thing as everyone else,' says Sophie. 'We visited many growers [outside Champagne], and they all had their own way. And that's what's great. Here, it is different, and we need our own inspiration in order to find our own path. We also were lucky enough to try some great wines on our visits, and these tasting experiences were a great encouragement for us to try to make some great wines ourselves.'

Pierre makes a further point: a grower can have the best intentions, but this alone will not be enough. 'What you need to know is how much cost and labour is involved in this approach. Without investment and without risk you cannot succeed.' And here, he spells out one of the major barriers to quality viticulture in the Champagne area: familial – usually paternal – resistance.

Pierre Larmandier's mother gave him free rein to run the estate as he chose. Anselme Selosse's father did the same. Jérôme Prévost had no one to stand in his way. But for many children who take over an estate, the father remains present and controlling and will in many cases not agree to radical change, an increase in costs or risk taking. There are often other siblings, and uncles and aunts as well, who can equally inhibit change. In such a scenario, progress of the kind we are discussing here becomes almost impossible – or, at best, it will come only slowly and after enormous struggle.

I ask Pierre if he thinks that this is the reason why the move away from industrial agriculture and towards a sustainable, quality and terroir-focused approach in the vineyard has been so slow in the Champagne area. 'This, and because the current system works so well.' He is making the same point as Pascal Agrapart when he said, 'When things are easy, it's hard to change.' Growers can make good money by farming conventionally, which is both easier and safer than farming without chemicals. Today, a Côte des Blancs grower can get €7 per kilogram for their grapes. At a yield of 14,980 kilograms per hectare, which was the average harvest between 2000 and 2009,[64] a grower will receive €104,860 per hectare of vines, even when they are farming conventionally, cropping high and picking early, even when they are not taking any of the risks that are required to produce the finest quality fruit.

'I have a very nice neighbour with 4 hectares of vines who loves to drop in to share a bottle,' says Pierre. 'He really enjoys our wines, and he says, "Pierre, it is marvellous, what you are doing!" But he sells all of his fruit to the co-operative. He says, "I will not change. It is too hard for me, what you are doing. Too complicated!" So he's happy. Happy with how he works and also happy to see and understand what we are doing.'

'But there are others who are not so happy,' adds Sophie. 'Some are jealous of our success and Anselme's success and so on, and they think that if we are successful it is because we have good communication, and they don't

Pierre the riddler

realise that they can make a different product. That they can act, change and also make better wine if they choose.'[65]

'But don't forget that most of the growers only sell fruit,' says Pierre. 'They do not make wine.' Again, we are reminded that the majority of growers will never taste a wine made exclusively from their grapes, so where is their incentive to produce higher quality fruit?

We can see why most growers are naturally resistant to change. It would mean having to work harder and to gamble with their (and their family's) income. The price they would receive for each kilogram of grapes would be exactly the same, but they would have less fruit to sell and therefore less income: achieving riper fruit in Champagne typically means lower yields, while later harvesting and avoiding chemicals often means more loss to rot. You can see the problem. Although the system may work well commercially (extremely well, it must be said), it has led to ever more poor-quality Champagnes being marketed (even by very prestigious brands).

Back to the Larmandiers' conversion. Step by step, beginning in the early 1990s, they removed chemical inputs from the vineyards, left natural yeasts to do their work in the cellar and introduced large format oak for maturation. The Larmandiers stopped using herbicides in 1992 and were fully organic by 1999. It was also from 1999 onwards that they fermented all the wines using wild yeasts and started to introduce biodynamics. The farm was fully biodynamic by 2002, and in 2004 the Larmandiers achieved organic certification.

The Larmandiers did not introduce biodynamics for any ideological reasons; their motivation was only to explore new tools that might improve the health of the vineyard and produce higher quality grapes. 'Biodynamics involves a lot of observation,' says Pierre. 'It isn't simply organics, where you say, "I won't put anything on the vineyard." Rather, you *can* add something. You can try to help your vines. You have to look for balance. It is really about the global health of the vineyards, which is the way we think for our bodies.'

Although they follow biodynamic practice, they are no fans of the bureaucracy and politics involved in the biodynamics world. 'There are different schools, and they compete with each other,' says Pierre. 'We have had certain suppliers of products complain to us because we have bought things from another supplier with another ideology. The correct product but the wrong ideology. It's completely crazy.' They are also keenly aware that biodynamics does not guarantee quality, particularly in Champagne. Anyone who sticks to the biodynamic rules in their vineyard can have the vineyard certified even when they farm a poor terroir, crop high, pick their fruit unripe, aggressively filter, add a lot of dosage and so on.

As hinted at earlier, there are those who follow biodynamics like a religion, or at least adopt its methodology and ideology as incontrovertible dogma. Many consultants encourage this approach by behaving like high priests. 'I remember asking my [biodynamics] consultant a direct question,' says Pierre, 'and he shook his head and told me that I was not yet ready to know the answer. "Next year," he said. "Next year we should be able to discuss this."'

My experience of the great growers of Champagne who use biodynamics is that they view it pragmatically and have little time for its mystical elements. For these growers, it is simply another suite of practices to be explored, picked through, trialled. Some practices will be adopted if they show benefits, others discarded. 'It was Pierre Morey [the former manager at Domaine Leflaive and owner of Domaine Pierre Morey, in Burgundy] who showed us that biodynamics could be something serious, not just ideology,' says Pierre.

Despite breaking with the conventional practices of the region, Pierre Larmandier has refused to be an outsider and has long played a key role in the CIVC. As we have seen, he is a former president of the GJVC, and, until a recent bout of ill-health, he was vice president of the Commission Communication et Appellations Champagne.[66] This part of the CIVC is charged with managing all the organisation's offices around the world, monitoring any illegal use of the term Champagne and overseeing the CIVC's communications. It was originally named the Commission of Propaganda. I kid you not. But somewhere along the way, the CIVC realised that this name might be a little too revealing, so it was changed.

You might think that a producer who has gone down the biodynamic, terroir-focused path, who has not only thrown out the official *How to Grow Champagne* handbook but has also helped develop an alternative path for the region, might also steer away from Champagne's establishment and bureaucracy. That is not Pierre Larmandier's way. 'You have to be involved to show that you are normal. To show that you are nothing special and to hopefully influence your region for the better,' he tells me. Better also to be there to defend yourself, and those like you, against the false accusations that you are some crazy sect or that you are successful simply because of some clever marketing. Better to be on hand to argue for a superior, more quality-focused path when such an opportunity arises. Better to be inside the tent than outside.

I think it's fair to say that Larmandier's time in the CIVC has mellowed him. 'In the past, I used to tell everyone that we needed to improve the general quality and strive to improve what was happening in the vineyards,' he says. 'But many would confront me and tell me that I was in another world, a niche world, and that I always wanted to go too far. Now, I think that perhaps they were right. Moët is a success. Whatever you think of their quality, they are still a success. What is bad in Champagne is not the Grandes Marques, but rather it is all the cheap, low-quality Champagnes being produced. I realise now that what the Champagne region needs is two things: the quality growers who make quality wine and the big houses with their prestigious names. What is bad is all the rest [the poor-standard growers, co-ops and négociants who sell on price alone], because they don't know where they are, and they make wine that is bad for the reputation of the region.'

I ask Larmandier how he would describe Champagne to someone who had never heard of it.

'What is Champagne?' he asks. 'It is a crazy wine, in that it can represent many things to many people. In the simplest terms, it is a wine with bubbles, but sometimes we forget it that it is a wine first of all. And this is something we should never forget.' Amen to that.

The wines of Champagne Larmandier-Bernier

Thanks to biodynamic viticulture, balanced yields, minimal fertilisers, precise pruning (done exclusively by their team) and having the nerve to wait, the Larmandiers are able to harvest fully ripe grapes – which is to say, grapes with fully ripe flavours. The wines all ferment naturally and mature mostly in oak – not for oak character, something assiduously avoided here, but because the Larmandiers believe, like all of the great growers of the Marne, that careful oxygenation is required for the wines to truly express their personalities. They purchase only new oak, to be sure of the quality, and they have sourced it almost exclusively from the cooper Stockinger since 2007, as they find this oak to be the most respectful to their wines. While most Champagne producers rack and filter their *vins clairs*, the Larmandiers prefer to age theirs for an extended period, between eight and twelve months, on their natural sediments. All of these details and countless others combine with the terroirs of the Côte des Blancs to produce some of the purest and most transparent wines in the region.

Each of the wines produced by Larmandier-Bernier, apart from the Rosé and the Coteaux Champenois Rouge, a Pinot Noir, is a Blanc de Blancs, so 100 per cent Chardonnay. The range begins with two non-vintage Blanc de Blancs blends: Latitude and Longitude.

Latitude is the richer, more textural wine and comes from the southern part of Vertus (and surrounding villages), where the soil is deeper and richer in clay. This was once Pinot Noir country, with 80 per cent of the vines planted to this variety. Now, it's nearly all Chardonnay, but the wines retain the richness and texture of the soils. It's called Latitude because the vineyards here run in a largely latitudinal direction, as opposed to the vineyards that supply Longitude, which run north to south along the Côte des Blancs, roughly following the fourth meridian (east). Latitude is broader in the mouth, filling it latitudinally, so to speak, whereas Longitude is far more linear, running the length of the palate and reflecting its chalkier soils. The vineyards that supply Longitude are located in Cramant, Avize, Oger and northern Vertus. In these sites, there is very little topsoil, and the vines tap directly into the chalk, resulting in a more mineral, racy, crunchy wine. Both the wines have between 30 and 50 per cent reserve wine (a blend of wines that goes back to 2004), while the dosage is around 3 grams, so they are in fact Extra Brut. They spend two to three years on lees.

Then there are four single-terroir, single-vintage wines. First is the remarkable Terre de Vertus, which we encountered in the Prologue to this book. It's a wine that comes from three neighbouring plots, mid-slope, on the northern side of Vertus. An incredibly pure, salty, mineral wine with citric, chalky notes as well as white pepper spice, Terre de Vertus can be very subtle and delicate, almost bony when it's young, but it blossoms with a year or two on cork. It is always the wine of a single vintage (though in the past the vintage was not always on the label), and it could not come from anywhere but the slopes of Vertus. Aged in *foudres* (large oak vats), it is a zero-dosage wine and was first produced in 1995.

Vieille Vigne de Cramant (now labelled as Vieille Vigne du Levant after the specific vineyard – *Bourron du Levant* – where the vines for this wine have always been situated) was the first single-terroir wine produced by the Larmandiers, the first vintage being 1988. It comes from the estate's oldest vines – between fifty and seventy years old – from two adjacent plots in the Grand cru village of Cramant. It is a fleshy, rich and powerful expression of the Côte des Blancs (particularly in the context of the Larmandiers' wines), and some smaller barrels are used in the maturation. The wine spends a year in barrels (large and small), on its lees, and receives some gentle stirring. As for all the wines here, there is no fining or filtration, and the wine receives an additional five years on lees in the bottle before being released at seven or eight years of age. Typically, there is a tiny dosage of 2 grams (there was zero dosage for the 2003 vintage).

The latest single-terroir wine is Les Chemins d'Avize. The fruit for this wine comes, again, from two small plots right next to each other in Avize. The Larmandiers have owned these vines since the 1990s, yet at the time of writing we have seen only one release, the 2009. The reason for this is simple. The vineyard area that feeds this wine is very small, and the Larmandiers' traditional press was not able to process such a small amount of fruit separately. In 2009, they traded in their old press and bought two smaller versions, so since that time they have been able to press the Avize fruit alone. The first release is wonderfully intense and mineral, yet very fine, with serious structure as well as some spicy, oak influence. The second release (2010) is finer, with better oak integration. It is early days, but it appears that something special is emerging here. The wine is more powerful than the Terre de Vertus but more compact than the Vieille Vigne. Like all of the wines mentioned above, it is a Blanc de Blancs, made from 100 per cent Chardonnay, and, again, the dosage is a very low 2 grams.

Finally, there is the brilliant Rosé de Saignée, for me one of the great Rosé wines of Champagne. It is made from a single vineyard in Vertus and comes from a single vintage (although it is not aged long enough to be legally labelled with a vintage). It is almost 100 per cent Pinot Noir; a small quantity of Chardonnay and Pinot Gris is included in the fermenting vat. The colour derives from a three-day maceration on skins, as opposed to the usual practice in the region of colouring Rosé wines via the later addition of red wine. Because of this extended skin contact, very strict fruit selection is required, as is a gentle destemming that leaves a lot of whole berries. This is the only single-terroir wine that neither sees any wood (the maturation is in stainless steel and two 600-litre concrete eggs) nor carries a vintage on the label. There are only 3 grams of dosage. The Larmandiers also produce tiny quantities of still wine from Pinot Noir and Chardonnay (Coteaux) that are well worth seeking out by those interested in this style.

PART XIII

The continuation of our *histoire vraie*, where the author views advanced capitalism through the rosiest of glasses and perhaps takes the friendship too far by comparing the history of Champagne to that of Camembert and free-range chicken

It's popular these days to evoke the image of some idealised Garden of Eden in our past, where natural, high-quality wine and food were the norm until the evil forces of American globalisation rose up and corrupted everything. This story has often been used to blame the US and its companies, consumers and wine critics, for any modern or industrial tendencies in French food and wine. Jonathan Nossiter's film *Mondovino* is perhaps the best known example of this in the wine world. But the 'blame America for everything' view does not hold up to even the most superficial scrutiny and is highly patronising to the French. In reality, the French have been great innovators in the realm of mass-produced foodstuffs, and they have been at it for centuries. The story of Camembert is just one example of many.

Camembert was once a farmhouse cheese that had a blue-grey mould with rust-coloured spots (the result of the indigenous microflora of the Normandy area). Originally, it was hand-made on a small scale, in farmhouses, from the unpasteurised milk of local cows. Only through a vast range of technological innovations – most, if not all, of which were invented by the French themselves – was Camembert eventually able to become the mass-market phenomenon it is today. These innovations started in the late 1800s and included pasteurisation (to eliminate wild bacteria and guarantee a consistent, homogenous end product), a range of new technologies to transport milk safely over vast distances (thus enabling the blending of milk from countless farms and multiple regions), the isolation and commercialisation of the cultured *Penicillium candidum* (which produced a more consumer-friendly, snow-white mould), the mechanisation of many areas of production (most notably ladle moulding) and the development of cheap, sturdy packaging (individual, light-weight wooden boxes) that enabled the cheese to travel long distances without damage. Only through the invention and application of these and a number of other technologies was 'brand Camembert' able to become a global success.[67]

The French have shown a particular genius for the marketing of such industrialised foods, introducing the techniques of mass production while maintaining the language of the artisan. So, Camembert producers have continually talked up the attributes of 'Norman Camembert' while blending their batches of milk from across France. Similarly, many Champagne producers spend a lot of time extolling the natural wonders of their soil while farming their vineyards industrially and not bothering to visit many of the sites from which they buy fruit. They manage to talk of terroir while at the same time blending it away in the name of house style.

It is tempting to assume that the move from artisan to mass production is a natural and linear evolution. Yet, one of the least anticipated outcomes of advanced capitalism is its tendency to create spaces in which the finest artisan wine and food producers can thrive. So it is that after decades of domination by the homogenising forces of mass production and its promise of 'foie gras for all' (albeit tinned foie gras), we now see pockets of resistance all across our culinary landscape. In advanced Western economies, the produce of the finest food and wine craftspeople now sells very well, even in challenging economic times. This is despite the fact that such products are typically far more expensive than their mass-market counterparts.

This is perhaps best illuminated by the circular story of naturally reared, 'free-range', or farmhouse, chicken. Once, all chickens were free-range and grew at their own pace. Roast chicken was a luxury, as the birds were either reared slowly by those who ate them or purchased at a significant expense for a special occasion. Industrially reared battery hens changed all this by making chicken far less expensive. Suddenly, we could all enjoy a roast chook any night of the week. The pure, snow-white flesh of these birds and their lack of gaminess seemed somehow to make manifest the promise of the modern industrial food complex: an inexpensive abundance of perfectly refined products and the repression of the rural reality of life and death and dirt. But something was lost. Flavour. Character. Our connection to the land. In hindsight, it was as though the ghost of authentic farmhouse chicken was haunting all of our roast dinners until a lack or longing reappeared in the market that could only be filled by naturally reared birds. First, the demand was driven by the best chefs and their restaurants, and then, the public caught on.

In many markets, the best free-range, 'hormone-free' chickens are far more expensive than their frozen, mass-produced equivalents, and yet demand has been very strong. This is because the flavour and quality of such birds are simply better, because there is increasing cynicism towards mass-produced foods and because there is a growing belief that smaller, more artisanal production with fewer chemical inputs results in better standards, more humane treatment of animals and improved health for the consumer and the environment.

This market logic can be extended to a great many products. Yes, we are talking about niche markets, yet today, these markets are large enough to allow superior artisan producers to arise and flourish. They are also growing fast enough to influence the mass market, as evidenced by the major supermarket chains' adoption and promotion of organic foods and, in some cases, banning of cage eggs. In today's culture, where information travels at light speed, where there is an upsurge in the desire for 'natural' and 'artisan' foodstuffs and where there is an abundance of importers and distributors cultivating niche markets, the finest artisan producers are typically able to establish powerful and profitable markets for their goods.

It is worth noting that the finest artisanal French cheeses have not been able to capitalise on this movement, due to the restrictions on the importing and selling of unpasteurised milk products that exist in many countries. It has been this restriction, rather than any lack of demand, that has tragically denied French farmhouse cheeses a rebirth of the kind experienced by many other artisanal products.

The movement from mass market to artisanal, of course, relies on a class of affluent consumers who can choose to pay a higher price for what they believe to be a more natural, sustainable and better tasting product. It seems possible only in advanced, post-industrial countries, where a significant proportion of the population is wealthy. However, this does not alter my point. It is clear that the agricultural revolution that gave birth to modern, industrialised food production contained within it the seeds of its own destruction – or, at least, its own limitation. As we have touched on above, the prescriptive use of agricultural chemicals and heavy machinery indirectly led to the recent movement towards 'living soil' viticulture in Europe. In the same way, the ubiquity of mass-market foods, such as frozen pizza and battery hens, has stimulated the growing demand for artisanal, farmhouse, natural and authentic produce. This is the trajectory taken by many foodstuffs, including wine, and it speaks directly to recent events in Champagne.

MYTH VIII

The shape of things to come: Champagne should be served in flutes

The choice of which glass to use for a given wine is influenced by a host of factors, including fashion. In the 18th century, the narrow, tall, flute-shaped glass was the standard choice for serving Champagne. Then, throughout the 19th century, it started to become fashionable to serve Champagne in short, wide-mouthed coupes, even though they are quite impractical glasses: the wine loses its fizz and aromatics quickly.

Despite its obvious shortcomings, the coupe became fashionable for reasons that we can only speculate on today. Some have argued that its popularity followed the rise of Rosé styles of Champagne, the coupe being considered a better vessel to showcase the colour of the vibrant pink liquid. Its shape was also perfect for building the Champagne towers that became a symbol of the early decades of the 20th century, and it was party tricks like this that helped to build Champagne's popularity at that time. There was also the legend that a pair of Champagne coupes had been moulded from Marie Antoinette's breasts, which certainly helped give this type of glass historical gravitas. As it turns out, the Marie Antoinette story is yet another Champagne myth. While there is some historical evidence to suggest that Marie Antoinette and her husband, Louis XVI, did commission a set of ceramic, breast-shaped bowls, there is no evidence that these were modelled directly from the teen queen's own breasts or that they were intended to be used for Champagne. In fact, the coupes are believed to have been a propaganda piece designed to encourage French noblewomen to breastfeed their babies.

Regardless, the rise of the coupe, a vessel that radically limits the taster's ability to appreciate the wine, reminds us that Champagne was, for much of its history, very much a party drink, a wine appreciated for its sweet, foamy attributes and its association with wealth, hedonism and good times. It was in this context that the coupe became the official Champagne glass. It probably didn't hurt that it was also a good shape for dipping cake or biscuits into.

Eventually, the flute made a comeback as the Champagne glass of choice, and we have been living through the era of the flute ever since. Yet, the times they are a-changing, once again.

The use of flutes has typically been justified by the idea that tall, narrow glasses help preserve bubbles for longer than more open-mouthed glassware, because the surface area of the wine exposed to the atmosphere is smaller. As most of the carbon dioxide in a glass of Champagne escapes from the surface of the wine as invisible vapour, without forming bubbles, it follows that the greater the surface of wine exposed, the faster the gas dissipates. This turns out to be correct. Tests have shown that the traditional flute holds its bubbles for around 30 per cent longer than a coupe, and my own admittedly rudimentary tests have revealed that a classic flute is more effective at keeping its bubbles going for longer than an open-mouthed, tulip-shaped glass. Yet, these test results only have relevance if you are going to leave your glass sitting there for ten minutes or more, as this is the time frame in which the glass shape starts to make a difference to the number of bubbles in your glass. I would venture that most glasses of Champagne are consumed in a far shorter period.

On the other hand, traditional flute-shaped glasses radically limit the drinker's ability to smell the aromatics of a wine (the small mouth of the glass again being the key factor) and therefore limit the potential pleasure offered. If you want to really appreciate a quality Champagne, you need a glass with a wider mouth. The good news is that many of the better known glass companies are now offering Champagne glasses with wider mouths that function almost as well as a white wine glass, as long as you fill them no more than halfway.

My suggestion? Don't worry about the bubbles! You get plenty of them, no matter what glass you use. Do, however, worry about the wine and maximising the pleasure it can give you. If you have a real wine in your glass, the kind of wine that I am advocating in this book, it deserves a real wine glass that will showcase the quality that is on offer.

Keep in mind that a number of growers (and, I am told, a number of larger houses) are dropping their levels of *tirage* to produce finer (and fewer) bubbles, while others are encouraging drinkers to decant their wines before serving. Again, we come back to our opening lesson: great Champagne is a wine first and *sparkling* wine second. If we agree with this adage, we must always prioritise the appreciation of the wine itself over the bubbles and serve it in a quality wine glass. To this end, a traditional, small-mouthed flute or a coupe will not do. After that, there are no hard and fast rules. You can be as creative as you like with the shape, so long as the glass gives you the opportunity to fully appreciate the wine's aromatics. I find a quality, mouth-blown, tulip-shaped white wine glass is the most versatile shape but I also use larger glasses when I feel the wine could benefit from more air.

PART XIV

In which we travel from Vertus to the historic market city of Troyes, all the while grappling with the ideologies of Champagne's separatists

In order to depart the Côte des Blancs and head to Troyes, the ancient capital of the Aube, we will need to get back onto the D9 and head due south. Surprisingly, perhaps, we have about 80 kilometres to travel, even though we are starting from the southernmost point of the Côte des Blancs. Just as surprisingly, we will arrive in a totally different area (the Aube) but remain in the same region (Champagne).

For a small detour along the way, we could do a lot worse than heading towards the village of Congy, only a twenty-minute drive west of Vertus. Congy is situated on the Coteaux du Morin, in an area that is difficult to pin down. Although some official maps place Congy in the Côte des Blancs, it actually sits quite some way westwards of the slopes that have historically defined this area. North of the Côte de Sézanne and west of the Côte des Blancs, Congy is in a historical no-man's-land, and yet there we will find another superb grower, Olivier Collin, of Ulysse Collin, who is making superb, authentic and delicious wines from a unique terroir that includes black flint, or onyx, as part of the soil composition (a rarity in Champagne).

But today, we are heading directly to Troyes. This great mediaeval market city is, with Reims, one of the mighty bookends of Champagne, which, along with Épernay, have helped shape the region. Yet, to speak of Troyes, or the Aube in general, as a vital player in the history of the Champagne region is to court controversy. There remain many voices in the region that argue that the Aube (the southernmost zone of Champagne) should never have been included in the Champagne AOC. The voices have been heard for as long as sparkling wine has been made here, and they typically come from the Marne, the Champagne department north of the Aube that includes the majority of Champagne's vineyards (over 67 per cent) and the most famous subregions: the Côte des Blancs, Montagne de Reims and Vallée de la Marne. The Marne

Olivier Collin of Ulysse Collin points us towards the Aube

department also contains the cities of Épernay and Reims, where most of the famous Champagne houses are based.

At face value, the argument is quite straightforward and rational: the vineyards of the Aube are simply too far away from the Marne to be meaningfully included in the same region. After all, Troyes is closer to Chablis (71 kilometres) than it is to Reims (126 kilometres), and the Aube has a completely different geology from that of the Marne (more limestone than chalk), as well as a different climate (sunnier, more southern).[68] It makes sense, then, that the two areas produce quite distinct styles of wines. From a terroir perspective, this argument would seem to have merit, but when it comes to the history of the region, it doesn't stack up. First, the Aube was always a part of the province of Champagne pre-revolution, and its vineyards have been a part of the official zone of Champagne since the passing of the law defining and delimiting the region in 1927.[69] More significantly, the Aube has always supplied a great deal of fruit and wine to the large Champagne houses; this drove its inclusion in the AOC of Champagne. Today, the Aube represents 20 per cent of the vineyards of Champagne and is also one the region's hotspots for terroir-driven wines.

The truth is that the Champagne AOC was never delimited by terroir, which is why there is only one AOC to cover such a vast area of land.

The black flint of Congy

Champagne has always simply meant a sparkling wine made according to the rules of the Champagne AOC from the areas that are included in the AOC. The wines of the region have nearly always been blends from many villages and therefore from many, very different, terroirs. Of course, a bottle of Champagne from the Aube will be different from one grown in the Marne, but then, a bottle from Vertus will be different from one grown in Ambonnay, even though both of these villages are in the Marne. You can't have it both ways: separate terroirs should have their own AOC or regional status, or it's difficult to justify singling out one area for marginalisation.

If those who make the argument above truly want a Champagne region that is defined along terroir and wine-style boundaries – something I would welcome – they should be calling for a change in the AOC laws that would enable Champagne to be sold according to the village or vineyard, à la the Burgundy AOC model, or perhaps along sub-regional lines (Côtes des Blancs, Coteaux du Morin and so on), rather than debating who deserves the right to the regional title of Champagne. This would, in turn, encourage the growers to produce their grapes in such a way as to magnify the expression of terroir in the final wines. The market could decide which of these sub-regions, villages or vineyards, should be more prized. The great growers have shown that such a movement is possible for an individual estate, but it remains highly unlikely for the region as a whole, for the reasons that I hope I'm making clear throughout this book. Even if the region did move in this direction, it would take a long, long time.

Of course, today, we do not require such a change for wine lovers to make choices along terroir, or subregional, lines. They can, for example, buy wine from a quality grower within the Aube knowing that what is in the bottle will reflect the specific terroir in which it was grown. If they prefer the wines from certain growers in the Marne, or from certain terroirs in the Marne, they are free to choose accordingly.

There is no question that this debate has led some in the Marne to look down their noses at their southern counterparts, viewing them as poor cousins. Those in the Aube have naturally felt this criticism keenly, and it remains a raw nerve today, as we shall see. Nonetheless, long before there was any talk of an appellation, or of delineating a Champagne AOC, the Aube was playing a major role in the development of the greater Champagne area. Although Troyes was not the only city in Champagne to attract European traders, it was a major draw, and its historical contribution was significant in other ways; it helped cultivate the mercantile culture of the Champagne region as a whole, and it was this culture that, in turn, ensured the international success of the region's wines.

Today the Aube is one of the most dynamic Champagne areas when it comes to the grower Champagne movement. There are a number of fascinating growers here, but the wines and stories of three of them have truly moved me, and I try to visit them regularly. They are Jacques Lassaigne, Vouette et Sorbée, and Cédric Bouchard.[70]

PART XV

Where the author discusses the problems with the term 'grower revolution' and then offers the reader a choice between two radically different worlds of Champagne

Today it is commonplace to hear talk of a 'grower revolution' in Champagne. Certainly, the Terre de Vertus I was served on that night in Châlons was a revolutionary wine for me. It was like an electric shock, a revelation, a call to arms. It ignited my interest and shattered all of my assumptions. It was the vinous equivalent of a 19th-century factory worker hearing the words of *The Communist Manifesto* or a biologist of the same era reading *On the Origin of Species*. All of a sudden, there was a radical alternative that called into question the current dogma and explained why so much Champagne had failed to excite me. All of a sudden, Champagne was interesting again. Yet while 'grower revolution' seems to capture the radically different paths being followed by the finest growers and those following in their footsteps, and the radically different wines that result, the term is misleading in several ways.

First, it suggests an explosion of high-quality, artisanal, vineyard-owning producers who are fashioning wines of a standard to challenge the pre-eminence of the big brands. The reality on the ground is a little more sobering. Certainly, the 'golden decades' of Champagne's recent history have encouraged those growers with a calling to start making their own wines. It is also true that there are now a reasonable number of growers working in a similar vein to the producers we are visiting in these pages and who are striving to produce quality wines of place. And yes, demand for the finest grower Champagnes has increased significantly in recent years, especially among knowledgeable wine buyers. Yet grower-producers of this kind are still only responsible for a tiny percentage of Champagne's overall production.[71] In fact, grower Champagne in general, regardless of quality, comprises only around 5 per cent of the Champagne exported from France. And, according to the CIVC, the number of grower-producers is actually shrinking. It seems that today's grape prices are so high (€5–7 per kilogram at the time of writing) that some grower-producers have been encouraged to stop making wine and to simply sell all of their fruit. It is, of course, much easier and less risky for a small landholder to sell grapes than it is for them to make and market wine. They also get paid far more quickly. If they can make the same return, faster, by just selling grapes, it's obviously very tempting.

In fact, most growers who do make wine themselves from their own vineyards typically make extremely basic, conventional wines following the practices and ideologies of the large houses (or what they believe these to be). This makes sense; the large houses were, until very recently, the only models of a successful Champagne business that the growers had to follow. The large houses have always been prosperous and are internationally revered. This is why the vast majority of Champagne growers don't believe that the grape-growing and winemaking practices that still dominate Champagne need to be challenged. Those practices have, after all, been key factors in the commercial success of the region, a success in which the growers now share.

Having said this, things are definitely changing and there are increasingly more quality growers appearing, but progress is slow. On the one hand, it does feel to many of us in the trade that Champagne is nearing some kind of turning point at which consumers will demand more of the excellence and uniqueness being offered by the best growers. And yet, for the reasons that we have already covered, the Champagne region still has a long way to go before it could deliver on such demand. The great growers, and those who are striving to emulate them, have certainly started a revolution in quality, authenticity and terroir expression, but in terms of significant change, in terms of the volume of wine being produced, the revolution is occurring only at the fringes.

The term 'grower revolution' is also problematic in that it seems to suggest that the finest grower-producers are doing something radically novel, something revolutionary. This is true only in the context of Champagne. When it comes to quality French wine in general, working with nature as much as possible to encourage life in the soil and working with balanced yields and ripe fruit in order to produce the finest quality, terroir-rich wines is not a revolutionary approach; it's normal. It's the modus operandi of all the greatest winegrowers in every other French region. Only in Champagne does it seem exceptional.

It's also true to say that most of the finest growers do not see themselves as revolutionaries, in that they have little desire to 'fight the system'. On the contrary, they are openly grateful for the work that the large producers and Champagne's regional bodies have done in creating the international market for Champagne, a market that they now benefit from. These growers see themselves as simply returning to historical vineyard practices that were the norm in their region prior to the 1960s. Nothing so revolutionary in that, they argue. On the other hand, we must not forget that the term 'revolution' has the same root as the word 'revolve'. It comes from the Latin *'revolvere'*, meaning 'turn back' or 'revolve around'. It was originally used in the context of celestial bodies. In this sense, a return to traditional practices is in fact revolutionary, and it is especially so in a region like Champagne. Further, the 'terroir first' approach of the best growers – where the vineyard and cellar practices are specifically designed to bring out the personality of particular vineyards and villages or soil types – is certainly something completely new when it comes to the history of sparkling wine in Champagne.

Perhaps the most misleading aspect of the term 'grower revolution' is that it seems to suggest (or, at least, it seems to have given many people the idea) that Champagne growers generally make better or, at any rate, more interesting wines than the larger houses, by simple virtue of the fact that their production is smaller and because they control their own vineyards. This is not at all the case. Although owning your own vines and making smaller quantities of wine are certainly advantages when it comes to striving for the highest possible quality, as the vast majority of grower-producers mimic the practices of the large houses, their potential advantage is lost. Their problems are further compounded by the fact that they don't typically have the same skills or resources that are available to the large houses. For these reasons, few 'conventional' growers manage to produce wine of the same quality as the négociants themselves. The truth is that grower-producers (*récoltant-manipulants*) in Champagne who use all of the fruit they grow to produce their own wines are still rare. Those who do this and also make high-quality wines are exceptional. And those who make terroir-driven wines that can sit comfortably alongside the finest still wines of France can be counted on your fingers and toes.

For these reasons, when trying to understand Champagne, it isn't meaningful to divide the region's wines into categories of 'grower-producer' and 'négociant' (or 'grower' and 'house'). This will tell you little about style or quality. What *can* be useful is to make a distinction between 'conventional' or 'house style Champagne' and what we could call 'terroir-driven Champagne'

On the road in Champagne

or 'Champagne of place'. Conventional Champagne, as produced by all of the large négociants and co-ops and by most growers, starts with the idea of producing a house style, typically with the expectations of the market in mind. It makes use of conventional viticulture, the customary high yields of the region, earlier harvesting, austere base wine, blending and winemaking to a house style and so on. Terroir-driven Champagne, on the other hand, is successfully produced by only a very small number of the finest growers, who pull out all the stops to maximise both the potential quality and the expression of the vineyard in their grapes and then seek to capture as much of these attributes as possible in the final wine. They do not seek to create a wine in the cellar or search for a house style; rather, they look for ways to mature the wine that will maximise the potential and personality already in the fruit harvested. In short, any apparent house style from a great grower will in fact be a reflection of their vineyards and of the choices made, in the vineyards and in the cellar, to allow these vineyards to express themselves. It will be a terroir style rather than a house style.

Of course winemaking is important, and of course there are different paths that can be taken in the cellar; yet, for these growers, the quality and ripeness of the fruit are the most significant factors in terms of determining the final quality. To this end, they make use of the kinds of viticultural practices already discussed, yields that are at least one-third to one-half less than a conventionally farmed Champagne vineyard (and sometimes far less than that), riper fruit (often 1.5–2.5 degrees of potential alcohol riper – a massive difference), minimal-intervention winemaking (no fining, filtration, enzymes, commercial yeast and so on) and little or no dosage.

They will also need outstanding terroir if they are truly to succeed. Everyone agrees that great wines of place need great vineyard sites, but this logic is very often conveniently ignored in Champagne, where blending is the dominant ideology and where there is no official hierarchy of vineyards, only of villages. Regardless, the two philosophies outlined above now separate the majority of Champagne producers from a tiny, marginal group of the finest, artisanal growers.

Not only is the number of exceptional grower-producers terribly limited; the growth in new producers joining their ranks has been frustratingly slow. Since the early 1980s, when the great grower movement was just beginning to take its first, tentative steps in Champagne, Burgundy has undergone a quality revival of monumental proportions. The same cannot be said for the Champagne region. Perhaps we are still witnessing the beginning of what will become a full-blown revolution? Some great Champagne growers cautiously hope this may be the case. Others have doubts and point out that the pressure on the limited number of great growers is mounting and that the defence of their approach rests on too few shoulders. Some growers have a great fear that the 'industrial forces' that drive the region, to quote one prominent vigneron, will seek to marginalise the best grower-producers, claiming that their wines are not 'true' Champagnes. These fears are magnified when producers are attacked for being 'charlatans' or for 'saying one thing and doing another', accusations I have heard directly from key négociants and other growers. As one grower told me, 'Before, they could just say that we were mad. Now we are successful it is much more troubling for them.'

Despite the limitations of the term 'grower revolution', it is obviously true that today there is a small but slowly expanding band of terroir-obsessed growers whose viticultural and winemaking practices, and the wines that result from them, depart significantly from those of conventional Champagne. It is also true that those growers are finding a loyal market across the globe. It may not be a revolution in terms of scale, yet the producers and their methodologies have raised serious questions about what should be accepted as 'good practice' in Champagne and have ignited a passion for their region in many who, like your author, had long ago ceased to consider Champagne one of the truly great wines of the world. Thanks to these great growers, I now know that I was wrong. The great growers may be reluctant to be labelled as revolutionaries, yet they are without doubt producing revolutionary wines for their region. For this revolution to become mainstream, there will need to be much more support and pressure from the broader trade and the wine-buying public.

Until I encountered the wines of the finest growers of Champagne, I assumed that Champagne's typical modus operandi was pretty much immutable, that the winegrowing and winemaking practices of the large Champagne houses, with all the limitations outlined above, were simply inherent in the production of a decent sparkling wine in the region of Champagne. I assumed that these elements were part of what defined Champagne, that they were, if not the only way to make such a wine, then surely the best way. Hadn't these practices evolved over time in order to produce the best quality? The leading wine books on the region said as much; as did the marketing spiel of the leading producers and regional bodies. I did not really spend that much time thinking about it, because, as I indicated early on in this book, I was not really that keen on Champagne.

With hindsight, I can see that my travels in the region in the early 2000s had led me to stumble upon an alternative world of Champagne, one that had been previously hidden to me and to many others. In fact, it was too small to be called a 'world'. It was more a satellite orbiting around a world. A small meteor hurtling through a universe of conventional Champagne. Subsequent visits to the region and regular contact with a good number of terroir-focused growers helped me to comprehend what I had been missing. Coming to understand these producers, their methods and their wines taught me that my assumptions about the region, and those of many of my colleagues and friends, had been, if not false, then at best simplistic. Most infuriatingly, it became clear that the story of Champagne, as I had previously understood it, was a careful and deliberate construction by the powerful marketing and PR arms of the large négociant houses and the regional bodies of the Champagne AOC. Sadly, I had accepted this version verbatim and without question.

Over time, I have come to understand that the structure of the Champagne region, as well as the typical Champagne viticultural and winemaking practices, did not evolve because they produce the finest wines, as we have so often been told. Rather, they came about either as a response to specific historical conditions that in many cases no longer apply, or simply as a result of the négociants' and growers' drive for growth, greater efficiency and higher profits. It has also become clear that the story of Champagne is far from finished and, in many ways, is just beginning. Finally, to my astonishment, I have discovered that Champagne is a region that can make wines that are every bit as great, as complex, as terroir rich, as delicious and as moving as the finest Burgundies. Such wines are being made today, although admittedly in tiny quantities and by only a small band of producers. Such wines will always be the exception to the rule, unless there is a paradigm shift of monumental proportions, which, for reasons that I am outlining here, is highly unlikely to occur.

The good news however, is that there is now a choice between two 'worlds' of Champagne: the vast and dominant world of conventional Champagne as practised and produced by almost all négociants, co-ops and most grower-producers and the tiny world of remarkable, terroir-driven wines being produced by a small bunch of the very finest Champagne growers. That this choice exists is a revolution in and of itself. The difference between the two worlds is not simply a question of quality; there are good wines on both sides. It is more a question of approach, of methodology, of what attracts you to serious wine in the first place.

PART XVI

In which we visit our first Aube grower and learn what it means to be an outsider in your own region

If you drive from Troyes in the Aube for only a few kilometres west, along the D660, direction Auxerre, you will soon see a small, isolated, vine-covered hill appear in the landscape a little way off to your right. Perched on this hill, overlooking Troyes and the Vallée de la Seine, is the tiny township of Montgueux. This is our first destination in the Aube. On the slopes here, we will find the vineyard of a small yet significant grower by the name of Emmanuel Lassaigne, who produces wine under the label Jacques Lassaigne – his father's name.[72]

Montgueux is possibly the only Champagne village or terroir that sits completely on its own – a hilly outcrop of vines in a vast agricultural plain. All the other villages of Champagne seem to form part of a subregion or a continuous collection of vineyard villages, such as the Côte des Blancs, Côte de Sézanne, Montagne de Reims, Côte des Bar, Vallée de la Marne, Vallée de la Vesle, Vallée de l'Ardre and Coteaux Sud d'Épernay. Montgueux is part of the Aube department and is officially grouped with other Aube vineyard areas, but this is an artificial, bureaucratic classification: the village is isolated, on the other side of Troyes from the Côte des Bar (home to the rest of the Aube growers), and has a completely different geology.

As Emmanuel Lassaigne tells it, the soils of Montgueux are in fact closer to those of the Côte des Blancs than to those of the rest of the Aube. 'Montgueux is the geological continuation of the Côte des Blancs,' he says. 'The same soil, chalk, but fifteen million years older. In fact, it's the bottom part of the chalk, and this creates some differences that are important. We don't have the same fossils, and we have a little bit of *silex* [flint] in the chalk, which does not occur in the Côte des Blancs except in a small area near Vertus called Le Mont Aimé, at the very edge of the Côte des Blancs.'

Montgueux's unique isolation (in terms of both location and geology) has been important in its history, its late development and its lack of recognition. Even today, and even with a well-respected grower located here, most maps of Champagne do not include it, and many articles on Champagne – even articles on the Aube – do not refer to it.

Although Montgueux has always been a part of the AOC of Champagne as it was formalised in 1936, it did not truly emerge as a winegrowing area until the 1950s and 1960s when négociants started to look for grapes outside their traditional sourcing zones and encouraged the growers of the village to plant vines.[73] Prior to this era, very few vineyards were located here. It may be hard to imagine today, but before World War II, Champagne was for the most part a poor region (certainly for those on the land), and grapegrowers generally struggled. So it was only in the late 1950s and early 1960s that enough incentive arose to plant vines in Montgueux, and Jacques Lassaigne and his brother and one other family, the Beaugrands, were the first to do so.

Initially, the new vignerons were farming only to sell grapes to the négociants, but in the 1970s Jacques Lassaigne began to make some wine to sell directly. The family managed to survive with this structure, selling both fruit and bottles of wine, until the late 1990s, when it suffered financial difficulties and began to contemplate selling out. The thought of losing the family estate was one of the key factors that brought Emmanuel Lassaigne home to help his parents. This was no easy decision: Lassaigne had already forged a successful career outside of wine, with an international manufacturing firm. Yet, the idea of his parents losing the farm they had worked so hard to establish disturbed him. And there were other motivations. For example, Lassaigne had long felt a strong sense of frustration at the lack of recognition that Montgueux received in the world of Champagne.

To understand this lack of acknowledgement and Montgueux's lowly position in Champagne's pecking order, we need to look over our shoulder at history. We have already seen that for as long as sparkling wine has been made in Champagne (and even longer, in fact), there has been a strong tradition of viewing the Aube as a poor cousin, an area that does not really belong in the AOC. Although it is difficult to justify such bias today, many in the Aube feel like they are still looked down upon by the more famous villages of the north. And if the Aube in general has struggled against bias from the north, imagine what a little outpost that is not even part of the Aube's best known, historical vineyard area (the Côte des Bar) has had to contend with. At least those vineyards in the Côte des Bar can point to centuries of vinegrowing tradition. Montgueux can't, and so it has been a singular outcast from the start.

Large houses have denied sourcing wines from Montgueux even when they have begrudgingly acknowledged that they sourced some from the Aube, and the few local growers who sold bottled wine did not put the name of the village on their labels, because they felt that the poor reputation (or lack of recognition) of the area would discourage sales. For an intelligent, educated and keenly sensitive local like Emmanuel Lassaigne, who grew up in Montgueux, this was more than frustrating.

One incident in particular crystallised Lassaigne's sense of injustice on this issue and finally motivated him to do something about it. Around the time that his parents started to consider selling their vineyards, Lassaigne found himself on a tour of the Veuve Clicquot facilities. He was not visiting as a winegrower; rather, he was there thanks to his previous career, chaperoning a group of Heineken executives who were interested in viewing Clicquot's bottling technology. One of the senior men at Heineken knew Lassaigne well so asked the Clicquot people, 'Do you work with grapes from Montgueux?'

The response was short and sharp. 'Montgueux? Oh, no! We only work with the grapes of the Marne!'

In fact, during that period, Veuve Clicquot was the largest purchaser of the grapes of Montgueux, buying the fruit of 40 out of a total of 200 hectares.

'At the time, I said nothing,' Lassaigne tells me. 'I was there with another job. But I knew that this was not right. You can say you don't like our fruit. You can decide not to buy our fruit. But to buy so much of it and then deny it? This is not right. This is not fair. So I thought, we must put Montgueux on our bottles and say that we are proud of our terroir. Our terroir is not better, it is not worse, but there is a typicity here, and I wanted to show it. That was the beginning for me. I was born here. If people say where you were born was shit and you disagree, well, you are motivated to do something about it.'

Not everyone in the north was reluctant to acknowledge the role Montgueux played in their blends. In the 1980s, one of the main buyers of Montgueux grapes was Charles Heidsieck. The *chef de cave* there at the time was the renowned Daniel Thibault, who was once quoted as saying, 'If there is a Montrachet in Champagne, it is in Montgueux that we will find it!' He was referring to the richness of the Chardonnay wines that can be produced on the hillside slopes of this village that face southeast (or, sometimes, southwest).

Emmanuel Lassaigne of Champagne Jacques Lassaigne

This statement must have been viewed with scepticism and surprise in an era when most négociants denied they sourced wine from the Aube at all. (Some still do deny it.) Yet, Thibault was onto something. Locals today talk of their wines as having a *'meursette'* personality (Meursault-like – that is, rich and textural) with age, a characteristic that is evident even in wines raised purely in stainless steel.

So Lassaigne quit his job and returned to the family estate in 1999. His first priority was to save the business, but soon he was making radical changes that involved a great deal of risk. The estate used to sell all the wines it made at the domaine (via the cellar door, if you like), directly to the public, but Lassaigne stopped this and decided to sell the wine only to the best retailers and restaurants. 'By the end of 2002, I only had two customers! So it was not very easy.' You still can't buy a bottle at Lassaigne's cellar, a policy that is very rare in Champagne. He also began immediately to make changes in how his family's vines were managed and then in how the wines were made and packaged. Not everything happened at once, of course. Many changes were small and have been implemented on the basis of Lassaigne's experience over the journey. The point has been to constantly strive for improvements in quality and in revealing the Montgueux terroir. As Lassaigne puts it, 'Each step is a detail. One detail doesn't change anything. But all the details together make a big difference.'

Today, the Lassaigne methodology reads like a model for great grower behaviour. In the vineyards, he works organically, cultivating between the vines and rolling the grass flat inter-row (rather than cultivating). No fertilisers, herbicides or pesticides are used, even those allowed under organic regulations. 'I have never understood organic pesticides: you kill, but you do it kindly,' he laughs. Crop levels are regulated via pruning and the absence of fertiliser, and the fruit is picked ripe. In the winery, he keeps each parcel of grapes separate and produces cuvées according to the vineyard origins. He avoids sulphur, adding only a little at the press and none during the *élevage* or at bottling. He doesn't fine or filter, disgorges by hand and no longer adds any dosage. He doesn't feel he needs to. In the hands of a genuine grower like Lassaigne, the south- and southeast-facing slopes of Montgueux can produce opulent, layered Champagnes that have ample fruit and texture.

One significant point of difference between Lassaigne and the other great growers visited in these pages is that Lassaigne is officially classed as a

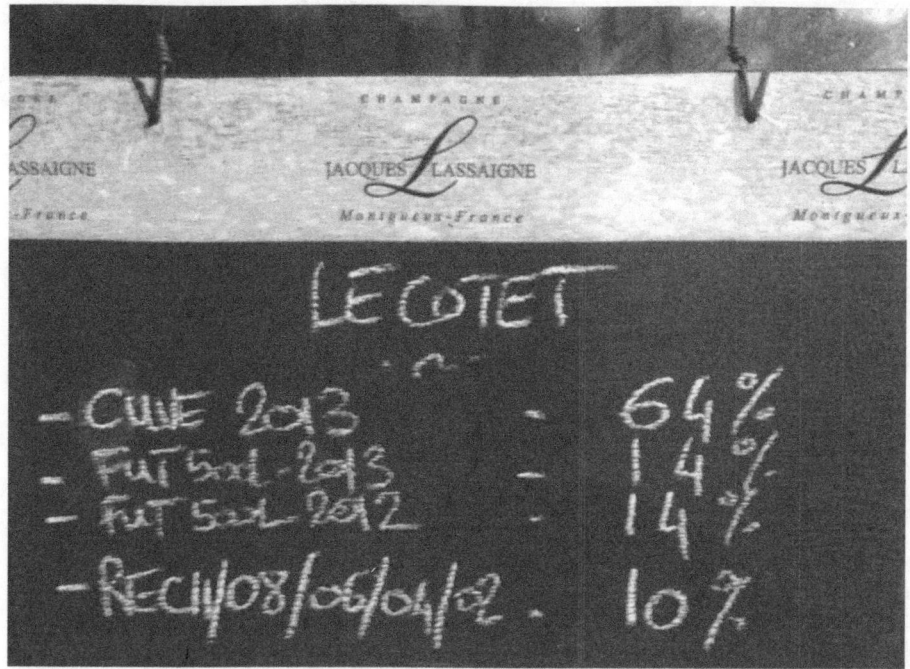

The blend of Le Cotet is marked clearly on the tank

'*négociant-manipulant*' because he buys some fruit from a few small growers in Montgueux. It is important to stress that Lassaigne makes these purchases following very strict criteria: his source vineyards are only in Montgueux and must be old vines – more than forty-five years of age. Then, they must have very chalky soils and enjoy a south or southeastern exposition. Finally, they must be managed by good growers who work well. Also, he buys only grapes, not juice or wine, and he presses the fruit himself. These purchases add another 30 per cent to his production.

Lassaigne purchases fruit in order to give his estate access to the other significant terroirs of Montgueux that he does not own, at least for the moment – his estate is tiny, just 3.5 hectares in one block, in the *Le Cotet* vineyard. 'The point of me being a négociant is not to make more wine. It's to have additional terroirs to work with so that I can make true Montgueux,' he says.

Although Lassaigne initially worked only with stainless steel, today he ferments and ages his wines in both steel tanks and barrels. He explains it this way: 'I do both; I like both. Diversity is always interesting, but I would say this: each barrel is different, each tank is the same. And also, it is possible to

Vine work at Jacques Lassaigne

make a good wine from a bad terroir in wood, with the make-up that the wood brings. In tank, you cannot. In tank, you need a great terroir to make a great wine. That is why we put the Millésimé only in tank. The oenologist will say that you should only raise a basic cuvée in tank. I am the opposite. Well, not the opposite, as I also raise my basic cuvée in tank, but I am different, as I do both my basic cuvée and my Millésimé in tank.'

It is fascinating, in a cellar like this, to be able to taste the same cuvée from both tank and barrel. It is clear that by the passing of time in oak, elements are both lost (something of the precision and clarity) and gained (another kind of expression, more textural and more complex). Lassaigne likes to play with both types of vessels for this very reason, as they give him different expressions. 'The only goal here is to catch and keep the aromas of the terroir. That's the only focus. I don't know if we succeed, but my focus is this. That's why we don't add [much] sulphur, why we don't do filtration and things like this.'

Once a year, Lassaigne pays workers to come in and clear his soil of *gadoues*, the city waste once used as fertiliser in the region. There wasn't much used at Montgueux, but Lassaigne is determined to rid his soils of whatever is there. He is the only producer I know who does this.

Lassaigne's story is a remarkable one that in many ways shows what is possible in our modern world. Here is a grower from a village that is still so poorly known that it generally does not appear on regional maps, where hardly anyone expected high-quality wines to be born. Here is a grower who took many risks, strived for greatness, refused to compromise and today is very successful. And he has achieved this in just over a decade. The lesson for Champagne growers seems to be this: as long as you have a terroir that can produce high-quality wines with personality, as long as you strive for excellence in your vineyard work and winemaking, and as long as you know what you are doing, there is a market waiting for you.

Lassaigne is grateful for his success and talks freely of his debt to those who came before. 'We are here because of two reasons. The first is the Grandes Maisons – Moët, Veuve Clicquot, Laurent-Perrier, etcetera – that created the market. We have to say thank you to these people. We are not competitors. Rather, it is because of them that we are able to be Champagne makers. The second reason is Anselme Selosse, because he pushed the vignerons to be at the same level as the Grande Maison. I know him a little bit, and when I see him I say, "Thank you for what you did over the last thirty years." Today, it's very easy for us because of these two.'

The wines of Champagne Jacques Lassaigne

Emmanuel Lassaigne produces four regular cuvées, with a fifth permanent cuvée on the way, along with his rare and experimental bottlings. None of the wines are fined or filtered, they do not receive any dosage, and they are all disgorged by hand. All of the wine is made from roughly one-third purchased fruit, with the exception of Le Cotet, which is 100 per cent estate grown.

The first cuvée is Les Vignes de Montgueux, a non-vintage Blanc de Blancs made from selected terroirs and mostly tank matured (15 per cent in wood). Lassaigne uses the last three vintages in the blend and mostly the last two. In the end, the wine is over 50 per cent reserve wine. Lassaigne calls this his 'aperitif wine', as it can be enjoyed without food. It is also his least expensive cuvée. It's a racy, salty, iodine-noted wine that is deliciously refreshing but also has good depth and some exotic notes – characteristics that highlight the potential opulence of Montgueux Chardonnay.

Then there is Le Cotet, another Blanc de Blancs, but this time the grapes come exclusively from a single-estate vineyard of the same name and, specifically, from a plot of old vines on the slope within *Le Cotet* planted in 1964. This vineyard is known for producing very racy, mineral, citrussy wines, and that's what you get here. A lot of complexity comes from the way Lassaigne introduces his reserve wine to this cuvée via a 'perpetual blend' (a concept discussed on page 130). This is a wonderful wine and often my favourite from Lassaigne.

The third regular cuvée is the Millésimé, a powerful Blanc de Blancs that, as we have already heard, is exclusively tank reared. The fruit can come from a selection of the *Le Cotet*, *Les Paluets* and *La Grande Côte* vineyards, depending on what works in each given harvest. Typically the oldest vines are used.

The last of the regular cuvées is La Colline Inspirée, again made from several parcels in Montgueux and from two vintages. It is now all fermented and aged in barrel and matured for four to five years before release. This is the most Burgundian style of wine, with a creamy texture and aged complexity, yet it nonetheless remains crunchy and energetic.

The new cuvée is called Clos Sainte-Sophie, for the vineyard of the same name. This is a vintage cuvée, and the first vintage, the 2010, was scheduled for release in 2016. It spent six months in barrel and two months in tank before bottling.

Lassaigne used to do a Rosé and still does a little for fun, but not for commercial release. He also produces a number of experimental cuvées, some of which will be released in the future and some of which are sold off on the bulk market if they do not work. Two of Lassaigne's experiments are yielding excellent results. First, he is ageing the same cuvée (a single pressing of 2012 from *La Grande Côte* vineyard) in barrel, on lees, for three different time periods. The pressing gave him three 500-litre barrels, and each of these was bottled separately: one in 2013 (which will spend five years in bottle), one in 2014 (which will spend four years in bottle) and one in 2015 (which will spend three years in bottle). All the bottles will be disgorged at the same time and released in three-packs containing one bottle of each, in 2018. Each bottle holds wine from the same terroir, the same vintage and the same pressing and will be disgorged on the same date. The only difference will be the time spent in barrel and bottle. Lassaigne has done this only once, so there will be no follow-up.

The second experiment is an extraordinary Le Cotet cuvée that he has been ageing in a Jura barrel for roughly three years. The barrel previously aged a Savagnin for a decade. Lassaigne admits that, with this wine, 'we do not talk about the terroir; rather, we talk about the vinification', but it is truly delicious, nonetheless. The sweet and sappy notes from the Savignin-cured wood bring a lot of complexity and energy. It really tastes of the Jura, with a strong presence of nutty, oxidative notes. It will be put in bottle with a very low pressure (18 grams of sugar for the *tirage*) and will therefore have a very gentle *mousse* (foam or bubbles).[74]

Finally, Lassaigne makes a little Coteaux Blanc and Rouge 'for drinking, not selling' and a rare Pinot-dominant *mousseux* called Les Papilles Insolites.

PART XVII

The final instalment of our *histoire vraie*, where the true grower revolutions are revealed – and yes, there were more than one

The oldest written account of winemaking is found in the Bible, but, as I discuss in Myth IX (page 195), there's nothing in the Good Book on *sparkling* wine. Bubbles are the work of man, it seems, not God. The Bible also famously tells us that the meek shall inherit the earth, a prediction that has certainly come true in the case of the Champagne region, where 88 per cent of the land remains in the hands of those who work it: the growers. Of course, it's one thing to inherit land and quite another to reap the profit that it generates. Until recently, most of Champagne's profit has gone to the large négociants of the region – those who bought the fruit of the growers and converted it into the international wine phenomenon that we know as Champagne and who still account for over 85 per cent of the wine exported from the Champagne region today. The profit discrepancy between those who owned and worked the land and those who made and marketed the wines has led to many of the defining moments in the history of Champagne, including what many call the 'grower revolution'.[75] In fact, there were several 'grower revolutions' in Champagne.

The first of these occurred in the 1950s. It was at this time that many grapegrowers decided to take control of their wine production by creating co-operatives or striking out on their own. This movement was driven by the frustration that growers felt at the increasing wealth of the large Champagne houses and their own inability to secure adequate prices for their fruit. There were even vintages in which most of the négociants refused to buy any fruit at all. Some co-ops had been founded prior to this era, but it was in the 1950s that the movement developed genuine momentum. This period also saw the establishment of a number of *récoltants-manipulants*, or grower-producers, a trend that continued through the 1960s and 1970s. If a négociant rejected the fruit of a grower or refused to pay a fair price, what was the grower to do? The new solutions were for the grower to sell their fruit to a local co-op at a pre-agreed rate or to make it, or have it made, into wine that the grower could then sell themselves.

As collectives, the co-ops had the resources and scale to invest in winemaking equipment and to pay trained winemakers. They could develop and export their own brands and produce 'buyers' own brands' for large trade customers like supermarkets. The co-ops were able to negotiate with large producers more effectively on behalf of their members and still supply them with a significant portion of their requirements. From the perspective of the négociants, the co-ops also offered some advantages: now there was a one-stop shop (and sometimes more than one) in each commune that was far more efficient to deal with than a vast number of small growers.

The amount of growers joining co-ops increased drastically during the petrol crisis of the 1970s, when the négociants again sought to drive fruit prices down and to reduce their purchases. The co-ops were strengthened enormously during this period, and many new grower-producers emerged.

Not all of the motivations that drove the growers to become more independent were positive. Many vineyard owners resented the fact that the négociants could examine and reject their fruit if it was not up to a suitable standard. Fruit sorting – known as 'triage' or '*épluchage*' – was also a standard practice with any green or rotten fruit given back to the grower.[76] In Champagne's marginal climate, where mildew and lack of ripeness can be major issues, rejections occurred regularly and obviously resulted in significant losses for the growers. One of the consequences of the increased independence and bargaining power of Champagne's growers is that négociants no longer have the clout to demand the quality controls of the past. On the other hand, the use of modern antifungal chemicals and the practice of picking as early as possible means that much of the fruit these days is delivered to the press houses reasonably clean (if green).

As the years passed, growers who had suffered at the hands of the négociants were motivated to sell increasing amounts of their fruit to the co-ops. Growers who were also able to sell at least some of their wine directly found that they could receive higher returns for their labour. These incentives, along with the factors touched on above, created the driving force behind the first grower revolution, a revolution that enabled many growers to strike out on their own. More significantly for our story, it enabled the rise of what we could call the 'superior grower-producers' (the distinction between typical grower-producers and 'superior grower-producers' has been touched on already and will be expanded further below), for although the co-ops and most grower-producers still mimicked the winegrowing and winemaking practices of the négociants, a tiny minority broke with the status quo or held on to traditions that differed from the common practices developed after World War II and in particular during the 1960s and 1970s. It seems self-evident that some of those who started making wine from their own plots would start to 'feel' their terroir and begin to take pride in the wines that resulted from their own labour. Perhaps this was what led some of them to adopt or retain certain quality-driven practices that differed from those of the mainstream.

Some of these historical practices have strong links with the present and have helped to inspire many of today's finest grower-producers. Anselme Selosse recalls precisely when his father moved away from cultivation (with horse and then tractor) and began using herbicides. This memory allowed him to question this evolution, and within two years of taking over his family's vineyards he had abandoned herbicide usage. It was the same for Pascal Agrapart. Francis Egly's father never used *gadoues* as fertiliser. Herbicides were never used on the vines that Jérôme Prévost's mother inherited from his grandmother. Pierre Larmandier's grandfather and father always picked later than their peers, believing that quality wine could result only from properly ripe fruit. In fact, this was a tradition that they themselves had inherited; before the modern era, there was a widely held belief in Champagne that very mature grapes were best for producing sparkling wine.[77] How things have changed. The Larmandier family also preserved and nurtured their oldest vines, much to the bewilderment of other growers, who knew that younger vines give larger crops and therefore more income. These traditional practices gave the new generation a reference point when they looked for alternatives to modern norms. And when they came into contact with great producers from other regions, they were able to put their parents' and grandparents' practices into context.

MYTH IX

In the beginning: Champagne is mentioned in the Bible

'Look not thou upon the wine ... when it bringeth its colour in the cup, when it moveth itself aright!' So roars the preacher in the opening scenes of Sam Peckinpah's *The Wild Bunch*.[78] Although it may seem like a stretch, the passage that Peckinpah's preacher is quoting, Proverbs 23:31, has sometimes been used to support the claim that sparkling wine is mentioned in the Bible. This is not only because the wine in the passage 'moveth itself', but also because 'when it bringeth its colour in the cup' has often been translated, as in the New Oxford Annotated Bible, as 'when it sparkles in the cup'.

In the King James Bible the full passage reads, 'Look not you upon the wine when it is red, when it gives its color in the cup, when it moves itself aright. At the last it biteth like the serpent and stingeth like an adder. Your eyes will see strange sights and your mind will imagine confusing things.' Leaving aside the complexities of translating ancient texts in general and the Jewish and Christian scriptures in particular, this passage obviously refers to a dark-coloured wine, and it also clearly warns us against drinking it. Naturally, the last two lines of the text are rarely quoted in the service of Champagne. In *The Wild Bunch*, the preacher is in fact proselytising to the local temperance society, which is why he has chosen a passage that speaks directly to the danger of drinking alcohol.

In fact, this passage and those preceding it warn of the dangers of *overconsumption* of alcohol. They speak against drunkenness rather than against alcohol per se. Proverbs 23:31 also seems to be warning the reader about a specific type of wine. The Hebrew word that is so often translated as 'aright' is בְּמֵישָׁרִים (b-mê-š-rîm) and would be better translated as 'smoothly' today. With this change we can begin to see that the passage is not describing Champagne or, perhaps, even wines in general. Rather, it seems to be warning the reader against the overconsumption of dark, viscous, strong wines, perhaps those that have not been watered down (a common practice in ancient times). To an ancient audience, the text would probably have meant something like 'Don't drink wines when they are viscous, smooth and so dark they stain the side of the cup; they'll give you quite the hangover!' It's advice that still has some currency today.

The other passage often cited as an example of sparkling wine's ancient history is Matthew 9:17, which is sometimes, as in the King James version, translated as 'Neither do men put new wine into old bottles: else the bottles break.' Bottles also often broke in the early days in Champagne, and so the idea seems to be that this passage is pointing out one solution to the problem: put the wine in bottle later, when it is not so young and there is less sweetness, and your bottles will not explode from the gas pressure generated by the secondary fermentation. This, then, is apparently held to indicate that the ancients had some knowledge of the secondary fermentation in bottle and of sparkling wine in general. There are obviously a number of objections that can be raised against such a reading. Perhaps the most significant is the use of the word 'bottles', here translated from the Greek ἀσκοί (as-koi), which actually means 'wineskins'; stoppered glass bottles were not used to store wine in biblical times as far as we know. The New Oxford version therefore offers a more precise translation: 'Neither is new wine put into old wineskins; otherwise, the skins burst, and the wine is spilled.' This line is in fact a metaphor that speaks of the need to introduce truth at the level that a listener is able to bear it – a metaphor that references the fact that wine should not be put into old, dried wineskins too soon after harvest, as it may continue fermenting and producing gas, and the resulting pressure may burst the hard wineskin. This is, of course, sound advice that the Champenois could have benefited from in the 18th century when they began to put their wine in bottle. But it has nothing to do with the production of sparkling wine.

Sparkling wine was a wine style that was completely unknown in biblical times. The Bible has many references to wine, including a number of passages about winemaking. But these passages relate only to still wines. This is because the Bible we know today was compiled from historical texts during the 4th century CE. The wine world had to wait another 1,200-odd years before all of the conditions were in place for bottled sparkling wine to become a reality, and it was around 1,400 years before all the technology existed to produce sparkling Champagne via the *méthode traditionnelle* (as we now call the method of producing sparkling Champagne), with the secondary fermentation in a sealed bottle.

Any link between the holy book and a wine region or wine style has long been a marketing boon, and the Champenois, who rarely miss a trick, did not miss this one. An association with religion once lent a wine region gravitas and opened up markets. This is one of the reasons why the Dom Pérignon myth has been so important to the Champenois. It should therefore come as no surprise that the CIVC has at times made the claim that the Bible makes mention of sparkling wine. It doesn't.

PART XVIII

In which we visit a vigneron farmer
– or is that a farmer vigneron?

Now we need to return to Troyes, as we will be travelling to the other side of the city in order to reach the Côte des Bar, the area most people are thinking of when they talk about the Aube. We are heading to the little village of Buxières-sur-Arce, where we will find a unique grower by the name of Bertrand Gautherot, of Vouette et Sorbée. If we had the time, we would stop for a bite and a glass of decent Champagne at the popular wine bar and bistro Aux Crieurs de Vin, in the centre of Troyes. But we must press onwards, driving along the E54, which skirts around the southern edge of Troyes, taking the exit for Châtillon-sur-Seine and joining the D443. Several minutes later, we turn onto the D104 and follow this road all the way into Buxières-sur-Arce. The whole trip will have taken us around three-quarters of an hour.

Bertrand Gautherot is a quietly spoken, humble man who is always quick to remind me that he is the student rather than the master, that he is only the current caretaker of his land – that there were many before and there will be many after him. He is thin and pale skinned with soft eyes and a gentle smile. Today, he is wearing a lumberjack-style checked jacket, and a beanie on his head.

We stroll up the hill behind his house to the *Vouette* vineyard. He speaks slowly, softly and deliberately. I ask him if we can talk about his terroirs. 'No,' he says definitively and then chuckles heartily. Then, more seriously, 'But it is difficult to talk of terroirs. First of all, because I do not fully understand them. Then, because they are not fixed. They are in a constant state of change. They move, the subsoil and also the surface. Then, there are the seasons and the management of the land. I can modify my surface by working the soil or by how deeply I work it. Or if I incorporate manure carefully, like the cow manure I prepared yesterday. With these practices, I have modified the soil so it is not exactly the same terroir. It will be very different from a parcel where herbicide has been used. There are many who speak of terroir and yet douse their soils in herbicides. It's completely crazy.' He shakes his head. 'No, "terroir" is a word that is overused. Better that we talk of *"climats"* [a specific terroir or site], or, even better, *"lieux-dits"* [again, a specific site, yet one with a historical name – *"lieux dits"* literally means "named places"], as here there is a historical name underneath that can be discussed along with the geology and the aspect.'

Gautherot works six identified *lieux-dits*, but there are two in particular that have literally created his name. They are, of course, *Vouette* and *Sorbée*. These are not the largest vineyards Gautherot owns, but they are the sites at the historic heart of the domaine. They are also the two vineyards he inherited from his father. *Vouette* sits immediately on the slope behind the cellars and the house. It has a mother rock of Kimmeridgian limestone with a little transition of Portlandian limestone. The exposition is south, with just a nod towards the southwest. *Sorbée* is on top of the same slope and is almost pure Portlandian, something not at all common in Champagne. It is almost flat, with again a slight exposition towards the southwest. *Sorbée* is planted to Pinot Noir, as was *Vouette* until recently. After the 2014 vintage, Gautherot grubbed up the vines in *Vouette* to replant to Chardonnay; he was not happy with the rootstock that he had in this vineyard and believes that Chardonnay is better suited here. *Vouette* had represented 8 per cent of Gautherot's total production and 15 per cent of the blend for the Fidèle cuvée. It will now grow fruit for the Blanc d'Argile bottling.

Sorbée is the vineyard that gives Gautherot the least stress. The vines here are between twenty-eight and forty-five years old and the soils have always been cultivated, going back to the 19th century; no herbicides have ever been used. Gautherot feels that this made it easier to transition the site to his biodynamic practices as the vines were already comfortable being worked (or ploughed). Historically, Gamay was grown in the vineyard to make red wine for the family. The name may derive from '*sorbier*', a type of tree that can be found in the Beaujolais (but also in other places). Until the 1960s, this site produced a light-bodied red wine for the farm, so it was not pushed to produce high yields in the way it would have been if the fruit was being sold. Gautherot tells me, 'The peasant works the soil differently to the vigneron, and the soil has a memory of this work. So it is a soil that is today very easy to work with. For me, it's a terroir that is both interesting and easy.'

Vouette is on the slope and south-facing, so it has always given good ripeness, but the work here has been more delicate. *Vouette* was treated with herbicide in the past, and although this stopped in 1993, Gautherot felt it made the vines more fragile. For this reason, he started to work the site with a horse. Interestingly, he stopped after three years, as he found the horse moved too quickly on the slope, and therefore the work was rough and shocked the plants. He then moved to an old tractor, which he felt did a better, more precise job. Now that the replanting program has begun, he should end up with a much more resilient vineyard. Fruit from the new Chardonnay vines should begin to come on stream from the 2019 harvest, and, if everything goes to plan, *Vouette* will be back in full production by 2022.

The other sites of the estate include the nearby *Biaunes*, the largest parcel at 2 hectares and one that shares the same geology as *Vouette* but is west-facing, colder, wetter and very late ripening. There is more forest influence here, and the vines are young. Within *Biaunes*, there is a small parcel of Chardonnay that Gautherot planted wild amid the native vegetation, without preparing the soils, and it is this very low-yielding parcel that gives the Chardonnay for Blanc d'Argile. Then there is *Tirmy*, a site of Pinot Noir vines almost thirty-two years old that was forest until the end of the 1960s. This is, again, more westerly and a little bit wetter, but it dries out quickly, and the fruit ends up in Fidèle. *Tirmy* is not a historic name; Gautherot came up with it. It was inspired by his neighbour, Remi (or Petit Remi). After that, there is *Fonnet*, whose name suggests the wind, which it gets plenty of. Its soils are Kimmeridgian yet rich in clay, and it is situated in a closed valley that is both sunny and warm during the day yet fresh at night. Mostly Pinot is planted here, with a little Chardonnay. Finally, we come to *Chatel*, where the soil is very rocky and full of large chunks of white limestone. There is a little château here, hence the name. The site is very sunny and dry; again, it is planted to Pinot Noir only. Taking into account all of the sites, the total vineyard area is a tiny 5 hectares.

The small size of Vouette et Sorbée allows Gautherot to treat the property as a self-contained unit, following a system that could be said to approach a kind of permaculture. His own cows provide him with compost, and there are also chickens, with both playing a role in the system. Gautherot feels as closely connected to his animals as he does to his vines. He seems to consider himself a farmer as much as a vigneron. He inherited this outlook from his father, a traditional farmer who understood the farm as a unit where everything could be produced that was required for both the continuation of the farm (what we call 'sustainability' today) and the provision of most of the items

Bertrand Gautherot explaining where it all begins

Some of the amphorae at Vouette et Sorbée

needed by his family: vegetables, meat, milk, cheese, wine and some income to source what they needed to buy externally.

We have already discussed the continuation of old ways with Pascal Agrapart. However Agrapart inherited seventy tiny parcels spread across a number of villages; the original Gautherot farm was far simpler, smaller and more unified. All of the land was in the tiny village of Buxières-sur-Arce, and there were only two parcels of vines (*Vouette* and *Sorbée*), right next to each other. Today, as mentioned, Gautherot works six parcels, five of which are in his home village, with *Chatel* in the neighbouring Ville-sur-Arce. Such a unified, compact estate, where all the vineyards are so near to the cellar – a rarely achieved ideal for many growers – makes it far easier to strive for quality and to work without chemicals. The other two Aube growers covered in this book – Jacques Lassaigne and Cédric Bouchard – have similar advantages, in that they have small estates confined to modest geographic areas. Gautherot's situation allows him to be idealistic about both his estate and his region in general. On a number of occasions, when I have discussed Gautherot's practices with growers further north, they have responded with something like, 'Yes, but

Vineyards in Buxières-sur-Arce

that's fine for Bertrand. He has all of his vineyards in his backyard! We could not succeed working exactly the same way.'

Although Gautherot did not begin his career in wine, he always had an interest in his family's vines and worked in the estate every year during his summer holidays, for vintage, pruning and when it was time to plant new vines. He was always a vigneron in his head, always '*double-actif*', as he puts it. There was an enduring passion for the vineyard, no matter what he was doing. He also grew up, as we have seen, on a true farm, a traditional, mixed farm, where all the family pitched in and ate and drank what they grew. He had always wanted to return to the land, but the estate was split up between all of his father's children, so it was not immediately apparent whether he could form a domaine.

Like a number of the great growers of his region, Gautherot initially prepared for, and worked in, another trade before coming back to the vines. Ironically, he worked in luxury goods, as a designer for Girlan, Chanel and Dior, and his experiences there, to some extent, informed his views on the Champagne region. At the famous fashion houses, he learnt that luxury was supposed to mean maximum effort – not just the best marketing but also the best ingredients and the best practices. The luxury goods he worked with cost more to produce and this was one of the reasons that they were aspirational. But when he looked at Champagne – also touted as a luxury product – he found the opposite. Champagne was mostly about the marketing, and the raw materials mattered much less.

In 1993, he returned to take over the family estate and not long after joined the GJVC and became friends with Pierre Larmandier and Jérôme Prévost. He began to work biodynamically in 1998, and his vines were certified in 2001, but it took the encouragement of Prévost and Anselme Selosse for him to start making his own wines. Farming and growing grapes were activities he was very comfortable with; making Champagne was another thing altogether. But he had some pretty handy mates to give him advice when he needed it, and his first vintage of Vouette et Sorbée was 2001.

When you meet Bertrand Gautherot today and watch him with his cows or in his vines, it's very difficult to imagine him at Dior or Chanel. He seems so much at home as a farmer. Self-effacing, unpretentious, dressed in the worn, mud-spattered clothes of a working man, he is missing only a piece of straw hanging from the corner of his mouth. Whatever complexities lie below the surface, Gautherot is clearly a man who has returned to his origins, to what he grew up with. And it suits him well.

The wines of Domaine Vouette et Sorbée

It has been suggested by other writers that the wine of Vouette et Sorbée may not be for everyone. This is just as well, as there is so little produced. I personally don't see why these wines shouldn't have quite broad appeal. It is true that the ripeness of the fruit, the oft-described minimalist winemaking and the Aube's sunnier clime and limestone soils combine to produce wines rich in both character and flavour, yet I've never found these traits confronting. These are generous yet savoury and complex wines without a drop of dosage. They are wines that make us think of Bertrand Gautherot the farmer – a farmer who works very closely with nature. They are wines that could not be more authentic or uncompromising. Yet, at the same time, they are textural, generous and delicious. Like the man, and like the farm on which they are grown, these wines are unique; they should be sought out by those searching for true wines of place.

There are three main cuvées. The first is Fidèle, a Blanc de Noirs (100 per cent Pinot Noir) that comes from Kimmeridgian soils, with *Fonnet* providing the 'heart' of the cuvée and *Biaunes* and *Vouette* (up to the 2014 harvest) giving the balance. Gautherot describes this as 'a dangerous wine', as it is so damn easy to drink. It has vibrant red and blue fruits and a racy acidity and minerality running the length of the palate, with some cleansing grip as well.

Then there is the Blanc d'Argile, a wine based on ripe Chardonnay from low-yielding vines that grow in the cold *Biaunes* vineyard. It will include some fruit from *Vouette* from the 2019 harvest onwards. It is a super-mineral, nutty, stone-fruited wine that also often carries some red fruit notes (rhubarb in particular). It is also quite salty and smoky, but always lovely and long with good texture and a twist of pleasant astringency.

Finally, there is the famous Saignée de Sorbée, a deliciously sappy, peppery Rosé that can be thought of as a light red. It has lots of crunchy red fruit notes as well as some resinous, stemmy characters. The spicy white pepper notes are the Portlandian soils of *Sorbée* coming through. It's an endlessly fascinating wine that demands food. Try it with fish (sea bass, John Dory, fresh water trout or cod), veal, pork, chicken and even sweetbreads.

Gautherot also makes minuscule quantities of a Pinot Blanc from the *Fonnet* vineyard that was originally called Dans le Vent and is now called Textures. This wine is at least partially raised in amphorae, and the first vintage was 2013. There is also a vintage cuvée called Extrait and an experimental cuvée called Sobre, made without any sugar additions whatsoever (including for the *tirage*). Bear in mind that this is a domaine still in its early days of evolution: we can expect the style of wine to evolve and the quality to improve even further.

PART XIX

Where we delve into the remaining key factors that led to the development of Champagne's current batch of great grower-producers

Around the time that Anselme Selosse's methods began stimulating debate in the region, a new generation of Champagne vignerons were taking over their family domaines from their parents. For a handful of this new generation, a life in wine growing in which the only goal was the highest possible yields was simply not engaging enough. These youngsters were also starting to become aware of the difference between industrial and artisanal winemaking, and they had their own ambitions. They wanted to improve their respective domaines, but they did not have the opportunity to significantly increase their land holdings (an option that had been open to their parents), as land in Champagne was now simply too expensive. They had to find new ways to progress, other than through expansion, so they began to look inwards.

In the mid-1980s, a small group within the CIVC called the Groupe des Jeunes Vignerons de Champagne (Young Growers of Champagne), or GJVC, began a program called Valoriser (to add value, or to develop). Pierre Larmandier was president of the GJVC at the time; he was later replaced by Jérôme Prévost, who was in turn followed by Bertrand Gautherot. All three, as we have seen, have become icons of the great grower movement. The idea of Valoriser was for small groups of young growers to come together to learn how to best manage and improve their estates. To this end, economists, bank managers and marketing specialists were invited to present to the growers.

At the same time, the GJVC commissioned Dominique Denis, my dining companion from the beginning of our journey, to organise some tastings for Valoriser. Denis is a particularly French character, a man who has woven a career out of wine without actually producing or directly selling any. He is a broker, a taster, a confidant, a crusader for what he considers authentic wine: terroir driven, organic, non-interventionist. He is a friend (and sometimes a former friend) of many of France's greatest wine producers and wine writers, and he was the instigator, along with Jean-François Coche, of the Rencontre Fête de la Qualité, a strictly private gathering and party that is held each year, with many of France's greatest vignerons in attendance.

Although I have known Denis for close to fifteen years, he had never mentioned anything to me about his involvement with Valoriser. He had vaguely talked about once teaching a course in Champagne, but that was about it. I knew that he was personally acquainted with many of the finest grower-producers in the region – this was why I approached him in the first place when I wanted to visit them – but it was only through my interviews with members of Valoriser that I became aware of the role he played in this story. Selosse told me that Denis was also one of the key people to influence his thoughts in the early days, although I think it is fair to say that, in this case, the student quickly became the master.

Denis was invited to help the members of Valoriser understand more about the wines and winemaking practices of other regions and to discover how those regions marketed themselves. This was the official line. In fact, Denis had zero interest in marketing. Rather, he had his own agenda and agreed to conduct the 'courses' only because he felt that he might be able to influence the young growers to produce more authentic wines. To this end, he organised masked tastings for the attendees in which supermarket wines were served alongside quality wines from the same appellation. As Prévost put it to me, 'These tastings were considered something extra that we could do, something not very serious or important. But for us young people, it turned out to be something very significant, as we were able to taste wines we had never tasted before.' In the tastings, Denis encouraged the vignerons to describe what they were tasting and helped them to see that the aromas, flavours, structures and energy levels that they found in the wines were related to the soils in which they were grown and to how the soils had been managed. 'This was fantastic for us,' said Prévost. 'We learnt that what we could taste and smell in quality wines was not the product of some laboratory, like in Champagne, but it was the product of the soil. It may sound incredible, but this was the first time we made this connection between the wine and the soil.'

The success of the tastings led to members of the group visiting regions such as Burgundy and Alsace. Revered producers such as Léonard Humbrecht and Dominique Lafon were also invited to present to Valoriser. On these excursions, the group encountered many of the practices that we associate today with the greatest domaines of France: balanced yields, rejection of herbicides and pesticides, cultivation, preservation of old vines, massal rather than clonal selection, minimalist winemaking and so on.[79] The producers that Valoriser visited spoke of their obligation to care for the soils and to produce the finest wines possible, wines that were rich in terroir and that were therefore unique. The young growers of Valoriser already believed that they were working with great terroirs. Now they were being told, directly or indirectly, that great terroirs should be managed with integrity and authenticity and that they should ideally not be blended away.

You might assume that meeting some of the most revered French producers would have had quite an impact on all the members of Valoriser. How could their eyes not start to open? How could they not begin to feel, as Selosse had done before them, that there was a clear alternative to the conventional approach? Remarkably, and much to Denis' disappointment, not everyone got the point. Of the initial members of Valoriser, Larmandier, Christophe Mignon (a quality grower from the Marne Valley), Prévost and Gautherot saw the light, but all of these were already well on the way to being 'converted', which was one of the reasons they had put up their hands to become members of the founding group. Eric Coulon (of Roger Coulon) was also in Valoriser and was clearly influenced by his experiences: today, Coulon is a member of the Trait-d-Union, a tasting group that includes Selosse, Larmandier-Bernier, Egly-Ouriet, Prévost and Jacquesson. Subsequent groups were more traditional and resistant to change, but all the members mentioned above went on to better things. Mignon is a very good biodynamic producer, and Larmandier, Prévost and Gautherot joined Selosse at the vanguard of the new Champagne. While the other, unnamed members of Valoriser may have tempered some of their former excesses, they largely continue producing grapes and wine via conventional methods.

Denis' role in the story can be explained quite simply using his own words. He once told me how the young growers often complained to him that the négociants were too strong. '"It is not that the négociants are too strong," I told them. "It is that you growers are too weak. You do not play to your strengths: the knowledge of the soil, the detailed work in the vineyards, the respect for the land in order to produce wines of terroir. Champagne is also, and above all, a wine! Everything flows from this obvious truth." It was not so difficult to see the way forward. There was already the example of the best growers of Burgundy. Burgundy was, and still is, the universal model. The university of terroir. And it was this model I had in mind.'

While all this was going on, Selosse was beginning to have more and more commercial success, receiving increasingly positive press and even finding time to encourage his peers. In the last of these he was only having limited success; on one occasion, he organised a public discussion on biodynamic viticulture, and only a handful of growers turned up. Nonetheless, many in the region were taking a very close look at what he and other similarly minded growers were up to. They were not always happy with what they saw. After all, associating lower yields and 'living soil' viticulture with quality wine was a damning indictment of the practices followed in the rest of the region. Selosse received threats after the airing of a Channel 4 interview in England in which he spoke honestly and critically about the region. From that point, he was viewed as a pariah by many in Champagne and at times felt the weight of the region's bureaucracy as a result, while like-minded growers were often confronted in regional meetings. Bucking the trend was considered a highly controversial and unnecessarily risky strategy in a region that was, after all, tremendously successful from a commercial perspective. Financial interests were potentially being threatened, and certain growers and négociants reacted with fear and aggression.

It was, of course, a mistake to consider the challenge being thrown down by the quality growers as dangerous to the region as a whole. On the contrary, the growers were (and are) proposing solutions to structural flaws that could one day undermine Champagne's popularity. Things have now changed significantly, and although there remain many growers and a number of houses that still respond negatively when the names of the finest growers are raised in conversation, many are supportive and see the work of these producers as a positive evolution for the region. And so they should. Today, the wines of these 'upstarts' are engaging many who had lost interest in Champagne or who had ceased to consider it a genuinely great wine. Every great wine region needs its great artisans, and at last Champagne has some.

MYTH X

Bursting bubbles: Smaller bubbles are a sign of a high-quality Champagne

One of the most persistent myths about Champagne is that the smaller the bubbles, or 'the finer the bead', the better the quality of the wine. In fact, bubble size and wine quality are two completely separate elements that are not at all interdependent. Today, thanks to the work of physicists like Gérard Liger-Belair of Reims University, we know definitively that the size of the bubbles in a glass of Champagne is almost entirely due to the gas pressure in the wine and, further, that the gas pressure is something that Champagne producers can easily manipulate, regardless of the quality of the wine itself.

How does this work? As we have already seen, it is the interaction of sugar and yeast that creates the gas pressure in a bottle of Champagne (and therefore the bubbles in the glass): in short, the yeast feeds on the sugar and creates carbon dioxide and alcohol. The more sugar added for the second fermentation, the more alcohol and carbon dioxide (and therefore gas pressure) produced. Less obvious is that the gas pressure in a bottle of Champagne determines the *size* of the bubbles in the glass. As a Champagne bubble forms and rises towards the surface of the glass, it gets larger and larger, because the gas pressure in the liquid forces more gas through the bubble wall, or membrane, swelling the bubble like a tiny balloon. The greater the gas pressure, the greater the amount of gas forcing its way into the bubble as it rises, and therefore the larger the bubble by the time it reaches the surface of the wine.

Yes, there are other factors that impact bubble size, such as the level of surfactants (compounds in the liquid that lower surface tension and stiffen the bubble wall) and the height of the glass (the higher the glass, the longer the bubble takes to reach the surface, and the more time there is for the gas pressure to swell the bubble). But these are minor or variable factors. It is ultimately the gas pressure in the bottle that dictates the size of the bubbles in a glass of Champagne, and this can be easily manipulated by the winemaker. Simply by adding less sugar for the secondary fermentation in the bottle, the winemaker can create a wine with less gas pressure and therefore finer bead.

You don't need a laboratory or a white coat to prove this claim; you can conduct a simple test. Pour a glass of Champagne and note carefully the size of the bubbles that form. Do not drink or swirl the glass; simply leave it undisturbed on a bench and watch what happens. As the gas dissipates from the surface of the liquid (from where most of the carbon dioxide is lost, even though this is not visible to the naked eye), the bubbles rising in the wine will get progressively finer and smaller. This can be easily brought into focus by pouring a second glass beside the first after several minutes. The bubbles in the second pour will be larger, reflecting the greater gas pressure. So, if you ever find yourself with a Champagne that has bubbles that you wish were smaller and finer, simply wait a few minutes and your wish will be granted. You could even carefully decant the wine to get a similar, and more rapid, effect.

Historically, quality in wine has been associated with the quality of the grapes harvested – where and how the grapes were grown and how they were processed. Bubbles are a secondary, technical process that can be mastered and applied, regardless of the standard of the initial wine. So how did the two separate elements – bubble size and wine quality – become conflated? In his book *Uncorked: The Science of Champagne*, Gérard Liger-Belair puts forward a plausible theory.[80] As sparkling wines age in bottle, they naturally lose some of their carbon dioxide pressure through the cork. Therefore, very old Champagnes have smaller bubbles than younger wines when they are first poured. And wines that are put aside for longer ageing are typically the best quality examples. After repeated contact with such aged, high-standard wines and their fine bead, people may have developed an association between higher quality wines and smaller bubbles, without necessarily understanding the mechanism that determined the smaller bubble size in the first place.

PART XX

In which we visit the last of our growers in the Aube
and learn that, no matter how seriously we take it,
wine's main work is to make us happy

I first met Cédric Bouchard outside his father's cellars in Celles-sur-Ource, in the Côte des Bar, where he used to make his wine. With gaunt, angular features, a mop of dark hair and matching beard, and loose clothes and sandals, the man looked positively messianic. The zeal with which he outlined his philosophies and practices to me only served to support this initial impression. Bouchard no longer works from his father's cellars, and from 2012 he has been based at his new property, a beautiful villa and cellar that he is restoring in nearby Landreville.

In a number of ways, Bouchard is the most extreme of the great growers we have visited in our travels, in that he pushes many of the agreed philosophies of quality and terroir as far as they will go – and then a little further. He does this with the aim of satisfying his almost fanatical desire to produce wines of the greatest purity, to transfer the personality and quality of the grapes he has worked so hard to produce into the glass. The lengths he will go to in order to achieve his goal seemingly know no bounds.

Bouchard's methodologies reveal a great deal about his perfectionist and uncompromising personality, and they are also the keys to understanding his wines. The first key of many is that there is no blending here. Every Bouchard wine is the lucid reflection of one vineyard parcel, one grape variety and one vintage. It's an anti-blending philosophy that flies in the face of traditional Champagne lore. He also works with insanely low yields (typically, 26 hectolitres per hectare – lower than any other Champagne producer I know). 'I work with low yields because we are in a northern region that gives very high acidity,' he says. 'With high maturity you have the richness to give pleasure and the acidity to give energy.'

Bouchard farms without chemicals and picks his grapes very ripe, a ripeness he easily achieves thanks to his low yields. Most base wines in Champagne would be lucky to make it to 10 per cent alcohol without chaptalisation – 9 per cent is typical. Bouchard's base wines usually achieve between 11 and 12 per cent natural alcohol and have even reached 13 per cent, and he never chaptalises. In other words, these are real wines, wines that can be drunk with pleasure even before their secondary fermentation. There is also a strict fruit selection in the vineyards at harvest time. And Bouchard sells off any wine that he does not feel has reached his very high expectations.

Bouchard's primary fermentation occurs with wild yeasts, and the final wines are not fined, filtered or cold stabilised and have no dosage added (they are all zero-dosage wines). So there are no additions at all, save the *liqueur de tirage*. 'I try to touch as little as possible,' he says. Even with the *liqueur de tirage*, Bouchard is as minimalist as can be, adding less than 20 grams of sugar, whereas 24 grams is normal, to prompt the secondary fermentation in the bottle. His wines therefore end up with a gas pressure of around 4.5 atmospheres, as opposed to the standard 6, resulting in a gentle *mousse* that often dissipates quickly. In some ways, the ripeness of the wines forces him down this path; the secondary fermentation not only creates the bubbles but also brings additional alcohol, and the more sugar added, the more alcohol will result. However, his approach predominantly reflects his desire to have the most delicate, subtle bead possible. (As described in Myth X, on page 212, lower levels of sugar in the *tirage* result in fewer and finer bubbles.)

Bouchard is not the only great grower working in this way, as we have seen. But he would like to go even further and be done with the secondary fermentation altogether. He once told me that he was not, in fact, a great fan of sparkling wines; that for him, 'the bubbles get in the way'. That is quite something for a Champagne producer to admit. For a number of years, Bouchard has been seeking to produce a great still wine from his vineyards. As yet, he has not been able to succeed in producing one that meets his high standards, so his trial wines remain unsold. I have the distinct impression that if he had been able to succeed in producing great still wines from his terroir and could justify asking the same prices for them, he would have ceased making sparkling wine altogether. He wants to produce wines that are as close as possible to their terroir, and so, if he can avoid the secondary fermentation in the bottle (the only point at which he has to add anything to the wine) and if he can get rid of bubbles, which for him simply get in the way of the terroir expression, he will be one step closer to his goal. Whether the extreme, northern climate of Champagne will allow him to produce still wines whose quality is anywhere near that of his best sparkling wines remains to be seen. I have my doubts, although he has not let me try the still wines he has produced. (There are also rumours that he is planting a vineyard outside the Champagne AOC, in order to produce still wines.)

Bouchard uses no wood at all in the *élevage*, only stainless steel, believing that wood marks the wines in a way that has little to do with terroir. We have already encountered, with Emmanuel Lassaigne, the belief that wood interferes with the transmission of true terroir expression, as it brings something that wasn't already present in the fruit. Further north, the great growers believe quite the opposite: that wood, if handled properly, helps to reveal the terroir. Bouchard and Lassaigne beg to differ. Yet, while Lassaigne likes to play with both wood and stainless steel, depending on the terroir, Bouchard is a purist. He says, 'I do not want to work with wood for many reasons. I do not believe in the idea that wood nurtures the wine. I also find, and this is my personal idea, that bubbles do not work with wood. The oxygen that the bubble brings when it bursts is already superior to wood. I am also not a fan of oxidation unless it is in varieties or regions that demand it, like in certain Jura wines. But in Chardonnay and Pinot? No. For me, oxidation is a fault, and it creates an imbalance. There are people that say it brings complexity, but for me, this is false. For me, it's not interesting, what it brings. Stainless steel, on the other hand, brings nothing. It simply guards the power of the fruit. That's what interests me. The wood brings something that was never there in the fruit.'

Perhaps this is a question of terroir. Is it a coincidence that the two growers in our story who have argued passionately against the impact of wood are both in the Aube? But it is also a question of how you rationalise these things. Naturally, when you put a wine in a wooden vessel, even an old wooden vessel, it causes the wine to change, to evolve. Some of the changes are to do with the wood itself; others are to do with what wine does when it spends time in this environment. Some say it is slowly oxidising, but why not say it is being oxygenated? Is the wine being marked by the wood, or is it revealing something inherent in its personality? It's surely a combination of both. We also need to acknowledge that wooden vessels were the historic fermentation and storage vessels in Champagne prior to tanks. Stainless-steel tanks are a relatively new phenomenon, so the style of wine they produce is also relatively new. Can we really say that all Champagnes that were made before the introduction of stainless steel were not true wines of terroir? It's also a question of degrees. How long the wine is aged in wood, the size and age of the barrel, how much sulphur is in the wine, how often the barrel is topped up: all these factors will influence how, and how much, the wine is affected by its time in wood. And, of course, this same discussion could be applied to other elements of winemaking. Does the secondary fermentation reveal or distort the true terroir? Does ageing on lees? Does racking?[81] What we can hopefully agree on is that the wines being produced purely in tank by Lassaigne and Bouchard are first rate but that there are also many glorious examples of wood-matured Champagnes being made by the other great growers.

Cédric Bouchard got his start in 2000, when his father, very much a traditional, conventional grower, transferred to his son a small parcel called *Les Ursules*. His father believed *Les Ursules* to be his worst parcel, because of its naturally low yields. Bouchard thought it was one of his father's finest, for the very same reason. On the one hand, this difference of opinion was fortuitous. On the other hand, it signalled that the son would take a direction that was diametrically opposed to his father's. From the very beginning, Bouchard's work reflected this divergence, and this led, perhaps understandably, to some tension between *père et fils*. Imagine that your son took up the same métier as you yet completely disregarded your practices and experience. Father–son relations are always complex, but Bouchard junior's approach must have taken this complexity to another level.

Sometimes, great things can come of familial conflicts. Bouchard senior challenged his son by questioning the radically new practices he had adopted. Bouchard junior found himself in a highly charged environment where he had something to prove. As he says, 'Without the friction between my father and me, without that sense of competition, I doubt I would have been able to create Roses de Jeanne [his estate].' Hopefully, such friction is now in the past, as *le fils* is producing some of the most interesting and sought-after wines of the region.

Bouchard is passionate, evangelical and uncompromising. But he also understands that wine is ultimately about pleasure, and he keenly wants to produce wine that is delicious and gives people joy. He tells me, 'I always have the same aim, the same politics, the same philosophy with my wine: to produce a wine that is pure, straight, long, complex and also a wine of pleasure. It's like when I leave a restaurant, I want to be able to say, "Wow! That was great!"

When I make my wine, I aim for the same thing. I want a wine that will make people happy. If the wine doesn't make people happy, then I haven't done my job well.'

On the state of the region in general, Bouchard has this to say: 'The great problem with Champagne is very simple. You have an over-production and it's a great pity, because we have a crazy terroir, an enormously important terroir that can make very, very beautiful things. But it's a terroir that has been undervalued, and so you have over-production. It's a real shame. When people have in their minds mostly money, when this is what's motivating them, then, sadly, it's hard to see this situation changing.'

The wines of Roses de Jeanne (Cédric Bouchard)

Bouchard has in the past produced two sets of wines under two labels: Inflorescence (two wines) and Roses de Jeanne (five wines). The wines released under the Inflorescence label were classified as *négociant-manipulant*, but now that Bouchard has his own cellar and does not purchase any fruit from vines that he does not fully control, he has no need of that designation; from the 2012 harvest, all of his wines have been classified as *récoltant-manipulant*, and all are now labelled under the Roses de Jeanne *marque* (label). Now, as Bouchard puts it, 'everything is clean'.

Bouchard produces wines that could be described as anti-Champagnes. They are wines trying to break free of the shackles imposed by the history and conventional wisdom of the area. All come from individual parcels and individual grape varieties, and all are vintage wines, regardless of whether or not they carry a year on the label. If a vintage is not stated on the back label and the cork, it will be marked on the label as 'V10' (for 2010), for example. Also on the back label are the month and year of disgorgement.

Although Bouchard produces seven cuvées, his production remains tiny, at only around 15,000 bottles in total. He believes that if the volume was much larger, he could not achieve the same standards. Four of the wines are Blanc de Noirs from Pinot Noir, there is one Rosé from Pinot Noir, and there are two Blanc de Blancs wines (one from Chardonnay and the other from Pinot Blanc). The Pinot Noir wines from the Aube have nothing to do with those from the Montagne de Reims; they have a much more delicate structure. From Bouchard, they are textural, flowing wines with plenty of fruit sweetness yet also vibrant freshness. The whites are delicious and speak as much of Burgundy as they do of the Marne. Perhaps that is only fitting, as the Aube is located between the two areas. None of the wines, white or red, suffer from the absence of dosage; they simply do not need it.

Côte de Val Vilaine (until the 2011 vintage known as Inflorescence Blanc de Noirs) comes from Pinot Noir vines planted in 1974 in the village of Polisy. In total, the vineyard is 1.41 hectares, faces plain south and is on clay and limestone soils. When this wine was released, under the Inflorescence label, Bouchard cropped the vines at around 50 hectolitres per hectare. Now that it has joined the Roses de Jeanne range, it is cropped at an average of 26 hectolitres per hectare. Naturally, this makes for a much deeper, more powerful and structured wine. Like all Bouchard's wines, there is no chaptalisation, fining, filtration or cold stabilisation, and the fermentation is with natural yeasts. The first vintage, under the Inflorescence label, was 2003. Bouchard believes that this is one of his finest cuvées. It is released earlier than the other cuvées, however – after twenty-four to twenty-eight months in the cellar – as he does not think it gains anything from further ageing. It is a great introduction to the line-up, with a fleshy texture, wonderful purity and intense, smoky minerality.

Côte de Béchalin (prior to the 2007 release labelled as Inflorescence La Parcelle) derives from a Pinot vineyard of the same name, of which Bouchard owns a 0.73-hectare slice. Planted in 1981–82, it faces southwest and is on the clay and limestone soils that dominate the Aube. It's the wine Bouchard keeps the longest in his cellars – for seven years. Again, the yields have dropped to 26 hectolitres per hectare to make a far deeper, more serious, more complex wine. And, again, it has the wonderful flesh and texture of all the Bouchard wines, with plenty of complexity from the time on lees.

Les Ursules is the original Roses de Jeanne wine, from a relatively flat site that sits on top of a slope in Celles-sur-Ource. It is a Blanc de Noirs Pinot Noir from vines planted in 1974. The soil is clay and limestone, and Bouchard's parcel is 0.97 hectares. From 2010, the vintage has been listed on the front label; prior to that, it was marked on the rear label as indicated above. It's a super-concentrated and deep Pinot Noir with all kinds of ripe, dark fruits and the smoky complexity typical of Bouchard's Pinot-based wines.

La Haute Lemblé is a Blanc de Blancs Chardonnay from a tiny 0.11-hectare, south-facing, clay and limestone parcel planted in 2002 (although you wouldn't know it from the depth and complexity of the wine). It is a rich, creamy, nutty wine with great texture – think of a full-flavoured white Burgundy with bubbles. The Chardonnay vines are on five different rootstocks, resulting in a diverse expression of the terroir.

At the time of writing, Presle was the latest and most experimental of Bouchard's wines. It comes from a tiny Pinot Noir plot of only fifteen rows in Celles-sur-Ource. Bouchard not only planted it relatively densely for Champagne (2,400 vines on a 0.25-hectare parcel) but also utilised ten different rootstocks. Caring for ten different vine types in a tiny vineyard makes management of the site complicated. He also allowed the natural vegetation to grow and compete with the young vines; typically, the soils of young vineyards are cultivated to give the vines a chance to establish themselves without competition. The result was that he lost a third of the vines: 800 of the original plantings. On the flip side, those that survived were the strongest specimens. Bouchard has progressively replanted. It is a west-facing site that has never seen any herbicide or pesticide, as it was a *petit bois* (little forest) before Bouchard planted it. The first vintage was 2010, released in 2014. It's a wine with Burgundy-like finesse and a deep, earthy, mineral complexity.

La Bolorée is a rare bird deriving from a south-facing parcel of Pinot Blanc vines planted in 1960 at an altitude of 230 metres. So not only is it an extremely rare example of a 100 per cent Pinot Blanc Champagne; it is also one from old vines. *La Bolorée* is the only Bouchard vineyard that is not on clay and limestone soils; the soils here are chalky marl – lots of chalk but also some sand. You can feel the chalk in the vibrant minerality in the mouth. The wine offers a completely different personality from that of Bouchard's other wines – yellow fruits with a saline freshness and hints of lanolin and bees wax. It is an absolutely fascinating and delicious wine – but one that can be very hard to track down.

Finally, Le Creux d'Enfer derives from a small, west-facing parcel that is planted to both Pinot Noir and Chardonnay. In the right years, when the stems are fully ripe, Bouchard makes a Rosé from the Pinot Noir, foot stomped and macerated on its skins (and stems) for up to four days, in order to extract its colour. It's a fabulously pure, silky and yet energetic expression of Pinot Noir, with crystalline red fruits and subtle nettle and herbal notes. It is a wine of remarkable finesse and surely one of the finest Rosé wines of the AOC.

EPILOGUE

A short manifesto in which the author asks you, the wine lover, a simple, somewhat rhetorical question: 'What sort of Champagne do you really want to drink?'

The wines of the finest grower-producers serve to remind us that Champagne is a wine, first and foremost, and so it should taste like one. We all know that wine is made from fermented grapes, so if the liquid in your glass does not have any flavours or aromas that resemble those origins, then it is a product that has more to do with wine*making* than wine*growing*. That doesn't mean that you won't like it, but it does raise questions about what I call 'authenticity'. For me and many other wine travellers, a great part of what makes a wine authentic is that it speaks loudly of where it was grown. Without fruit clarity, without vinosity, without aromas and flavours that predominantly reflect the soil and climate in which the vines were grown, it is hard to see how this is possible.

For too long, we, the wine community, have gone easy on Champagne. We have bought into the countless myths espoused by the marketeers of the region, and we have ignored the shortcomings of many of the wines. Time and time again, I have seen Champagnes dominated by overtly sweet, toasty, biscuity dosage characters described by experienced wine professionals in glowing terms without any critical comment. Time and time again, I have tasted very expensive prestige cuvées that lacked any of the breed, length, purity and clarity of terroir expression that we would expect of even the most basic Burgundy. In fact, the majority of even the most prestigious wines of the region derive almost all of their character from winemaking artifice, or what the French call '*maquillage*' [make-up].

To be fair, Champagne is easily the most difficult wine to taste critically. The froth of the bubbles, the sweetness of the dosage, the often-used narrow, flute-shaped glasses and the typically ice-cold serving temperatures all present major challenges to critical assessment. The flavour characteristics derived from the Maillard reaction, autolysis, the impact of special yeasts, enzymes and so on can also easily distract and seduce the taster (even the professional taster) and can mask many shortcomings. This is precisely what the 'art of the blender' is designed to do: to summon 'a wine that is greater than its parts', to quote the web site of the CIVC. It takes a lot of experience and effort to separate dosage sweetness and texture from fruit sweetness and ripe acidity (refreshing yet not austere) from green acidity (steely and gum numbing after several glasses) that has been 'balanced' or masked with added sugar. The same goes for separating winemaking from fruit complexity. Yet, it *is* possible, especially if the wine is served in wine glasses rather than flutes, and if you take the time to give the wine some air and to taste it at a variety of temperatures (as it naturally warms up in the glass). And, of course, context is important; knowing the specific terroir or terroirs from which the wine has derived, something typically hidden in Champagne, and knowing the producer's viticultural and winemaking approach certainly help us gain a far deeper understanding of any wine.

Perhaps the primary message of the great grower-producer movement is this: we should judge Champagne according to the same criteria that we apply to all other great wines. How fruit intense is the wine, how balanced, how pure, how mineral, how long on the palate? How deeply does it speak of where it was grown, rather than of how it was made? These are all questions that professional tasters instinctively apply to Burgundy, say, but that most fail to apply to Champagne. In fact, Champagnes are often marked down for characters that we celebrate in wines from other regions: intensity, concentration, structure (critical for ageing and food matching), vinosity, fruit richness and savouriness. We owe the remarkable terroir of Champagne more respect than this.

It may at first seem counter-intuitive, but Cédric Bouchard reinforces this point when he says, 'I really don't like Champagne,' by which he means *sparkling* Champagne. Bouchard wants to make the greatest possible wine from his terroir, and he feels that the bubbles get in his way. So, he creates wines with the least amount of bubbles possible, and, like Selosse before him and now many other growers, he encourages his customers to decant his wines and to serve them in wine glasses as opposed to flutes. I don't agree with Bouchard on his point that bubbles get in the way of terroir, by the way, but his position helps remind us that what is most important is the wine itself, not the bubbles – that great Champagne must be a great wine first, and a great Champagne second.

Earlier in this book, I said that very few growers were making the kinds of wines I have championed here – that, in fact, most grower wines are no better, and are often less interesting, than those available from the best négociants. So, can I put forward a concrete definition of a quality grower-producer and say how they differ from other growers, co-ops and the négociant houses? I think I can.

Obviously, quality grower-producers will almost always own and certainly manage the vineyards that supply their grapes, and they will make outstanding wines.[82] They start with the desire to grow unique wines that speak loudly of the commune or vineyards in which they were grown. This is in fact their key point of difference from other Champagne producers and informs all of their subsequent methodologies in the vineyard and the winery. To this end, the wines of these growers are often from single vineyards or single villages. If they are blends, they are often an assemblage of similar terroirs that produce wines with comparable personalities, as opposed to being from radically different terroirs that 'complement' each other.

Quality grower-producers' vineyards are managed with little or no synthetic chemical inputs, using what are often referred to as 'organic' or 'biodynamic' methods. Some will prefer to use synthetic fungicides in high-pressure years rather than a lot of copper, yet herbicides and pesticides are never used. Cultivating the soil is standard practice. Yields are far lower than those in the rest of the region (typically at least one-third less), resulting in more intense, more expressive, riper fruit, which in turn enables a lower level of dosage to be used, if any is used at all. Fruit is picked only when it is fully ripe – typically between 1 and 3 degrees of potential alcohol riper than their neighbours' fruit – because that is when genuine flavour ripeness occurs. When dosage *is* used, it's in small quantities (typically around 0–4 grams per litre – the level of Extra Brut – and very rarely above 5 grams). Even then, dosage is used only to subtly balance the wine or to discreetly lift the terroir, never to mark the wine with any aromatics or flavours or to balance a lack of ripeness.

There are no enzymes, special yeasts or any other secret 'herbs and spices' used in the cellar. In general, the ultimate ideal for these growers is to produce fruit and wine that do not require any additions at all. A number of the growers in this book have achieved just that. Finally, the wines of the finest grower-producers are matured more slowly than those of conventional producers, and they are not fined or filtered.

These choices are made simply because the growers believe they lead to more expressive, terroir-rich grapes and higher quality, more authentic wines. The growers want to start with intense, perfectly ripe, balanced fruit and base wines, rather than seeking to create balance and interest via blending and the winemaking process. This is no different from the great growers in other regions of France who work hard in the vineyard in order to do less in the cellar.

As we have seen, this approach is opposed to that of almost all other Champagne producers, including the co-ops and most grower-producers, who start with the objective of producing a house style or a wine to suit a particular market and whose techniques (high yields, neutral or high-acid base wines, blending across a wide range of sources to achieve 'balance' and complexity, yeast additions, enzyme additions, maturation techniques, dosage additions, fining and filtration) are designed in order to, or justified by, their ability to produce a consistent, homogenised product according to a predetermined goal that satisfies commercial ends.

The styles of wines produced by the finest growers are drier and more vinous than the regional norm. They often remind the drinker of their base wines, especially when young. They taste like exceptional wines that just happen to have bubbles. They are sometimes, although not always, more full-bodied, and they do not have the slippery texture or simple, toasty, biscuity, caramelised aromatics and flavours of dosage-dominant Champagnes. Any apparent sweetness is fruit sweetness and is noted in the mid-palate rather than marking the finish, which is the case with wines of high sugar additions. They are clean, pure, mineral and long. They can often age magnificently on cork (in fact, many demand such ageing), and because they are wines first, they are typically better with food. They can also be enjoyed at various temperatures with equal pleasure and can even be served as still wines once they have lost their bubble.

Of course, it will be you, the drinker, who decides which wines you like and how you wish to serve them. There is nothing stopping you serving a great grower Champagne chilled in a champagne flute: it will still deliver a far better drinking experience, in my opinion, than a conventional Champagne served in the same way.

All the great growers discussed in this book follow the parameters above and are now successful on every level. The (admittedly limited) availability of their wines in many markets means that knowledgeable drinkers have a clear alternative to the conventional, large house style, while those Champagne growers with the vineyards, passion and winemaking skill to produce high-quality, terroir-rich wines have an alternative and successful model to follow. While many are trying to do just that, the great grower-producer movement remains, for the moment, limited by its small number of successful members and the necessarily small amount of wine they offer. These growers typically produce between 1,000 and 10,000 cases each – a drop in the Champagne ocean. Yet, their wines can often be tracked down if you follow the best merchants and the finest restaurants.

Sometimes, the wines are available in the most surprising places. At one of my favourite spots to eat in Piemonte, a tiny, humble *enoteca* called Centro Storico in Serralunga, I often find the wines of Selosse, Larmandier-Bernier, Agrapart, Chartogne-Taillet, Ulysse Collin, Egly-Ouriet and Prévost, among others, all on offer on the compact yet excellent wine list. Then, only 300 metres from my home in suburban Melbourne, a tiny yet lively wine bar offers wines from almost all of the producers mentioned in this book. Less than one kilometre in the other direction is an independent retailer who has stocked and promoted Larmandier-Bernier and Egly-Ouriet for close to a decade. Across Australia and the rest of the world, there are many excellent restaurants, bars and retailers doing the same.

Of course, there are still many wine lists in top restaurants across the world, including France (especially France!), where the Champagne selection is based on either brand recognition or kickbacks, (large Champagne houses routinely pay restaurants 'marketing' dollars to list and pour their bubbles.) When I visit such restaurants, I no longer let the wine list get me down. I simply remind myself that the same world that has given us Camembert that tastes like rubber and the kind of Champagne that Scarlett Johansson and Roger Federer are paid to drink, has also bestowed upon us the wonders of Larmandier-Bernier's Terre de Vertus and the many outstanding wines we have touched on in this book. And I happily select a still white wine to start the meal.

NOTES

Disclaimers

1. When I began researching this book, I was working with only four of the eleven producers mentioned in these pages. By the time of publication, I was receiving an allocation from nine. The only two producers covered in detail here that I do not work with today are Cédric Bouchard and Jacques Lassaigne.
2. 'Négociant' is a legally defined French term used to classify wine producers who purchase at least some – typically most – of the grapes they need. In contrast to this, the term 'grower' or 'grower-producer' is typically used to describe those producers who make Champagne from the grapes of their own vineyards.

Prologue

3. The term 'dosage' is used here to refer to the legal addition of sugar to Champagne. The controversial and often misunderstood role dosage plays in Champagne will be discussed in more detail later in our travels.
4. A wine 'bracket', or 'flight', is a set of wines served in several glasses lined up in a row, for comparative tasting. Wine tastings and dinners tend to be organised into several 'brackets' of wines.
5. Here and throughout the book, I use 'Burgundy' to refer to the Côte d'Or region of Burgundy.
6. Becky Sue Epstein, *Champagne: A Global History*, Reaktion Books Ltd, 2011.
7. Thomas Brennan, *Burgundy to Champagne: The Modern Wine Trade in Early Modern France*, Johns Hopkins University Press, 1997, pp. 252, 253.
8. All these ingredients were 'usually present in the liqueur d'expédition' for Champagne and were listed by the chemist and doctor Edme-Jules Maumené in his 1873 work *Traité théorique et pratique du travail des vins*.
9. The term 'grower-producer' is used throughout this book to indicate a Champagne producer who grows the grapes for the wines they make. In the rare instances that they do buy fruit (we only visit one grower who does this: Emmanuel Lassaigne), it will be a minority of their requirements and will come from vineyards they either manage themselves or that are managed by other growers who work to the same standards.
10. Of course, this assumes that your vineyards have the same potential for quality as your competitors' and that you have the same winegrowing and winemaking skills. It is an 'all other things being equal' argument. This is why I speak here of 'great growers'; the overwhelming majority of Champagne growers (vineyard owners who also sell wine under their own labels) produce very ordinary wines, often considerably lower in quality than even the basic cuvées of the large houses. Regardless, the argument above is one that experienced wine people accept without question when it comes to the wines of other European regions of renown. When it comes to Champagne, however, this logic somehow manages to get repressed.

Part I

11 Benoît Musset, *Vignobles de Champagne et vins mousseux: histoire d'un mariage de raison, 1650–1830*, Fayard, 2008, p. 62.
12 Prior to the mid-19th century (at least), breadmakers would have used starter dough (*'levain'* in French) rather than modern baker's yeast (*'levure'*) as we know it. Although the fermentation process was not understood at this time, it was known that adding a *levain* to fresh dough made it 'rise', hence the origin of this word.
13 Thomas Brennan, *Burgundy to Champagne: The Modern Wine Trade in Early Modern France*, Johns Hopkins University Press, 1997, p. 248.
14 Tom Stevenson & Essi Avellan, *Christie's World Encyclopedia of Champagne & Sparkling Wine*, 3rd edition, Absolute Press, 2013, pp. 10–12.
15 ibid., p. 9.
16 Brennan, p. 249.
17 'Contemporary explanations for the region's commercial stagnation [in the mid-18th century] tended to emphasize the declining quality of its wines': Brennan, p. 244.
18 Don Kladstrup & Petie Kladstrup, *Champagne*, Kindle edition, HarperCollins, 2005, location 634.
19 Before the rise of sparkling wines, the still wines of Champagne were often rated according to the source village, with Aÿ, Ambonnay, Bouzy and Hautvillers being among the most highly regarded. Whether all the grapes that went into these wines were exclusively from these villages we cannot know.
20 All of the historians I spoke to while researching this book work directly or indirectly for the large houses or regional bodies. For this reason, I have decided not to name them, as I do not want to implicate them in the conclusions of this work.
21 Musset, p. 369.
22 Rod Phillips, *A Short History of Wine*, HarperCollins, 2000, p. 138.
23 The oldest records we have for Blanquette de Limoux date from 1531 and are found among the papers of the Benedictine community at the Abbaye de Saint-Hilaire. These documents outline the method of production for Limoux's sparkling wines in cork-stopped bottles. *The Oxford Companion to Wine*, 3rd edition, Oxford University Press, 2006, pp. 402–3; 'Première Bulle', *Wine LR*, no. 21, December 2013 – January 2014, www.winelr.fr/numero/n-21_article_premiere-bulle.html.
24 Musset, p. 88.
25 Kolleen M. Guy, *When Champagne Became French: Wine and the Making of a National Identity*, Kindle edition, Johns Hopkins University Press, 2003, locations 610, 619.

Part II

26 A *'beguine'* was a woman who entered a convent by donating all of her belongings to the church. Presumably, this parcel was once one such donation. Prévost also farms a tiny, second plot in a vineyard that borders *Les Béguines* called *Le Languet*.

27 '*Closerie*' is an old French term, used in the Middle Ages, that signifies a small 2-hectare property. Such a property did not generate enough income for the farmer to be able buy the cows to plough the soil, and so all the work had to be done by hand. The name has nothing to do with a '*clos*', an enclosed or walled vineyard, as has sometimes been suggested.

28 Peter Liem, 'Jérôme Prévost, Gueux', Besotted Ramblings and Other Drivel, 11 June 2008, www.peterliem.com/2008/06/jrme-prvost-gueux.html.

29 Almost all of the sulphur used in the wine industry is also a by-product of the petroleum industry; mined, elemental sulphur is hard to source and rarely used.

30 'AOC' stands for '*appellation d'origine contrôlée*' (the laws that govern regional produce in France). Products that carry an AOC must come from a delimited area and must be produced according to a range of regulations that, in theory at least, ensure a regionally unique product.

31 As mentioned in the notes to the prologue, by 'dosage' here I simply mean the legal addition of sugar to Champagne. In fact, there are two types of dosages in Champagne production. The first, officially known as '*liqueur de tirage*' and often called '*tirage*' for short, is a dose of sugar and yeast that is added to the base wine in order to begin the secondary fermentation in the bottle – the process that will create the bubbles in the wine. The second type of dosage, the one I am speaking of here, is officially called the '*liqueur d'expédition*' and is the addition of a dose of sugar at the end of the winemaking process, prior to the Champagne being released to market. This is the addition that is normally referred to as 'dosage'.

Part III

32 'Chaptalisation' is the process of adding sugar to grape juice or fermenting wine in order to stimulate and extend the fermentation and increase the alcohol and texture of the final wine.

33 'Lees' are the dead yeast cells and other micro-particles of grape matter that settle out of a wine following fermentation.

34 Rod Phillips, *A Short History of Wine*, HarperCollins, 2000, p. 243.

35 Kolleen M. Guy, *When Champagne Became French: Wine and the Making of a National Identity*, Kindle edition, Johns Hopkins University Press, 2003, location 169.

36 Champagne was not the only region, nor France the only country, that tried to satisfy the demand for sparkling wine that arose in the 18th and 19th centuries. Champagne was also far from being the only region that coveted the mantle of 'world's finest sparkling wine producer'. Other French areas like Burgundy, the Loire, Alsace and the Languedoc were also very dynamic producers of *mousseux*. In terms of other countries, Germany was perhaps Champagne's greatest competitor in the early days, having a very well established sparkling wine industry in the early 19th century. Austria and Italy were also producing significant quantities of sparkling wine in the 19th century, when production of this wine style kicked off in Spain, Chile, Australia and the US.

37 *The Oxford Companion to Wine*, 2nd edition, Oxford University Press, 1999, p. 407; 'Première Bulle'.

38 Tom Stevenson & Essi Avellan, *Christie's World Encyclopedia of Champagne & Sparkling Wine*, 3rd edition, Absolute Press, 2013, pp. 10–12.
39 James Crowden, *Ciderland*, Birlinn, 2008.

Part IV

40 The estate is named for Francis Egly's paternal grandparents. His grandfather was Monsieur Egly, while his grandmother was Madame Ouriet. Together, they started Champagne Egly-Ouriet.
41 Michel Bettane & Thierry Desseauve, *The World's Greatest Wines*, Stewart, Tabori and Chang, 2006.
42 Out of 319 villages in Champagne, there are only 44 classified as Premier cru (often written as '*1er cru*') and 17 as Grand cru (the highest classification). While these classifications give us a rough guide to the potential quality of the villages, they are not necessarily very useful when it comes to assessing individual wines, as we will discover in Myth III (page 68).
43 Wines aged in barrel are often aged 'on lees' (although this practice is rare in Champagne), and lees also form in a bottle of Champagne after the secondary fermentation. Ageing the wine in the bottle, on lees, following the secondary fermentation is a key element of the Champagne process. Later, the lees are removed via the disgorgement process, so that a bottle of clear wine can be sent to market.
44 'VP' stands for '*vieillissement prolongé*', which means 'long aged'.

Part V

45 Becky Sue Epstein, *Champagne: A Global History*, Reaktion Books Ltd, 2011, p. 31.
46 One bottle every two seconds adds up to some fifteen million bottles of Moët a year, a figure that is close to half of what Moët is widely held to produce. Moët does not publicly divulge its production figures, but looking at the amount of vineyard land it controls and the average yields, we can do some basic arithmetic and arrive at a safe estimate of the volume of wine Moët makes each vintage. Unless it is selling off a large portion of this wine in bulk (highly unlikely in a world in which Champagne demand exceeds supply), we can conclude that, incredibly, a bottle of Moët is popped somewhere in the world almost every second of every day.
47 'Champagne bubble myth burst: Forget the silver spoon', news release, Stanford University, 21 December 1994, news.stanford.edu/pr/94/941221Arc4008.html.

Part VI

48 Jamie Goode, *Wine Science*, Mitchell Beazley, 2005, p. 16.
49 I cannot say with any certainty that this logic necessarily applies to vineyards everywhere in the world, but my gut instinct tells me that it does. Many Australian wine professionals argue that Australia's soils are too fragile and its rainfall too irregular for cultivation to have a positive effect. I am involved in an Australian vineyard project that is currently testing this hypothesis.

50 Note that we are talking about superficial and limited cultivation here, a working of the soil where only the very top surface layer is broken at specific times of the year, as opposed to the aggressive, deep cultivation associated with broad-scale agriculture.
51 Andrew Jefford, *The New France: A Complete Guide to Contemporary French Wine*, Mitchell Beazley, 2002; Tom Stevenson & Essi Avellan, *Christie's World Encyclopedia of Champagne & Sparkling Wine*, 3rd edition, Absolute Press, 2013.
52 'Biodynamics' is a form of organic farming (farming without any synthetic chemical inputs) that also takes into account the lunar calendar and makes use of a range of homeopathic (plant-, compost- and mineral-based) treatments. The practice is somewhat controversial, as many of the treatments have no scientific explanation or evidence, and some of the beliefs and practices seem to border on the religious.
53 This is now changing, with the recent updates to the European Union laws that allow producers to seek organic and biodynamic certification both in the winery and in the vineyards. The winery certification at last puts restrictions on what can be done in the cellars.

Part VII

54 In France, as in much of the wine world, yields are measured in hectolitres. One hectolitre equals 100 litres. Under Champagne's regional laws, 160 kilograms of fruit can produce a maximum 1 hectolitre of juice. So 16 tonnes of grapes are required to produce 100 hectolitres, and 15.7 tonnes will yield 98.4 hectolitres, the permitted maximum.
55 It's an accepted truism in the wine world that as yields climb beyond a reasonable level, so fruit intensity and quality diminish. When you combine early harvesting with the cropping levels being discussed here, you lose much of the character of the grapes – certainly vineyard character and even varietal character. This is why it is so difficult, even for professionals, to accurately assess the dominant grape variety used to produce many a Champagne in masked wine tastings.
56 Of course, there are grape varieties other than these three being used in Champagne, as we will see on our travels and as I discuss in Myth V (page 77).

Part VIII

57 All stereotypes are historical. What is accepted today is not the same story that was told in the past; nor will it be the one told in the future.
58 The Albariza soil of the sherry country in Spain is also very high in chalk.
59 These two sites, *Les Champboutons* in Avize and *Les Bionnes* in Cramant, historically produced the Agrapart Millésimé, a wine that is again on offer. Agrapart now re-releases the Minéral under the Millésimé label after ten additional years of ageing on cork. Same wine, just ten years older and with a different label.

Part IX

60 Even Krug, the most revered négociant of Champagne, claims to blend wines from well over 100 sites, which are whittled down from more than 300 in their cellars, to try to re-create the famous Krug Grande Cuvée.

Part XI

61 A 'co-operative', or 'co-op', is a large-scale grape-processing and winemaking facility co-owned by a collective of growers from the same area. Co-ops first appeared in Champagne in the 1930s, but they became an increasingly significant part of the landscape from the 1950s.

62 I have researched the above history through direct interviews with surviving members of the Petitjean family and their relatives. The timeline that has resulted from these interviews renders the following claim, found strewn across the web and even on some LVMH web sites, a little problematic: 'Krug Clos d'Ambonnay ... has been one of Krug's best-loved terroirs for generations.'

Part XII

63 'Organic farming' is the name of a collection of practices that seek non-synthetic-chemical solutions to age-old agricultural challenges – weeds, insects, mildew, rot and other vine diseases. These 'organic' practices were simply the standard agricultural approach before World War II and until the 1960s and 1970s, in Champagne and across France.

64 Tom Stevenson & Essi Avellan, *Christie's World Encyclopedia of Champagne & Sparkling Wine*, 3rd edition, Absolute Press, 2013, p. 35.

65 The irony here is that the Larmandiers do not spend any money on promotion or advertising (save the costs of any travel and of attending those wine fairs that they feel are worthwhile). I believe that this is the case with all the growers we have visited in this book. As the Australian importer for a number of these producers, I have never received any marketing dollars, branded glasses, ice buckets or paraphernalia that I didn't pay for myself. Free samples are given only in very rare and exceptional circumstances. Such producers believe that all of their money should be spent in the vineyard and cellar – that is, on what ends up in the bottle – rather than on marketing. When you weigh this against the hundreds of millions of dollars spent by the Grandes Marques to promote their brands every year, you can start to understand why many people may not have heard of Larmandier-Bernier.

66 In fact, he was supposed to be co-president with Bruno Paillard, but Paillard would not accept this, so a compromise was reached, with Paillard as president and Larmandier as vice president.

Part XIII

67 Of course, this success has come at the expense of the quality and interest of the product itself. The type of Camembert found on supermarket shelves around the

world today is a bland, homogenised version of the original, and its commercial success has been a disaster for the region's artisanal producers, who have all but disappeared.

Part XIV

68   Regarding geology, in the Côte des Bar, Kimmeridgian limestone takes over from the predominantly belemnite or micraster chalk soils of the Marne, while another form of chalk, Turonian, takes over in Montgueux. Regarding climate, the Marne is less than 300 kilometres from the Channel, experiencing the influence of the ocean and more regular rainfall.
69   This was then ratified through the formation of the AOC of Champagne, in 1936, following the creation of the Institut National des Appellations d'Origine, or INAO (the organisation that regulates the production of French agricultural products), in 1935.
70   There are other quality producers of the Aube of whom I have a less intimate knowledge or whose wines have not moved me in the same way as those covered here. That does not mean they are not worthy of attention. Those most often cited include Fleury Père & Fils, Dosnon & Lepage, and Marie-Courton.

Part XV

71   The term 'grower-producer' means a producer who grows their own grapes for the wines they make; a producer that typically makes wines only (or mostly) from the fruit of their own vineyards. If they do buy any fruit, it will be from vineyards they manage themselves or from growers who work to the same standards.

Part XVI

72   Make sure you get the right Lassaigne – it's an old name in this village and there are at least six growers who carry it on their label.
73   There were previous laws and decrees prior to the founding of the AOC, most famously the 1908 legislation that included only the Marne and Aisne and excluded the Aube completely. But the AOC of Champagne was only passed into law in 1936. From that point onwards, the Aube, including Montgueux, has been a part of the Champagne region. There was obviously a great deal of politics involved in the 1908 ruling: prior to 1908 the courts had included the Aube within the boundaries of Champagne. This was ratified by the AOC laws.
74   The more sugar is added for the *tirage* – to stimulate the secondary fermentation in the bottle – the more gas pressure and the more frothiness will be produced. Also, the bubbles will be larger. The addition of 18 grams is extremely low; 24 grams is the norm in Champagne, this latter producing a gas pressure in the bottle of roughly 6 atmospheres (that is, six times the pressure of the atmosphere). Lassaigne typically uses 20 grams, an amount that gives him 1 atmosphere less pressure than an average bottle of Champagne.

Part XVII

75 When I use the term 'grower revolution' here, I'm not talking about those instances when the growers rioted against the large houses, which has occurred a number of times in the history of Champagne, most famously in 1910 and 1911. Rather, I am using the term as it is typically used today, to suggest those moments in history when growers took control of their own wine production.
76 Kolleen M. Guy, *When Champagne Became French: Wine and the Making of a National Identity*, Kindle edition, Johns Hopkins University Press, 2003, location 1361.
77 ibid., location 1344.
78 *The Wild Bunch*, film, Warner Brothers / Seven Arts, United States, 1969.

Part XIX

79 'Clonal selection' denotes the use of vines propagated from the same mother vine and purchased en masse from a nursery. Each of the vines has the same genetic material and therefore tends to behave consistently, producing fruit with a predictable and reliable expression. By contrast, 'massal selection' is the process of taking cuttings from the most successful vines within an existing vineyard and using them to replace any dead or poorly performing vines in that same vineyard or estate. This creates a selection that continually improves the quality of the vineyard, as the chosen vines are already excelling in that same place, and also creates a spread of genetic material that in turn is held to produce a more complex and complete expression of the terroir. As the parent material has already been proved to prosper in the soil, the vines will typically be healthier and the quality of the wine is also said to be higher.
80 For many more details and fun facts about the physics of Champagne bubbles, I recommend Gérard Liger-Belair's *Uncorked: The Science of Champagne*, Princeton University Press, 2004. It is a popular rendering of the latest in 'bubble science', has some remarkable images of the life and death of Champagne bubbles and contains many curious facts. If you're nerdy enough to wonder which planet in our solar system you'd need to be on to get the finest bead in your Champagne (spoiler alert – it's Venus) or why Champagne bubbles behave so differently from beer bubbles, this is the book for you.

Part XX

81 'Racking' is the movement of wine from one vessel to another, often with the deliberate intention of aeration.

Epilogue

82 Of the growers covered in this book, only Emmanuel Lassaigne breaks this mould, by sourcing from some Montgueux vineyards that are not his own. Why he does this and why it has not disqualified him from entry to this work are explained in Part XVI. I see no problem with a grower sourcing quantities of fruit from other vineyard owners, so long as the viticulture is of the same standard.

ACKNOWLEDGEMENTS

I would like to thank my entire team at Bibendum Wine Co. whose hard work, dedication and shared passion keeps me inspired. My mother, who always encouraged me to read and to write. Neil Beckett at The World of Fine Wine who was willing to publish articles on Champagne that were certain to challenge at least some of his readership, not to mention other contributors and advertisers; these articles were the starting point of this book.

I must acknowledge all the great growers and winemakers with whom I work and who have been a constant source of education and inspiration. Especially the artist, the rock, the teacher, the monk (and Sophie!) and the farmer. You are the reason this book exists.

To my immediate family who never once begrudged me the time and support I needed to write this book and often exhibited more enthusiasm for the project than I did. To Max Allen, who gave me invaluable feedback on the text and put me in touch with much needed contacts. To Karl French and Penny Mansley for their excellent proofing and feedback, Louise Sheeran for the wonderful map of Champagne that adorns the inside cover of the book, indexer Kyla Petrilli, who went above and beyond, and Phil Campbell for his design work, layout, all round production assistance and endless patience. To the talented duo of James Broadway & Nic Moghabghab who contributed a number of the best photos in the book and to all those who read some or all of the book and encouraged me to publish, especially Jesús Barquín and Andrea Frost, who provided quotes for the back cover. And of course to the great Andrew Jefford, who so generously wrote the foreword. Enormous thanks to you all.

BIBLIOGRAPHY

Bettane, Michel & Thierry Desseauve, *The World's Greatest Wines*, Stewart, Tabori and Chang, 2006.
Brennan, Thomas, *Burgundy to Champagne: The Modern Wine Trade in Early Modern France*, Johns Hopkins University Press, 1997.
'Champagne bubble myth burst: Forget the silver spoon', news release, Stanford University, 21 December 1994, news.stanford.edu/pr/94/941221Arc4008.html.
Crowden, James, *Ciderland*, Birlinn, 2008.
Epstein, Becky Sue, *Champagne: A Global History*, Reaktion Books Ltd, 2011.
Goode, Jamie, *Wine Science*, Mitchell Beazley, 2005.
Guy, Kolleen M., *When Champagne Became French: Wine and the Making of a National Identity*, Kindle edition, Johns Hopkins University Press, 2003.
Jefford, Andrew, *The New France: A Complete Guide to Contemporary French Wine*, Mitchell Beazley, 2002.
Kladstrup, Don & Petie Kladstrup, *Champagne*, Kindle edition, HarperCollins, 2005.
Liem, Peter, 'Jérôme Prévost, Gueux', Besotted Ramblings and Other Drivel, 11 June 2008, www.peterliem.com/2008/06/jrme-prvost-gueux.html.
Liger-Belair, Gérard, *Uncorked: The Science of Champagne*, Princeton University Press, 2004.
Musset, Benoît, *Vignobles de Champagne et vins mousseux: histoire d'un mariage de raison, 1650–1830*, Fayard, 2008.
The Oxford Companion to Wine, 2nd edition, Oxford University Press, 1999.
The Oxford Companion to Wine, 3rd edition, Oxford University Press, 2006.
Phillips, Rod, *A Short History of Wine*, HarperCollins, 2000.
'Première Bulle', *Wine LR*, no. 21, December 2013 – January 2014, www.winelr.fr/numero/n-21_article_premiere-bulle.html
Stevenson, Tom & Essi Avellan, *Christie's World Encyclopedia of Champagne & Sparkling Wine*, 3rd edition, Absolute Press, 2013.

INDEX

italic/bold denotes images

Agrapart, Pascal 99, 102–3, 104–12, *106*, 152, 194, 202
Alsace 92, 151
Ambonnay 57, *60*, 61, 66, 133, 134, 141–42, 168
Aube, the 166–69, 180–82, 198, 204, 220
Aubry, Pierre & Phillipe 99
Avenay-val-d'Or 111
Avenue de Champagne (Épernay) 71–74, 75–76
Avize 37, 80, 102–3, *105*, 107, 110, 111, 124, 125–26, *126*, 131, 132, 133, 146, 147, 156, 157
Aÿ 57, 133

Beaugrand family 181
Beaune 125, 126
Bergères-lès-Vertus 146
Bettane, Michel 58, 62
Blaise, Theirry 151
Bouchard, Cédric 99, 169, 202, 216–22, 225
Bourguignon, Claude 85
Bouzy 57, 61
Brennan, Thomas 24
Bubbles 15, 22, 24, 30, 46, 77, 143, 164, 212–13, 217–18, 225
Bugey-Cerdon 53
Burgundy 26, 28, 63, 92, 116–17, 125–26, 129, 138, 139, 141–42, 151
Buxières-sur-Arce 198, 202, *203*

Celles-sur-Ource 216, 221
Chablis 167
Châlons-en-Champagne 14, 48
Chamery 56

Chaptal, Jean-Antoine 48
Charles Heidsieck 70, 139, 141, 182
Chartogne, Alexandre 34, 129
Chartogne-Taillet 34
Chavot-Courcourt 80, *81*, *82*
Chiquet, Jean-Hervé 86, 87
Chiquet, Laurent 86
Chouilly 81
Clicquot-Ponsardin, Barbe-Nicole 49
Clos Rougeard 43
Coche, Jean-François 209
Collin, Olivier 129, 166, *167*
Congy 166, *168*
corks 25, 31, 49, 52
Côte des Bar 181–82, 198, 216
Côte des Blancs 63, 80–81, *87*, 102, 116, 146, 157, 166, 180, 181
Coulon, Eric 210
Cramant 80, 110, 111, 131, 132, 133, 156, 157
Crowden, James 53
Cuis 80

Denis, Dominique 14, 97, 208–9, 210–11
Duval-Leroy family 99
Drappier family 99

Écueil 56
Egly, Francis 57–67, *59*, 194
Egly-Ouriet 57–61, *60*, 63, 66–67, 132, 210
England 24–25, 53, 117, 118
Épernay 71–76, 80, 166

fermentation process 22–23, 42–43, 45, 48–49, 52–53, 94–96, 111, 143, 196, 212, 217
Foucault, Nadi 43
François, Jean-Baptiste 48–49
French Formula One Grand Prix 34–35, *35*, *37*
Gaillac 52, 53
Gautherot, Bertrand 99, 198–205, *201*, 208, 210; *see also* Vouette et Sorbée
Georges Laval 88
Germany 139
glass 25, *25*, 49, 163–64
Goulet, Joseph 56–57
Goulet-Turpin 56–57
Grossard, Dom 31
grower revolution 172–74, 176, 192–93
Gueux 34–36, *35*, 37, 40, 57

Hautvillers abbey 30–31
herbicides 39, 61, 83, 84, 88, 107, 127, 148, 151, 153, 184, 194, 199, 210
Humbrecht, Léonard 209

Jacques Lassaigne 169, 180–89, *185*, *186*, 202; *see also* Lassaigne, Emmanuel
Jacques Selosse 124, *126*, *129*, 131–34, *see also* Selosse, Anselme
Jacquesson 86–87, 210
Jacquesson, Adolphe 49

Krug 71, *115*, 120, 139, 140–41, *142*
Krug, Henri *115*

La Closerie 36, 46; *see also* Prévost, Jérôme

Lafon, Dominique 209
Laherte, Aurélien 80, 99
Laherte Frères 80
Landreville 216
Lanson 70
Larmandier-Bernier 14, 146–47, 148, *150*, 153–54, 156–58, 210
Larmandier, Pierre 116, 146–58, *149*, *153*, 194, 204, 208, 210
Larmandier, Sophie 146, 147–48, 151–53, 156–58
Lassaigne, Emmanuel 180–89, *183*, 218, 219; see also Jacques Lassaigne
Laurent-Perrier *72*, 187
Laval, Vincent 88
Le Mesnil-sur-Oger 80, 133, 134, 146
Le Phare 56
Liem, Peter 36
Liger-Belair, Gérard 143–44, 212–13
Limoux 31, 52, 53
Loire 53
Louis Roederer 70, 86, 87–88, 139
Louis Vuitton Moët Hennessy 31, 141

Macquer, Pierre 48
Mareuil-sur-Aÿ 133
Massif de Saint-Thierry 34
McGee, Harold 77
Meret, Christopher 24
Merfy 34
microbes 83-84
Mignon, Christophe 210
Moët & Chandon 16–17, 31, 71, 72, 73–75, *75*, *76*, 86, 87–88, 141, 187
Moët, Claude 27
Montagne de Reims 34, 56, 61, 111, 166
Montgueux 180–82, 185, 187
Morey, Pierre 154

Moutard family 99
Müller, Antoine de 49
Mumm 70
Musée de la Vigne (Le Phare) 56–57

Nossiter, Jonathan 160

Oger 80, 111, 131, 132, 156
Oiry 111
organic viticulture 85, 86, 88, 89, 150-51, 153–54, 184, 226

Parc Naturel Régional de la Montagne de Reims 56, 57
Pargny 56
Paris 26
Pasteur, Louis 23, 49
Peckinpah, Sam 195
Pérignon, Dom 23, 30–31, 72–73, 75, *76*, 144
Petite Montagne 34, 42, 56
Petitjean, Henri 141
Philipponnat 120
Phillips, Rod 50
phylloxera 35, 98
Piper-Heidsieck 17, 70, 139, 141
Pluche, Noël-Antoine 31
Pommery 71
Prévost, Jérôme 36–45, *41*, *45*, 129, 152, 194, 204, 208, 209, 210

Reims 27, 34, 57, 70–71, 166, 167
Rémy Cointreau 141
Rocheret, Bertin du 23
Roger Coulon 210
Roses de Jeanne 219, 220–22; see also Bouchard, Cédric
Rossillon, Stephane 102

Sacy 56
Saint-Aubin 14

Saint-Hilaire abbey 52
Salon 120
Saumur 43
Selosse, Anselme 37, 62, 63–64, 102–3, 124–34, *125*, 148, 150, 152, 187, 194, 209, 210, 211, 225
Selosse, Corinne 102, 134
Sermiers 34, 56
Spain 127, 130
Stevenson, Tom 24, 131

Taittinger 70
Tarlant, Jean-Mary & Benoît 99
Thibault, Daniel 182, 184
This, Hervé 77
Trépail 57
Troyes 27, 166, 167, 180, 198

Ulysse Collin 166, *167*; see also Collin, Olivier
United States of America 98, 160

Vallée de la Marne 80, 166–69
Valoriser 37, 150, 208, 209–10
Vertus 14, 81, 115–16, 146, 147, 156–57, 168, 180
Verzenay 56, 57, 61
Verzy 56
Veuve Clicquot 17, 27, 70, 86, 141, 182, 187
Vignes de Vrigny 66
Ville-sur-Arce 202
Villers-Allerand 56
Vin de Pays 92
Vouette et Sorbée 169, 198–205, *201*, *202*, *203*; see also Gautherot, Bertrand
Vrigny 56, 61, 66

Walfart, Armand 49–50